MYTH AND REALITY OF TERRORISM IN SOUTH ASIA

MYTH AND REALITY OF TERRORISM IN SOUTH ASIA

Rajkumar Singh

KALPAZ

Myth and Reality of Terrorism in South Asia

ISBN : 978-81-7835-950-2

Published in 2013 in India by
Kalpaz Publications
C-30, Satyawati Nagar,
Delhi - 110052
E-mail: kalpaz@hotmail.com

Laser Type Setting : Rajender Vashist, Delhi
Printed at : G. Print Process.Delhi

Dedicated to

Smt. Sunita Devi

Bhabhi

Contents

Preface

Myth and Reality of Terrorism in South Asia is an analytical piece of work with explanation of facts and issues involved in the different dimensions of terrorism – religious, cross-border and ethnic that we face in our everyday life as a reality. The region South Asia where terrorism is an experienced danger and not a false alarm consists of diverse societies and cultures with multi-religiousness. The tradition of violence which started in the form of bilateral wars, soon transformed into wars based on religion, ethnicity and ideology. Originally terrorism, as we see it in proliferated and diversified forms is a gift of world bipolar system of Cold War era, which for its strategic considerations, pushed the region in uncertainty and resulted in the Soviet intervention in Afghanistan and another superpower of the time invited the terror masterminds of the world to come and give the enemy a retreating defeat in the name of Jihad through guerilla warfare.

The year 1979 was the actual beginning of terrorism in South Asia sponsored by an extra-regional power via Pakistan and Afghanistan. In succeeding years a world-wide network of terrorism was formed with Islamabad as its capital that posed a direct threat to region's peace and security. A decade later the withdrawal of the Soviets and further the devastating attacks of 11 September 2001 made the impacts of terrorism largely felt in South Asia. In post–9/11 the United States of America launched its global war against terrorism and pressurised Islamabad to stop terror support and ban several terror outfits, who later took refuge in other South Asian countries, especially in Bangladesh and Nepal where they got at least moral support at social level and began to operate from there comfortably.

In South Asia religiously motivated terrorists have been operating for decades which led to the ominous developments such as rise in sectarian violence and Islamic extremism in Pakistan, upsurge of communal riots in India, Islamic factionalism in

Bangladesh, and polarisation of South Asian society on religious line. In so far as India is concerned the main purpose of terrorists is to damage the social fabric by injecting communal disharmony. This is done systematically through different channels that include ISI agents, Madrassas, direct contacts/agents, and professional criminals operating in the region. True is the fact that India being at the centrestage of South Asia can not avoid spill over effect in the neighbouring states.

I wish to thank the institutions and individuals for their encouragement, cooperation and good wishes that I received and staff of the central libraries at New Delhi and other places where I got a lot of information and analytical/critical views of different subject experts. They all concerned deserve cordial thanks.

I am deeply grateful to several persons and colleagues. Among teachers, Dr. D.N. Mallik, Dr. Kirtyanand Singh, Dr. R.N. Kumar and Dr. M.R. Kazami, retired Professors of the University Department of Political Science, BRA Bihar University, Muzaffarpur, have been constant source of guide and encouragement at every stage. Colleagues Dr. Dhirendra Narayan Singh, Department of Political Science MLT College, Saharsa, Dr. Chandra Prakash Singh, Department of History, Dr. Kumar Jyotivardhan, and Dr. Usha Sinha Department of Hindi, Dr. Ram Naresh Singh, Department of Maithili, West Campus P.G. Centre, Saharsa and departmental colleagues, Dr. Bijay Kumar Verma and Dr. Pawan Kumar are thankful for their cooperation and good wishes. Eldest brother the late Suryanath Singh, elder brother Bhuvneshwar Prasad Singh, father-in-law Shri Ramanand Singh, retired Professor and Head, University Department of Physics, BRA Bihar University, Muzaffarpur, deserve deep sense of gratitude for their sincere good wishes. I am no less grateful to Rajeev Ranjan who performed the painful task of composing the book, and to colleagues and staff of the B.N. Mandal University, West Campus, P.G. Centre, Saharsa.

I would be failing in my duty if I do not record my honest good wishes and gratitude to the family members including my wife Dr. Hemlata Singh, son Aditya Priyadarshi and Apurv Adarsh in the completion of the book.

However, for the facts, analysis, views and misjudgements contained in the book, I alone am responsible.

21 November, 2011 **Rajkumar Singh**

Glossary

Ahmadis	– followers of Mirza Ghulam Ahmed Qadiani; a religious minority in Pakistan
Ahimsa	– non–violence
Alim	– religious scholar
Amir	– a person holding authority, a ruler, head of an organisation
Aryavarta	– land of the Aryas
Bande mataram	– literally 'hail to the mother,' title of song in Bankim Chandra's novel
Deobandi	– belonging to the Muslim religious seminary of Deoband, India; an orthodox sect which abhors superstitions attributed to the Brelavi sect
Dharma	– appropriate form of moral and religious obligations in Hinduism
Fatwa	– a ruling by a jurist on the legality or otherwise of an action
Fidayeen	– suicide-squad tactics
Hindutva	– Hindu essence or political identity
Hudood	– plural of hadd, punishments under Islamic Law
Imam	– faith
Islamiat	– Islamic religious studies
Jihad	– striving for perfection; spiritual endeavour; holy war
Kafir	– one who refuses to believe in the unity of God, infidel
Karma	– action or deed; theory of future births being based on quality of actions in the present or previous lives

Lashkars – armies
Madrassas – religious schools
Majlis–i–Shoora – consultative council
Maulana – title given to Muslim religious scholar
Maulvi – title given to Muslim religious leader
Muhajir – Muslim migrant
Mujahid – one who participates in *Jehad*
Mujahideen – plural of mujahid
Nawab – title given to a nobleman or a king
Nizam – rule or ruler
Pakhtun or Pushtun – people of the Afghan race inhabiting mostly in the North–West Frontier Province in Pakistan
Pandit – title given to Hindu religious scholar
Qazi – a judge; judge of Shariah Court
Quaid–i–Azam – the great leader, a title used for the founder of Pakistan, Mohammad Ali Jinnah
Satyagraha – literally the way of truth; form of political agitation based on moral pressure pioneered by Gandhi
Sharia – literally 'a clear path,' set of moral injunctions constituting Islamic law
Sufi – Muslim mystic; the word 'sufi' comes from the coarse woolen garment, 'suf', worn by the early mystics of Islam
Sunnah – tradition of the Prophet
Tanzeem – organisation
Ulama – learned authorities on Islam
Ummah – community
Vedas – literally wisdom or knowledge; ancient Indian religious scriptures
Wadera – Sindhi landlord
Zamindar – landholder, large or small

Abbreviations

AIADMK	–	All–India Anna Dravida Munnetra Kazhagam
AL	–	Awami League
ANA	–	Afghan National Army
ANP	–	Awami National Party
APMSO	–	All Pakistan Mohajir Student's Organisation
BC	–	Before Christ
BNP	–	Bangladesh Nationalist Party
BSF	–	Border Security Force
CBM's	–	Confidence Building Measures
CENTO	–	Central Treaty Organisation
CFA	–	Cease Fire Agreement
CIA	–	Central Intelligence Agency
CISF	–	Central Industrial Security Force
CPIM	–	Communist Party of India (Marxist)
CPIML	–	Communist Party of India (Marxist– Leninist)
CRPF	–	Central Reserve Police Force
CSTO	–	Collective Security Treaty Organisation
DMK	–	Dravida Munnetra Kazhagam
E & P	–	Exploration and Production
EPRLF	–	Eelam People's Revolutionary Front
EROS	–	Eelam Revolutionary Organisation of Students
EU	–	European Union
FATA	–	Federally Administered Tribal Areas
FBI	–	Federal Bureau of Investigation
FDLs	–	Forward Defence Lines

FP	– Federal Party
FRD	– Federal Research Division
GFC	– Global Financial Crisis
HM	– Hizb-ul-Mujahideen
HuJI	– Harkat-ul-Jehad Islami
IB	– Intelligence Bureau
ICG	– International Crisis Group
IM	– Indian Mujahideen
INC	– Indian National Congress
IOJ	– Islamiya Okiyya Jote
IPKF	– Indian Peace-Keeping Force
ISI	– Inter Services Intelligence and Inter-State Intelligence
ISR	– I Sinha Regiment
JeM	– Jaish-e-Mohammad
JKLF	– Jammu and Kashmir Liberation Front
JI	– Jamaat-e-Islami
JMB	– Jamaatul Mujahideen Bangladesh
JMJB	– Jagrata Muslim Janata Bangladesh
JUI	– Jamiatul-Ulema-e-Islam
JVP	– Janatha Vimukthi Peramuna
LeT	– Lashkar-e-Toiba
LoC	– Line of Control
LTTE	– Liberation Tigers of Tamil Eelam
MCNC	– Media Centre for National Security
MCOCA	– Maharashtra Control of Organised Crime Act
MQM	– Muttahida Quami Movement
MUF	– Muslim United Front
NA	– Northern Alliance
NATO	– North Atlantic Treaty Organisation
NCS	– National Clandestine Service
NCTC	– National Counter Terrorism Center
NFZ	– No-Fire Zone

NIA	–	National Investigation Agency
NSA	–	National Security Act
NSG	–	National Security Guard
NWFP	–	North-West Frontier Province
ODNI	–	Office of the Director of National Intelligence
OIC	–	Organisation of Islamic Conference
OPEC	–	Oil Producing European Countries
PLOTE	–	People's Liberation Organisation of Tamil Eelam
PML	–	Pakistan Muslim League
PoK	–	Pak-occupied Kashmir
POTA	–	Prevention of Terrorist Act
PPP	–	Pakistan People's Party
PWG	–	People's War Group
RAW	–	Research and Analysis Wing
SAARC	–	South Asian Association for Regional Cooperation
SCO	–	Shanghai Cooperation Organisation
SDGT	–	Specially Designated Global Terrorist
SEATO	–	South East Asian Treaty Organisation
SIMI	–	Students Islamic Movement of India
SLFP	–	Sri Lanka Freedom Party
SNA	–	Social Network Analysis
TADA	–	Terrorist and Disruptive Activities (Prevention) Act
TC	–	Tamil Congress
TELA	–	Tamil Eelam Liberation Army
TELO	–	Tamil Eelam Liberation Organisation
TESA	–	Tamil Eelam Supporters Association
TM	–	Tehreek-ul-Mujahideen
TNT	–	Tamil New Tigers
TTP	–	Tehrik-e-Taliban Pakistan
TULF	–	Tamil United Liberation Front
TUF	–	Tamil United Front
UAPA	–	Unlawful Activities (Prevention) Act
UNO	–	United Nations Organisation

UNP – United National Party

UPA – United Progressive Alliance

USD – United States Dollar

USSOCOM – United States Special Operations Command

VoA – Voice of America

WMD – Weapons of Mass Destruction

WTC – World Trade Center

1

Characteristics of South Asian Terriorism

South Asia has seen inter-state wars and intra-state violent movements during most of its post colonial history, but its experience with terrorism by non-state actors is relatively recent as compared to other regions such as the Middle East. In the last decades or so, South Asia has, indeed, emerged as the centre – stage of international terrorism, with horrendous implications for countries - India, Pakistan, Afghanistan and Sri Lanka. Within South Asia, Afghanistan and Pakistan alongwith India have been victims of the decade-long wave of non-state terrorism. For the past over thirty years, Afghanistan has seen successive rounds of warfare, with Pakistan bearing the cost of engagement in each such instance.

By creating and conflagrating conflict in the region the terrorist organisations rationally hope to keep its three principal nations divided. This fact alone provides enough incentive for Afghanistan, Pakistan and India and the rest of the South Asian states to unite and offer a collective response to terrorism. What may be most significant for all countries of South Asia is a common goal that connects all terrorist organisations: that of creating inter-state conflict or sabotaging cooperative trends among them.

Such trends include the peace process between India and Pakistan, which is derailed each time an instance of terrorism occurs, or the recent improvement in Afghanistan - Pakistan relations, which terrorist organisations have spared no opportunity to sabotage. The emergence of terrorism as the most dominating form of conflict - generating activity in South Asia has put in jeopardy the whole regional quest for peace and progress.

The Indian subcontinent or South Asia incompasses today eight very diverse sovereign states of very different sizes: India, Pakistan, Bangladesh, Sri Lanka, Nepal, Bhutan, Maldives and Afghanistan. The terms South Asia and India refer, in the first instance, to a vast geographical space stretching from the Himalayan mountain ranges in the north to the Indian Ocean in the south and from the valley of the Indus in the west to the plains of the Brahmaputra in the east. The subcontinent carries the weight not only of its people but also of their ancient history, stretching back five millennia, and a modern history incompassing the experience of British colonialism compressed in tumultuous developments within the past couple of centuries.[1] It has 3 per cent of the world's area, 23 per cent of its population and 2 per cent of its GDP. Within that, India has 72 per cent of the area, 77 per cent of the population and 75 per cent of the GDP.[2] The geographical boundaries drawn by the highest mountain ranges in the world and encircling seas and oceans set the whole of the subcontinent apart from the rest of the world.

The region South Asia and its peoples present a picture of diversity in unity, indeed of immense diversity within a very broad contour of unity. Among them there is great diversity in natural attributes–imposing hills and mountains, lush green river plains, arid deserts and brown plateaus. The South Asian societies are marked by their plural character in terms of languages, cultures, regions and religions. The people of South Asia speak at least twenty major languages and if we include the more important dialects, the count rises to over two hundred. The very diverse languages and language families of South Asia have made enormous contributions to world literature from ancient to modern times. In a broad historical and cultural sense all states of the region may be viewed to be belonging to the Indian family of nations.

It is a fact that the major countries of South Asia share a common historical past in the form of the British colonial rule, however, in terms of political stability, economic regeneration and socio-cultural change they remained poles apart in post-Independence period with the exception that they cooperated each other both at the bilateral as well as multilateral levels under the umbrella of forums, such as Economic and Social Commission for Asia and Pacific (ESCAP), Non-Aligned Movement and Commonwealth. Years following their independence were full of internal characteristics of the polities comprising the region ranged widely from democratic, federal and parliamentary to monarchical and unitary. Over the decades, they have restructured, developed and maintained altogether different political traditions and with certainty none of the member states has fully succeeded in evolving in a 'nation state'.

Culture, as Spengler and Toynbee used the word, is the product of long tradition, of shared habits among people living together over generations; it reflects a particular way of life and a particular view of the world. Its characteristic is spontaneity, and it is often said that it can not be exported or imported.[3] Likewise the region South Asia share certain things in common and they are the religious – cultural heritage of the ancient and medieval times and the administrative, political, educational, economic institutions.[4] Adherents of major world religions, Hinduism, Islam, and Buddhism are found in the subcontinent. Hinduism with its ancient roots, modern transformation and multiple interpretations plays a vital part in the culture and politics of the subcontinent. The greatest cultural and political achievements of Islam have taken place in the subcontinent, where more than 400 million of the world's 1.3 billion Muslims live today. Each of the three most populous countries of South Asia – India, Bangladesh and Pakistan has nearly 140 million Muslims, next only to Indonesia as the largest Muslim countries in the world.[5] Buddhism, apart from the formal adherents in the land of its birth, continues to flourish in Sri Lanka and the Himalayas as well as in East and South-east Asia. South Asia has also significant number of Jain, Zoroastrian, Christian and Sikh minorities.

In spheres of culture, economy, politics and society the modern South Asian history witnessed a number of significant changes in which pivotal role was played by the intermediate social groups in the construction and continuation of British raj. As a result of this social group the colonial state succeeded in intervening the earlier communal and caste categories. They also refashioned the social relations of class by the linking of Indian economic regions to wider capitalist system and thus created a new group in subcontinent's society for their benefit. The states of South Asia emerged as sovereign entities after their prolonged struggle against colonialism. In the post-colonial era, nation building became an arduous task. It was all the more challenging for multicultural states to blend the diverse religious, linguistic and ethno-cultural groups into a national mould.[6] Majority of these states devised the mechanism of a secular democratic order to achieve this objective.

But lack of popular participation or the inadequacy of participation have, rather, contributed to political fragmentation. The absence of a political mechanism to settle who will get what and how has given rise to conflicts among ethnic groups.[7]

The withdrawal of empire leaves a legacy of uncertain frontiers and other disputes among the legatee states. It was complicated further by the lack of self-confidence in the leadership elites of the new nations who frequently direct the fears of their citizens against neighbouring nations in a mistaken belief that this will strengthen the spirit of nationalism and inspire internal cohesion.[8] Real problems among neighbours do exist and in the South Asian System we can easily discern two types of dialectical struggles that have in the past influenced the nature of ties in the region. One type of struggle is by India for a regional role of dominance, maturing into, either a sphere of influence or a hegemonic order. Another is primarily influenced by India's ambitious role, the struggle by Pakistan and others for autonomy, independence and sovereign existence.[9] Alongwith autonomy security perceptions of the South Asian states remained at the top they, however, have developed stronger economic links with the countries outside the region.

Terrorism has profoundly influenced inter – state relations in South Asia. With the world's fastest-growing markets, fastest – rising military expenditures and most serious hot sports coupled with a toxic stew of boiling religious, political, ethnic, strategic and historical animosities, made all the more volatile by endemic poverty, illiteracy and the sheer agony of daily existence, Asia holds the key to the future international security order. Much of Asia's terrorist violence is concentrated in its southern belt, which in the past decade emerged as the international hub of terrorism. This southern part of Asia, encompassing Afghanistan, Pakistan, Uzbekistan, Tajikistan, Chinese ruled Xinjiang and Tibet, India, Nepal, Sri Lanka, Bangladesh and Myanmar, is wrecked by terrorist, insurgent, and separatist violence in a manner unmatched elsewhere in the world.[10] The number of annual fatalities in terrorist – related violence in South Asia far exceeds the death toll in the Middle East, the traditional cradle of terrorism. The entire expanse from the Middle East to South-East Asia is home to militant groups and troubled by terrorist violence posing a serious challenge to international and regional security.[11] Developments in several parts of the world are prompting scholars and policy makers to re-examine old theories of terrorism. The terrorist slaying has belied the arguments that, 'Simply killing a lot of people has seldom been a terrorist objective. Terrorists want a lot of people watching, not a lot of people dead.[12] It, in general, challenges the secular fabric of South Asia.

Secularism, as a concept, is not new in the realm of politics of South Asia. In modern concept the term secularism was first used in 1851 by George Jacob Holyoake, a British protagonist of socialism. The term as practised in the West, meant as a concept that disqualifies religion as the basis for morality and education. For the first time the concept was coined against the excessive interference of Church in the governance of state. Although the concept was redefined by Saint Simon, Durkhiem, Comte and many others, however, it remained not the same as practised in this region. The South Asian philosophy of secularism in the realm of politics has been matured over several hundred years and is an age-old practice. This well-established socio-political culture of South Asia first reversed in 1947 when partition of India took place to create a separate homeland for the Muslims who have lived together in harmony with Hindus for centuries.

In the Indian sub-continent Jawaharlal Nehru defined secularism as peaceful co-existence of different religions without interference from the government and he was the first to propagate secularism in the Indian polity. He further explained that secularism refers to religious tolerance rather than disbelief in religious practices.[13] Religious tolerance as practised in this region is an ancient social tradition. Secular values have influenced social life of South Asia for ages. The concept of co-existence of human beings amidst the good and the bad and the beautiful and the ugly is hallmark of social and cultural life of this region. Needless to mention that the Royal British government was the first to sow the seeds of communal divide as an instrument of state policy to exercise political control over India.[14] Historically too, the South Asian society has been characterised by cultural diversity and religious perspectives rooted in tolerance and humanism. Conscious nurturing of these values and distinctive cultural features can go a long way towards making the region inhospitable for terrorism based on religious fundamentalism.

After the departure of the Britishers, the political leadership in this region did not come up to the expectation of the people. Like the British most of contemporary political leaders followed the same course to gain political mileage. In context of India-Pakistan relations religion has been the single most important factor for the recent sharp deterioration in their discourse.

However, in post-partition political development secularism emerged as an issue in both India and Pakistan. The Constitution of India has two main objectives to achieve through secularism. First, secularism is adopted as an ideology, which confers a well-defined identity to the nation and second as a state policy for governance.[15] In opposite the Government of Pakistan and the terrorists nurtured by the government agencies strongly believe that the Indian secularism is humbug. This perspective is probably because it defies the national aspiration of Pakistan and the communal agenda of the latter.

In the Constituent Assembly of India, its chairman Baba Saheb Ambedkar declared that the state will not adopt or uphold any religion of its own but protect all religious faiths. While the Pakistan, as it exists today is not what Qaed-e-Azam Jinnah had in his mind. His dream of making Pakistan a secular state was buried along with him. In his absence political leadership in the country became weak and fragile and the vacuum created by his departure provided fertile ground for religious clergies in Pakistan to intervene in the political affairs. This gave good opportunity to Islamic clergies and institutions to profit from the situation and manoeuvre towards making Pakistan an Islamic Republic. The clergies belonging to the *Deoband* School of Islamic thought and the *Wahabi Takfir* played their move cautiously but diligently to share political power along with the military dominated political system. They had the religio-political vision and the successive military regimes had the geo-strategic purpose. The combination of the two set right atmosphere for creating religiously motivated militant outfits to undermine the influence of Indian secularism. The creation of Bangladesh and later invasion of Afghanistan by the erstwhile Soviet Union brought the two schools further closer to each other.

The Soviet intervention that took place in December 1979 had posed not only a serious threat to India's security but to the entire South Asian region. As the intervention was done by the Soviet Union – a cold war ally of the United States of America, the latter took the event seriously and went with the single-minded purpose to teach the former the lesson of its life.[16] In the US war against the Soviets, Pakistan became the most important ally and this *Jihad* was waged with Pakistan's border regions with Afghanistan acting as a launching pad for Afghan and other militants from the Muslim world. The weapons for Afghan Mujahideens were passed on through Pakistan. It also enabled Pakistan to receive substantive military aid as well as quiet acceptance of its indulgence in nuclear technology extended by China. Be it the critical issue of Pakistan's tribal areas acting as safe haven for Taliban-led insurgents in Afghanistan or the worrying affair of the growth of extremism and its terrorist consequences in Pakistan, the root, cause lies in the globally sponsored Afghan *Jihad* of 1980s.[17] If that concluding event of the Cold War had not occurred, the conflict in South Asia might still be confined to traditional forms of armed versus the armed and not transformed into violence by the armed against the unarmed. The South Asia, which had experienced very low levels of organised terrorism until the early 1980s, has undergone a dramatic transformation to become the scene of the bloodiest terrorist violence in the world.

Building a strategic relation with Pakistan has been a persisting feature of US policy in South Asia and the new development in Afghanistan had precipitated its urgency. In the context of policy requirements Pakistan was used by the US as a conduit of arms supplies to the Afghan Mujahideens who were fighting against the Soviet forces in Afghanistan from their bases in Pakistan. These arms came mainly from America but also from China, European countries and the Muslim world. Besides supplying arms to the Mujahideen, Pakistan also provided them with training. Without all this assistance, the US objective of bleeding the Soviets while in Afghanistan could not have been achieved.[18] When in February 1989 the Soviet takeover in Afghanistan ended, the supply of US arms and assistance to Afghan Mujahideen also halted simultaneously. The Government of Pakistan very tactfully turned the face of Afghan rebels and others towards Kashmir. The pace of terrorist activities increased suddenly in Jammu and Kashmir and along the line of control.[19] Further the disintegration of Soviet Union marked the end of cold war between the two superpowers and made the US least interested not only in Afghan affairs but to the whole of South Asia strategically.

In the whole history of terrorism, the event of 11 September, 2001 was of immense significance as it had changed the entire Western approach towards terrorism. It was for the first time that terrorism attacked the mightiest of the powers. In the attack even more important was the fact that it challenged the prevailing hegemonic power structure of the world and a powerful statement that the dominance of the US in this power structure was not acceptable; that it could be challenged through the use of force and violence.[20] Obviously in post – 9/11 period Osama bin Laden, the mastermind and main culprit of the event became target of the US, and the latter had declared him to catch dead or alive. In retaliation, the US launched a war against global terrorism and as the attack on US installations came from within Asia, the suspected regions were bound to be hot seat of war against terror. In this war, Pakistan once again received top priority in US calculations and with the moral support of many countries US war against global terrorism began in October 2001. The United States of America, in particular, was determined to eliminate Al-Qaeda and the Taliban as was done in Afghanistan and the border regions of Afghanistan and Pakistan where the terrorists are suspected to have taken refuge. And about a decade latter on 1 May, 2011 Osama bin Laden, the most wanted face of terrorism, was killed by the US forces in a operation at Abbottabad in Pakistan.

Earlier in January 2009 when Barack Obama became the President of United States, started a correction exercise on both Afghanistan and Pakistan so as to remove the distortions of the past and help bring back the focus on the needs of the future. The new President was confident that the attacks in Newyork on 9/11 were planned from these areas and it is from here that new attacks are being plotted. He announced to pursue a military strategy that will break the Taliban's momentum and increase Afghanistan's capacity. Perhaps, in line, the US killed Osama bin Laden, the Al-Qaeda chief, and sent additional troops to Afghanistan.[21] The new US policy has put Pakistan in an uneasy position as its heart has never been with the US declared war on terror. First for the reason that it deems its interests correspond to re-installing the Taliban in power in Afghanistan. Secondly, its foreign policy is driven very largely by terror tactics and therefore, Pakistan can not at the same time be in the advance – line of any fight against terrorism.[22] Currently in post – bin Laden phase while the US is interested to deal militarily with Sirajuddin Haqqani group of Taliban, an ethnic Pashtun and former Mujahideen leader, Pakistan is resisting the pressure to act through mediation. While America is focussed on destroying the extremists, Pakistan, ostensibly a partner in the war on terror, is more concerned with preventing a pro-India government taking over in Afghanistan. The US is apprehensive of the powerful Haqqani Network, close to the ISI and operating both in Pakistan and Afghanistan and recently it had carried out the suicide attacks on the Indian Embassy in Kabul.[23] The new US policy is designed to break the backbone of Taliban Al-Qaeda surge in Afghanistan with a view to establish stability and peace not only there but in the whole world.

Current Status of Terrorism in South Asia

There is no uniform approach applicable to all South Asian countries for dealing with terrorism. What is needed is a differentiated country – specific approach. While in security terms India pursues the objective of zero tolerance to terrorism, in political terms it also believes that all solutions can not be found exclusively through the use of coercive power of the state. Political initiatives have to play a seminal role in complementing the security efforts including exposure of diabolical designs of the terrorists and building a strong civil society support for governmental initiatives. India has kept its doors open for peace initiatives provided the violence was abjured.[24] India's strategic response includes neutralising collaborative networks of terrorists like gun runners, operators of funding channels, smugglars, organised crime syndicates etc. Intelligence driven capabilities were developed to degrade these networks, most of them having trans-national linkages. In line, Pakistan, being the primary exporter of terror to India, occupied a high priority. Political and diplomatic pressures were exerted to make it abandon use of terrorism as an instrument of its state policy. Political engagements and initiation of confidence building measures did help but not to the desired extent.

With the fast radicalisation of Afghanistan, Pakistan and Bangladesh on one hand and erosion in the will and capability of the governments in power there the overall security scenario in the region stands highly vitiated. Taliban's ground entrenchment recruitment of new cadres, battle preparedness and increase in drug linked financial resources are a cause of concern.[25] From this perspective, South Asian countries of Afghanistan, Pakistan, Bangladesh and India have a special import both academic and empirical; the first three where the virus multiplied most prolifically and the last where it struck most lethally. Largest number of Muslims have fought and died in the name of Jihad from this region in last quarter of a century. Together, this region has one third of the world's Muslim population and has over 200 Islamic extremist groups and Jihadi organisations of various brands and sizes. Most of the Islamic terrorists who struck in different parts of the world have had some link or the other with this region. All the three states where Islamic radicals received state or civil society support are politically unstable, burdened with no or weak democracies, traped in slow economic and social growth and seen as near failing states. More importantly, though theocratic Muslim majority states, they themselves are facing vicious sectarian terrorism.

Especially after 11 September, 2001 the situation in Bangladesh has fastly deteriorated than is normally understood. When Pakistan and Afghanistan came under pressure, a good number of terrorists, reportedly with Pak intelligence support, found Bangladesh as safe haven. Using Islamic card for political gains the Bangladeshi society stands highly radicalised – most local groups working on the franchise of Pak-Afghan terrorist outfits including Al – Qaeda. Because of its social and cultural homogeneity, there is a larger margin of safety in Bangladesh with regard to all the forms of terrorism prevailing there. The collective strength of terrorist groups like Hakat-ul-Jihad Islami, Harkat-ul-Ansar, Okaye Jote etc. now is estimated in several thousands. While India is the principal target, the anti-US and anti-West outbursts are to shrill to be ignored. On terrorist front, India is living in an unenviable neighbourhood. Islamic terrorism in India is essentially of an imported variety.

In recent months a more promising trend is the start of the reconciliation process with Afghanistan in the lead and Pakistan and some other countries offering due assistance for the purpose. The reconciliation process in Afghanistan provided an opportunity for the forces of Afghan insurgency, especially Taliban, battered by long war to compromise on the pre – conditions for peace, including renunciation of violence, dissociation of links with Al-Qaeda and acceptance of Afghanistan's new constitutional and political reality. For Afghanistan's majority population, the pashtun, who primarily constitute the insurgents, overcoming post-Taliban marginalisation in the country's security, political and economic structure should be an important incentive to make peace. There was a counter-insurgency campaign launched in Afghanistan, which besides going after Al-Qaeda and Taliban operatives includes a broad plan to try to improve governance in Afghanistan, fight corruption, train the Afghan Army, wean farmers off the cultivation of poppies, promote women's rights and protect local population centres.[26] With Al-Qaeda losing relevance in Afghan insurgency and its leader Osama bin Laden dead, the justification for military engagement of foreign forces in Afghanistan has significantly eroded.

Likewise the country Pakistan has achieved some successes in the war against terrorism, which is far from over. It needs to build upon these successes for its own sake and that of the region, and not because of any pressure from any extra-regional power. The irreparable cost of terrorism for Pakistan's security, economy, politics and social fabric, particularly the chilling fact of nearly 40,000 innocent civilians and security personnel becoming a victim of the terrorism spree, leaves the country with no option except to exhaust all possible opportunities to deal with terrorism and extremism. In Pakistan the recent gains could be reversed by the deteriorating relationship between the Pakistani and American governments, which threatens to curtail cooperation in counter-terrorism operations and increase Pakistani opposition to drone strikes.[27] Given Pakistan's exceptional geographic, ethnic and historical link with Afghanistan, it was but natural for the ensuing anarchy in Afghanistan to seriously impact Pakistan's fragile security, economic, political and social situation.

However, still the original Saudi-Pak expansion design of Wahabism that started the radicalisation of the Muslim world several decades earlier remains intact. At some stage the radical elements will be able to lay their hands on Pak nukes.[28] In addition, the stakes in the Af-Pak region are enormous: stopping a second attack on American soil like that on 9/11; the future security of Pakistan's nuclear arsenal; the fortune of the NATO in Afghanistan and the fate of the war on terror declared globally. The mountainous terrain of the Pak-Afghanistan borderland which gives a safe shelter to the Taliban guerillas apart, one great obstacle to the operations of NATO forces under the USA in Afghanistan is the betrayal of the Pak military and especially its intelligence. Marvin Weinbaum, a Congressman, said before a Congress session about this ambivalence and commented, 'Despite the Pak Government's ban on the Lashkar-e-Toiba Pakistan's ISI continues to consider the organisation an asset. The ISI is believed to share intelligence and provide protection to the LeT. The current leadership in Pakistan should recognise the dangers that LeT and other terror groups pose to the State. But any attempt to reign them in will be impossible without the military's full commitment.'[29] In Washington US Secretary of State, Hillary Clinton also said before a Congressional hearing that Pakistani Government was abdicating to the Taliban by allowing the extremists to impose Islamic laws in parts of the country and added that Islamabad lacked credibility to the inhabitants of those areas.

The situation is increasingly perilous, according to the top US military officers and diplomats.

In the circumstances, the success against Al-Qaeda does not guarantee that its militants will not take root again in Afghanistan, particularly as the United States turns security over to a shaky Afghan government. And a fast reduction of troops could allow the Taliban, which is stalled but not destroyed, to regain power it lost to the surge. In June 2011 a summit was also organised by Shanghai Cooperation Organisation (SCO) for a neutral Afghanistan and the member countries were of the opinion that no peace deal in Afghanistan will stick unless the era of outside interference by its neighbours comes to an end.[30] They held the view that the biggest challenge in Afghan is to end its 35 years of civil war and only talks among all the Afghan stake holders and parties including the Taliban, can do that. Thus, there is a long way to go for peace in Afghanistan.

There is now a broad consensus in the international community that direct actions to combat terrorism can not be postponed until its root causes are eliminated. Therefore, combating terrorism should proceed side by side with actions designed to prevent it. However, counter-terrorism by itself can become a problem. First, given the nature of the modern technology of using violence against terrorists and the closely-knit character of modern economies, the collateral damage caused can only be really staggering. Every effort should, therefore, be made to minimise, if not avert, it. Besides, international arrangements should be put in place to pay due compensation to non-combatant nations and individuals. Second, counter-terrorism creates vested interests in the perpetration of terrorism, particularly when it serves domestic political purpose. Finally, it is very difficult to take effective counter-terrorist measures in the polarised societies of South Asia. There are formidable obstacles to revamping the law and order machinery in a divided society. In these conditions, dealing with the root causes of terrorism may become the pre-condition for ensuring the effectiveness of counter-terrorist measures. Economically developed, politically stable and conflict-free South Asia is conducive not only for the members of the region but can be an asset for the international community and sure guarantee for international peace and security.

References

1. Sugata Bose, Ayesha Jalal, *Modern South Asia-History, Culture, Political Economy* (New Delhi: Oxford University Press, 2004), pp. 3-4.
2. Verghese Koithara, *Society, State and Security: The Indian Experience* (New Delhi: Sage Publications, 1999), pp. 180-181.
3. Geoffrey Barraclough, *Turning Points in World History* (U.K. : Thames and Hudson, 1977), p. 80.
4. D.N. Mallik, *Post-war International Politics – A Quadripartite Survey*, (Muzaffarpur : Veena Mandir Publishers, 1973), pp. 594-95.
5. Sugata Bose, Ayesha Jalal, *Modern South Asia – History, Culture, Political Economy*, p. 4.
6. *The Hindustan Times*, 4 August, 1988.
7. Tahir Amin, *Ethno-National Movements of Pakistan: Domestic and International Factors* (Islamabad: Institute of Policy Studies, 1988).
8. Eric Gonsalves and Nancy Jetly (eds.), *The Dynamics of South Asia Regional Cooperation and SAARC* (New Delhi: Sage Publications, 1999), p. 11.
9. Shelton U. Kodikara (ed.), *External Compulsions of South Asian Politics* (New Delhi: Sage Publications,1993), pp. 24-25.
10. Rashed Uz Zaman, *WMD Terrorism in South Asia: Trends and Implications* (Dhaka: University of Bangladesh), p. 5.
11. Brahma Chellaney, 'Fighting Terrorism in South Asia: The Lessons of History', *International Security* (2002), p. 95.
12. *The Washington Post*, 22 September, 1988.
13. Kshitij Prabha, "Terrorism Challenges Secular Fabric of South Asia', in Mahavir Singh (ed.), *International Terrorism and Religious Extremism– Challenges to Central and South Asia* (New Delhi: Anamica Publishers, 2004), pp. 263-64.
14. D.D. Basu, *Constitution of India* (Delhi: Printice-Hall India, 1976), as quoted in *Ibid.*, p. 264.
15. *Ibid.*, p. 25.
16. Rajkumar Singh, *Contemporary India with Controversial Neighbours* (New Delhi: Gyan Publishing House, 2011), p. 128.
17. Dr. Ishtiaq Ahmad, *Terrorism in South Asia: Retrospect and Prospect*, 15 July, 2011.
18. S.D. Muni, 'The United States and South Asia: The Strategic Dimension', in Shelton U. Kodikara (ed.), *External Compulsions of South Asian Politics* (New Delhi: Sage Publications, 1993), pp. 68-69.
19. Manvendra Singh, 'Threshold of Patience', *The Hindustan Times*, 15 January, 2002.

20. S.D. Muni, 'Terrorism, 'Tectonic Plates' and Strategic Equations in Asia,' in Mahavir Singh (ed.), *International Terrorism and Religious Extremism – Challenges to Central and South Asia*, pp. 27-28.
21. Sudhanshu Tripathi, 'Obama's New Af-Pak Policy: Ominous Road Ahead', *South Asia Politics*, Vol. 8, No. 10, February 2010 (New Delhi : 2010), p. 6.
22. Sukumar Pathak, 'Obstacles to Afghan War on Terror – Pak's Hesitancy and Karzai's Apostasy,' in *Ibid.*, Vol. 9, No. 10, February 2011 (New Delhi : 2011), pp. 29-30.
23. Vikram Sood, 'Policy Sans Frontiers', *The Hindustan Times*, 5 December 2011.
24. Ajit Doval, *'Islamic Terrorism in South Asia and India's Strategic Response* (Oxford University Press, 2007), pp. 1-5.
25. *Ibid.*
26. Mark Landler and Helene Cooper, 'Al-Qaeda Woes Fuel Talk of Speeding Afghan Pullback, *The Hindu*, 20 June, 2011.
27. *Ibid.*
28. Vinod Saighal, 'USA – PAK Potentially More Menacing Than AF – PAK', *South Asia Politics*, Vol. 9, No. 1, May 2010 (New Delhi: 2010), p. 12.
29. Sukumar Pathak, 'Obstacles to Afghan War on Terror : Pak Hesitancy and Karzai's Apostasy', in *South Asia Politics*, p. 29.
30. Jonathan Steele, 'The Taliban's Wish List', *The Hindu*, 22 June, 2011.

2

Terrorism: Formation, Forms and Features

South Asia has been the major target areas of terrorism, insurgencies and separatist movements in comparison with other parts of Asia. Afghanistan, Pakistan, India and Bangladesh are facing serious terrorist threat. In South Asia, the number of fatal casualties in terrorist attacks is the highest in the world; internecine ethnic, communal and separatist conflicts pose a serious threat to stability and inter – state relations in this region. This part of the globe, in particular, witnessing multiple conflicts in which ideological, ethnic, communal and political issues are intertwined. Terrorism operates in this region under the façade of different terminologies and varies in its nature. It ranges from the practice of internal colonialism as manifested by contrast regional disparity as in Balochistan, Pakistan, to demand for political independence by the Sri Lankan Tamils in the north-east of Sri Lanka; and brutal and massive human rights violations ranging from social discrimination and disenfranchisement as in southern Bhutan to economic alienation manifested in naxalite movements in Andhra Pradesh, Chhattisgarh, Orissa, Bihar etc. The poor side of the river is that these South Asian countries have also been clearly involved in encouraging, hosting and aiding terrorists from neighbouring countries. The ULFA's presence in Bhutan, insurgents in Bangladesh and the well known support extended by Pakistan to terrorist activities in Jammu and Kashmir are blatant manifestation of cross – border abetment of terrorism. The worst part is that the increasing coordination of the terrorists, insurgents and radical groups with their counterparts in neighbouring countries has added a critical dimension to the entire management of militancy or terrorism in South Asia. It is said that violence-social, political or physical, perpetrated by the state or the agents of the state against other states or its own peoples is the womb of terrorism, humiliation its cradle and continued revenge by the state, the mother's milk and nourishment for terrorism. There is a desperate need to study and understand the deep-rooted causes that divide groups of people. The causes of these conflicts and the form they take, whether it be terrorism or otherwise, must be studied and understood in a scientific and objective manner.

Updating Terror Perceptions

The famous English poet John Milton once wrote 'The mind is its own place, it can make heaven of hell and hell of heaven'. The term 'Terrorism' has recently been defined by Paul J. Smith, a security expert at the Asia- Pacific Center for Security Studies, as a form of psychological warfare that is used to create extensive fear through the use of extensive force against non-combatant civilian military targets. It thrives in a milieu characterised by some festering and unresolved issue in an atmosphere of financial crisis and in situation where unlawful trade in narcotics and small arms.[1] The possibility of proliferation of Weapons of Mass Destruction (WMD) through the innovation of modern technology is more real today than it has ever been in human history. Weapons of Mass Destruction terrorism involves the most modern and the most extreme form of random violence. Nuclear, chemical and biological weapons are inherently terrifying; in most cases of their being used, the fear they would cause would dwarf the injury and death. Its dreadful nature creates its own dangers; of victims panic and try to flee, they spread contamination and disease still further. The effects of these weapons are also inherently random. The radius of injury depends on conditions that are impossible to control or predict with certainty.[2] The use of these innovations for terrorist activities is limited only by the imagination of the terrorist. Every one is a potential target and this creates a climate of fear and suspicion within a society.

Different scholars have tried to come to terms with terrorism depending upon their ideological moorings. Today terrorism is the new form of warfare then it is evident that politics for some states has become an offshoot of this deadly virus and has acquired its own autonomy.[3] For example, Yonah Alexander links terrorism with national security. To him, 'terrorism is the use or threat of violence against random or civilian threats in order to intimidate or create generalised pervasive fear for the purpose of achieving political goals'. But Paul Wilkinson makes a difference between political terrorism and other forms of violence. He defined political violence as "the systematic use of murder and destruction, and the threat of murder and destruction in order to terrorise individuals, groups, communities or governments into conceding to the terrorists' political demands".[4] While the United States' Department of State defined it as a, "pre-meditated, politically motivated violence penetrated against non-combatant targets by sub-national groups or clandestine State Agents, usually intended to influence an audience." In the state of terrorism, nation found itself in a condition in which it is very difficult to provide security and the environment of development to its citizens in terrorist affected areas. In so many cases terrorists also run their parallel government in specific part of territory, in this situation governments face so many challenges for safeguarding territorial integrity and preserving sovereignty of the nation state.

On the other hand, terrorism has been analysed by several social science disciplines, intelligence agencies, militaries, law enforcement agencies, IGOs and NGOs and legislatives and judicial bodies. They all use different type of framework, institutional perspectives, requirements and dimensions. According to them terrorism seems to possess four key elements – I. cause (generally political), II. non-state entities with group dynamics, III. chosen place and IV. indiscriminate use of violence.[5] When all these four key elements combine together they create an environment of psychological fear and terror, all these combined are known as terrorism.

In a nutshell, despite lack of consensus on what terrorism actually encompasses, there are, however, certain features common to all forms of terrorism. For instance, terrorism, in all forms, is aimed to generate fear, panic and terror in the minds of the general public. It may be politically motivated or may emerge because of obscure ideologies or beliefs, the acts of terror may be perpetrated for political ends or for changing the cultural norms or religious ethos of a targeted country or a segment of population. Further, terrorism, unlike ordinary violence, employs inordinate lethal force against civilian targets to erode the political will of the targeted country, undermine the morale of the people, spread despondency and panic through catastrophic terrorist attacks.[6] Moreover, terrorism is arbitrary and unpredictable as far as its effects are concerned. And it does not recognise any rules and conventions of war and geographical limitations.

Thus, a 'terrorist' is a person who indulges in criminal acts with manifestly political motive without exhausting legitimate remedies at his disposal for the redressal of his grievances. His acts may be organised or unorganised, sporadic or widespread, commanding public support or hatred. The decisive element is that he indulges in criminal acts without invoking legitimate remedies for his alleged grievance or suffering.[7] The terrorist hypothesis is that the system itself suicides in response to the multiple challenges of death and suicide. Neither the system, nor power, themselves escape symbolic obligation and in this trap resides the only chance of their demise (catastrophe). In this vertiginous cycle of the impossible exchange of death, the terrorist death is an infinitesimal point that provokes a gigantic aspiration, void and convection. Around this minute point, the whole system of the real and power gains in density, freezes, compresses, and sinks in its own super – efficacy. The tactics of terrorism are to provoke an excess of reality and to make the system collapse under the weight of this excess. It indicates that terrorist actions are both the magnifying mirror of the system's violence and the model of a symbolic violence that it can not access.[8] By using violence and terror, terrorists disturb communal harmony in society, create fear and suspicion between communities. That is why they pose and direct threat to maintaining domestic peace.

In its latest manifestations, terrorism is violence for a cause and terrorists always want the world to know about their existence, their causes and the power they wield.[9] From the ongoing discussions the theories of terrorism have been derived as the following:

(i) Terrorists are not born but created by particular sociological, economic and political conditioning processes.

(ii) Terrorism is not based on reason and is nothing but a series of senseless and mindless actions to create fear.

(iii) It is deliberate and systematic assault on civilians to inspire fear for political ends.

(iv) It is a method whereby an organised group or party seeks to achieve its avowed aims, chiefly through the systematic use of violence.

(v) It is a weapon of the weak employed against powerful opponent not with the aim to defeat but as an attempt to show itself as all powerful and a good force with a view to change the balance of power.[10]

To conclude terrorism is not an act, but, it is a thinking in which some people think that political objectives could be achieved by illegitimate use of violence. Its motivations are also changing. A new breeds of terrorist including ad hoc groups motivated by religious convictions or revenge, right-wing extremists and apocalyptic and millenarian cults, appear more likely than terrorist of the past to commit acts of extreme violence. Religious groups are becoming more common and are more violent than secular groups.

Terrorism: Analysed and Explained

Initial Phase

Basically, the concept of 'Terrorism' is as old as the civilization of mankind itself and has existed in all ages in some form or other which might be known anarchists, revolutionaries, fundamentalist or dissents against the established authority or even ruling tyrants having no tolerance or dissent. However, terrorism was not as widespread phenomenon as it is today in contemporary political system of the world. Terrorism has, in fact, become a global phenomenon with increasing and rather well identifiable links between different terrorist group and organisation. They use each other's areas for recruitment and training, exchange of illegal weapons, engage in joint planning and ventures and also provide administrative and other logistic support. This type of terrorist activities show a new dimension due to circumstances characterised by the advancement of science, technology and diverse social, economic, political and historical reasons conditioning it. It will remain a menace as long as there are people who are driven by fanaticism, paranoia and extremism. So long as there exists in the world poverty, strife, injustice and oppression, conditions will exist which terrorists can turn to their advantage.

The term terrorism comes from the French word terrorisme, which is based on the Latin verb terrere (to cause to tremble). It dates back to 1795 when it was used to describe the actions of the Jacobin Club in their rule of post-Revolutionary France, the so-called 'Reign of Terror'. Jacobins are rumoured to have coined the term 'terrorists' to refer to themselves. Terrorism refers to a strategy of using violence, social threats, coordinated attacks, in order to generate fear, cause disruption, and ultimately, brings about compliance with specified political, religious, or ideological demands. Traditionally, terrorism is a highly organised enterprise that fits into a clear political strategy. It has been filling the news for most of our lives and will doubtless go on demanding the attention of our children and grand-children as well.[11] What is new is how it achieves its goals these days.

Until today the world under UN has failed to come to an agreement about what is an acceptable definition for terrorism. It is still under debate despite attempts made by many experts. The effort to approach terrorism from a definitional perspective has thus become a never – ending effort. 'Terrorism is a term used to describe the method or the theory behind the method whereby an organised group or party seeks to achieve its avowed aims chiefly through the systematic use of violence. Terroristic acts are directed against persons who as individuals, agents or representatives of authority interfere with the consummation of the objectives of such a group.[12] In the sense it differs in several important aspects from such phenomena as mob violence, mass insurrection and governmental terror. Terror practised by a government in office appears as law enforcement and is directed against the opposition, while terrorism in its proper sense implies upon defiance of law and is the means whereby an opposition aims to demoralise a governmental authority, to undermine its power and to initiate a revolution or counter-revolution.[13]

Terrorism as a revolutionary technique was for many years an accepted tenet of anarchism. The writings of Bakunin with their emphasis upon violence as a method of achieving social change were the inspiration, if not the actual source of this doctrine. The idea of the propaganda of the deed was developed in the years following Bakunin's death by Kropotkin, Brousse and others, who stressed the failure of generally accepted methods and the educative and publicity value of acts of terrorism. This theory was translated into action principally in the last two decades of the nineteenth century. It was almost always part of the strategy of an armed national liberation movement, and in the colonial context it usually worked in the end. The reason terrorism worked so well in anti-colonial struggles was that you did not have to defeat the imperial powers' superior military forces in order to win. They were a long way from home and there was a limit to how many lives and how much money the imperial government would spend to hang into its possessions. But the early, easy successes of terror tactics in the anti-imperial context left everybody with a greatly inflated notion of what the technique could achieve against an established national government with local roots.

With its initial success in several spheres, the concept of terrorism also gained other valuable characters such as mass realisation and publicity. Even today terrorism as a method is always characterised by the fact that it seeks to arouse not only the ringing government or the nation in control but also the mass of the people to a realisation that constituted authority is no longer safely intrenched and unchallenged. The publicity of the terroristic act is a cardinal point in the strategy of terrorism. If terror fails to elicit a wide response in circles outside of those at whom it is directly aimed, it is futile as a weapon in a social conflict. In this phase and type of terrorism violence and death are not intended to produce revenue or to terrorise the persons attacked but to cause society or government to take notice of the imminence of large scale struggles. The terroristic act committed in secrecy by one person or several is conceived as the advance notice of what may be expected from mass action.

The fullest expression of the theory and practice of this terrorism is to be found in the functioning of the famous Russian revolutionary organisation Narodnaya Volya, formed in 1879. In the same year it made an unsuccessful attempt to shoot the Czar and in the following year a revolutionary workman, Khalturin, succeeded in dynamiting the Czar's dinning room at the Winter Palace, where the royal family was to entertain a large official assemblage. But in 1881 Alexander II was killed by a bomb. Such an effective start encouraged the Narodnaya Volya and its activity spread despite the efforts of the government to exterminate the organisation at all costs. The newly formed Party explained its method of action in paragraph 2, section D, of its programme, which defined destructive and terroristic activity as follows: 'Terroristic activity, consisting in destroying the most harmful person in government, in defending the party against espionage, in punishing the perpetrators of the notable cases of violence and arbitrariness on the part of the government and the administration, aims to undermine the prestige of the government's power, to demonstrate steadily the possibility of struggle against the government, to arouse in this manner the revolutionary spirit of the people and their confidence in the success of the cause, and finally, to give shape and direction to the forces fit and trained to carry on the fight.'[14]

Apart from this terroristic commitment, the organisation was crystal clear in matters of motivation and end. The motivation of the party was frequently stated in paragraph 1, section V, of the same programme which reads, 'By this overturn, in the first place, the development of the people will be to proceed independently and in line with its disposition, and, in the second place, many purely socialist principles common to us and the people will gain recognition and be supported in our Russian life. It also stressed that the use of terror was not an end in itself but only a means to effect the transference of power from the government to the people; that the party proposed to seize and retain power only until a form of popular government could be determined upon by a Constituent Assembly; and that it would not decree revolutionary reforms and impose its desires upon the people but on the contrary would aid the latter to express its own will, to which the party would submit. In later years, although it was revived in 1901 when the Socialist Revolutionary Party came into existence and in 1917, upon the cessation of the temporary political alliance of the Socialist Revolutionary party with the Bolsheviks, it however, never attained real success as a method of revolution.

The Present Devastating Phase

Current day terrorism has many faces. Its objectives are multifaceted and operations multi-pronged. The entire world is its stage, which has made it a prime concern for governments and societies around the world. No society is safe from its impact. It ranges from individuals to groups to international networks and thus poses a challenge to internal intelligence system of nation states round the world.[15] In the opinion of some analysts, it is indeed a world war, not the third one, but the fourth and the truly world war. The first two world wars were traditional wars, were classical wars. The first ended European supremacy and the colonial era. The Second ended Nazism. The third, which did not happen, as a dissuasive cold war, ended communism. From one war to the other, one went further each time toward a unique world order. But the fourth world war is elsewhere. It is that which haunts every global order and every hegemonic domination. Terrorism, like virus, is everywhere. Immersed globally, terrorism, like the shadow of any system of domination is ready everywhere to emerge as a double agent. There is no boundary to define it; it is in the very core of this culture that fights it.

The root cause of present devastating terrorism is religious fundamentalism. Every religion comes into existence in given society with its values, its ethos, customs and traditions. A religion tries to reform a society by providing certain ideals and values. But the human behaviour is never determined simply by the religion one follows. It is determined by several factors – personal or group interest and inspiration, social mores and traditions and tribal or national expectation.[16] Thus understanding religion varies according to tribal, national and ethnic considerations and one always finds a tension between the theological and the sociological. This tension could be creative or destructive, depending on the situation or approach of the people concerned. In fact any religion, particulary those that have existed over long periods of time and continue to be practised – speak to us in many voices. Their multivocality, which expresses the diversity of historical experience, allows for a degree of internal and external critique. Extremism in any religion propagates intolerance and hatred for other communities and that generally leads to violence that may take form of terrorism. Religious extremism driven by political motives invariably leads to terrorism, as the aim of the extremist groups is to capture or retain power. A fundamentalist sect or group may also want to isolate other sects or religious factions from national mainstream so that they are unable to compete with it politically or gain equal status.

The fundamentalists look upon scriptures as the word of God. Fundamentalist traits have uniformally appeared in all the major religions of the world in recent years. In the USA, there are the Operation Rescue Protesters. In Israel, there is the Gush Emunium, who claim that God has given the Land of Israel, with precise boundaries, to his children. In Sri Lanka, there are militant Buddhists. However, it is Islamic fundamentalism which has the broadest global sweep, stretching from the Mediterranean through the Balkans, the Black Sea, across the Caucasus and Southern Russia, through Western China enveloping Pakistan and Bangladesh, affecting India moving on to Southern Thailand, Malaysia, Indonesia and Philippines. It is, in fact the best organised fundamentalist force with a worldwide network.[17] However, of an entirely different variety, it emanates from extreme rigidity of beliefs and disdain for other religions though it is against the true tenets of Islam.

Originally, the term Islam means submission to God, and as such, designates a religion, preached by the Prophet Muhammad at the beginning of the seventh century A.D. It believes that in obedience of God, lies peace, prosperity, happiness and the salvation of man. According to Islam, the other prophets who preceded Muhammad were all true prophets, and Islam is nothing but a confirmation of the true faith taught by previous religions and teachers. Religion is certainly a vital force in every society and Muhammad made Islam a permanent force vitally by giving it a natural and rational basis.[18] It spread from Arabia to different countries of Asia, Africa and Europe. Thus, Islam could embrace diverse social and ethnic countries and it emerged as a universal religion from the very beginning.

The Quran is the scripture of Islam and the authentic source of its teachings. Its emphasis on the need for tolerance of diversity and the sanctity of life is worth nothing. God in the Quran requires the believers to show tolerance and respect to those who differ in their ways. It says: 'To every people we have appointed a way of worship, which they have followed. So let them not wrangle with you over the matter'.[19] It emphasised the universal concept of religion such as the unity of God and the unity of human race. As regards the sanctity of human life, the Quran says : 'Anyone who kills a human being if not in retaliation for a murder, nor for causing corruption in the land – must be accounted to have killed all mankind, and who ever saves a life it will be as if he had saved the life of all mankind'.[20] Islam's concept of the unity of man had very deep and far-reaching effects on the social, political, economic and moral way of life of the Muslims.

Islam started as a great revolutionary movement based on equality, human dignity and justice. These ideals were partly acceptable to the tribal society of Mecca. Equality and human dignity was acceptable in a limited way within tribal social boundaries. Members of a tribe could be accepted as equals, but not those of other tribes. Members of other tribes could be accepted only as a client, not as an equals. Radical Islam is what Prophet Muhammad is believed to have given to the citizens of Medina after his light from Mecca. He outlined an ideology, couched in religious terms, from which an escape was next to impossible. The ideology offered no accommodation except on its terms, ruled out all compromises, and demanded an allegiance any violation of which was declared blasphemous, inviting instantaneous annihilation.[21] As radical Islam spread far and wide beyond Mecca and Medina, often in the shadow of the sword, it did encounter powerful ideas which sometimes mellowed it and some times led to the emergence of new sprouts. In the circumstances, the concept of universal brotherhood and inter-tribal equality created social tension throughout the Islamic history. Even within Arab society these became explosive after the death of the prophet. By the time the prophet died, different tribes of Arabia had embraced Islam.

Thus the ideas of radical Islam are in contrast to the message of Quran that the mystery of divine mercy is also being experienced in other traditions. Prophet Muhammad accorded the world-view and encouraged the Muslims to approach non-Muslims with respect and know how the mystery of God found expression in older traditions. With their internationalist attitude and travelling to foreign countries either in connection with their overseas and overland trade or in search of knowledge, the Muslims became the pioneers in starting inter-religious dialogue. In fact, the desire on their part to understand what other cultures might have to offer enriched their cultural heritage. However, the lofty ideals of Islam received a setback when the tribe of Quraysh claimed the Caliphate quoting a 'hadith and superiority over other tribes.'

Islamic society soon transformed into a feudal society. The reasons for embracing a religion could be quite varied. Some embrace it collectively along with other members of the caste or tribe or nation; some embrace it for political or economic advantages; and some after studying the religion. In its historical march to its present expanse, Islâm has destroyed empires, countries, religions, cultures and people. In the process it even opposed the Sufi Islam which toned down the hard features of the original and introduced new concepts. Sufi Islam conditioned the Islamic mindset to acceptance of co-existence with other cultures and religions. Islamic extremism is invariably been politically driven and seldom a purely religious movement. It has no sanction either in Quran or in the practices of the holy Prophet of Islam. Distorted interpretation of various historical events by some Islamic clerics led to violence against non-Muslims in the past. The creed of tolerance, compassion, charity and civilised behaviour preached and practised by Prophet Muhammad were forgotten soon after his departure from the scene. The stern commands in the holy Quran pertained to particular situations such as murderous attacks on Muhammad and his followers by the pagan tribesman. These were later misinterpreted or used by vested interests to wage wars against political opponents. The terrible massacre of Karbala, in a battle for political supremacy and power illustrated for ruthlessness of the tribal customs to achieve political ends.

In course of its spread far and wide Islam came to India with Arab invasions, Sultan Mahmud, of Ghazni, in particular. Initially the Islam that settled down in India was not so radical. Its core got impacted by Hindu philosophy, bhakti movements which provided Islam a broad based co-existence with all religions of India.

For over 300 years, Islam remained peacefully as a religion and took its place among the many religions of India without trouble or conflict. Before Islam, Jainism and Buddhism had been absorbed by Hinduism. Also there were Christianity and the Hebrew religion which had reached India probably during the first century after Christ, had found a place in the country. Historically, Hindu society had shown a peculiar ability to absorb and culturally assimilate groups which entered its fold from outside, even with military power.[22] But Islam was the first exception. Islamic groups had much greater cultural self-confidence, and clearer self-recognition in terms of doctrines and observances. This prevented an absorption into Hindu society in the treacherously insidious way that had been the common fate of earlier intruders. The new approach produced powerful psychological reactions among the people and filled them with bitterness. There was no objection to a new religion but there was a strong objection to anything which forcibly interfered with and upset their way of life.

As a result of the industrial revolution more or less world over, large sections of the population unigratedfrom their original surroundings, resulting in a deep sense of dislocation and alienation. At the same time it fails to provide an alternative set of values and along with it, a sense of belonging to these people. To offset this deficiency they try to reclaim and assert their traditional identities more stridently. The alienation generated in the process of modernisation provided the material for the growth of orthodox religious forms.[23] It is said that this modern phenomenon of terrorist movement is born out of frustration and despair. Despair caused by social marginalisation, economic decline and political defeat. Leon Trotsky once described the two emotions central to terrorism as being despair and vengeance. The betrayed hopes one talks of, are as we are aware, the hopes of diverse communities to obtain their fair share of the cake.[24] In nutshell, the Islamic fundamentalism or pristine puritan Islam had lost its original dynamism and failed to meet the challenges of the time.

The continuous enjoyment of political power for over 1,000 years had given the Muslims a self-confidence which was based on a faith in Islam, which they believed would never let them down. But as a result of the renaissance in Europe, with the age of reason, the invention of gun powder, the geographical explorations, the industrial revolution and the colonial expansion of the European powers, Islamic glory became a thing of the past. The mainstream of the intellectual and creative section of the society fell into the grip of traditionalists who valued piety more than progress. Islamic decline became more apparent from the eighteenth century, when the French Revolution gave new concepts of democracy and nationalism to Europe and the Muslims were left far behind in every sector of human life. With them declined a civilization which had consistently flourished in the major areas of three continents, Asia, Europe and Africa. Even their political authority was seriously challenged by the British in India, the Dutch in Indonesia, the French in Western Africa and the Russian in Central Asia.[25] The question before Islam was not how to find few channels for its expansion, not even to retain the superiority they had enjoyed, but to survive and escape total annihilation and humiliation.

In the circumstances fundamentalist revival sought to strip modern, innovative and foreign influence from the Islamic faith. Earlier when Muslims were unable to meet the challenge posed by Western countries, the situation created fundamental doubts among the educated Muslims in Islamic values and ideas, and they were inclined more and more towards an appreciation of Western culture and outlook. The matter became much worse when not only the Westerners but also the Western-educated Muslims began to think the same way. Hence, Islam came under fire both from within and without. But this does not mean that the Muslims did not resist the European onslaught. They fought every battle in India, including the one in 1857. Apart from this several movements were started to revise the tenets of Islam, each in their own way.

The quest for such an identity can be identified with the efforts of Syed Ahmed Khan and Amir Ali, for calling upon Muslims to strengthen the bonds of community. These efforts were akin to that of Shah Waliullah who urged the glorification of Islam in the wake of the disintegration of the empire under Aurangzeb. Shah Waliullah (1703-62) who was celebrated in history as a Muslim reformer or a hardliner was of the view that the essence of the scriptures i.e. Quran, Sunnah and Hadith could not be diluted and the purpose of Islam must remain synchronous with the Prophet's vision. Two generations later, Waliullah's followers founded the Deoband seminary of theology. The seminary was not just a Madrassah for religious teachings. Its instructions were inspired by one larger purpose of avenging the 1857 defeat by the British of the Muslim Empire.[26] The Indian Muslims under the impact of the Wahabi movement preached the slogan, 'Back to the Koran, and sought to restore *Jihad* (holy war) for an Islamic ideal state.

There had been the movements of the Mujahideen, dedicated to the establishment of an ideal Muslim state in the North-West Frontier. Thus Islam became politically useful after the revolt of 1857 as aptly remarked by Abbas Rashid that the elite managed to foster a degree of general Muslim identification with issues like lack of education, discrimination in employment, inadequate political representation etc. He maintained that while their use of Islam may have been subjectively opportunistic, it was nevertheless effective given the context.[27] Later on, of course, the British policy of divide and rule widened the cleavages of Hindu-Muslim differences, encouraged the Muslim Leaguers and used them to counter the Congress to strengthen their rule.

However, within the Muslim community, in contrast to the westernised elite, the orthodox religious leaders or traditionalists who struggled to attain a position of leadership, regarded the credentials of the former to lead the Muslim Ulama with contempt. They considered the Muslim League a bunch of loyalist toadies and accused them of cooperating with the Satans of Europe against the Islamist Caliphate and Pan-Islamism. However, the foremost of the causes that ultimately led the Muslims to take to the gun was the betrayal by the imperialist powers of the West, to the Arabs after the first World War (1914-18). As a result of this French domination was established over Syria and Lebanon while Palestine was excluded from all obligations to the Arabs. In contrast to Palestine, the Jewish immigrants from the Eastern European countries and Russia were out of harmony with the local environment but went on turning it into their homeland on European pattern and at the cost of Arabs.[28] Further the creation of Israel and its recognition by the United Nations Organisation (UNO) shook the confidence of the Islamic world in this international organisation.

In post-World War II phase radical Islam's opposition to the West in general and the USA in particular continued unabated. No doubt the West has given the world science and technology and also introduced the concept of democracy and human rights. But it has also rubbished India, China and the Muslim world. They have imposed on these civilizations. Missionaries have been sent with foreign funds to subvert the religion and culture of those people. Muslims resent it more because they have recent memories of their power. Many Muslim countries were occupied. Even after independence their government were either toppled or turned into puppets. Their oil wealth still goes to enrich the West. Their oil revenues are diverted to arms purchases. Neighbouring countries are encouraged and armed to fight each other.[29] The recent militant image of Islam has come basically from the use of religion to generate political consciousness in the Middle East where external involvement, on account of oil and Israel, has not permitted democracy to take root. The fear of confrontationist Islam became a burning issue in the West with the rise to power of militant Islam in Iran and the resilience it has displayed in several countries including Egypt, Algeria, Sudan, Pakistan, Libya, Lebanon and Afghanistan.[30]

The end of second world war witnessed the beginning of cold war between the two superpowers of world politics – the USA and USSR. Initially the USSR was a territorial power against the nuclear dominance of the United States. At the height of Cold War for supremacy in world politics the USA blocked the USSR in Europe through the North Atlantic Treaty Organisation (NATO), and both the USSR and China in East Asia through alliances with Japan, South Korea and Taiwan. In early years with a view to pursue its policy of containing communism, it placed higher priorities on West Asia, where a Soviet military threat was perceived, and to South-East Asia where the Chinese were suspected of long-term expansionist ambitions. In response the USSR contained the vision of changing the world in direction of a particular ideology.[31] However, they both emerged comfortably dominant in its respective sphere.

World Context of South Asian Terrorism

At the close of the seventies the overall situation in world politics went against the US interest, especially after the fall of Shah in January 1979 followed by the Soviet intervention in December that year. The collapse of Shah's regime in Iran and the emergence of Khomeini in his place, marked a new revival of Islamic tenets. Further it caused a new surge of revivalism in Pakistan which was manifest in Bhutto's latter years and was culminated in General Zia's programmes of Islamic reforms. The new rising tendency, at least in general, was the result of the failure of the secular ideologies. The increasing hegemony of the two world political and economic systems as represented by the military, technological and economic domination of the United States and the former Soviet Union had left little room for the autonomy of the liberal/nationalist or Marxist/nationalist movements. They made the course of development a difficult one in Muslim countries.[32] In addition the exodus of vast numbers of traditional Muslim peasants to the cities in search of identity alongside a demographic revolution whereby those below the age of 20 make up 50 per cent of the population, have combine to create conditions ripe for revolution. The secular ideologies of progress, however, could not compensate these transient, alienated and exploited segments of population for the decomposition of traditional religious ontological securities and social identity.[33] The Western academia and media, particularly after the Iranian Revolution of 1979, had developed the segments to demonise Islam as a faith, and to depict Muslim societies, with varying degree of candour and crudity. In real politic terms the West has always been selective in its dealings with Islam. It has opposed Islamism in Egypt, Algeria and Saudi Arabia but has been supportive of it in Chechnya, Bosnia and Kashmir.[34] Singlling out Islam as a fundamentalist religion is clearly not a practical, long term proposition when it is the second largest religion in the world.

Thus, since 1979 the Soviet-Afghan war played a large role in reshaping ethnic identities towards larger identities. It may, however, be said that this process did not start suddenly in 1979; its roots are to be found in the creeping politicisation of Afghan society. But the process was precipitated by the state policy and external factors mainly resulting from confrontation with the USSR as well as from both Pakistan and Iranian policies towards Afghanistan. In post-intervention period Pakistan adopted its so called 'Islamic strategy'. By labelling the Afghan intervention as Islamic cause, Pakistan managed to receive financial support from Saudi Arabia and various other Muslim countries. Islamabad thought it to be an easy option as a means of promoting its strategic goals in the region, particularly in Afghanistan and India. Pakistan called it Jihad obviously the intension was to mobilise and motivate the Pakistani army and irregular armed forces of all kinds in the name of Islam.[35] The Islamic strategy got support from the United States and China merely because it was directed against the Soviet Union, and they are now reaping its bitter consequences as now they are finding difficult to contain this Frankenstein monster. Viewed in cold war perspectives the events in Afghanistan was an alarm for the countries of the region as a whole.

In fact the rivalry between America and Russia for world hegemony gave birth to the American Muslim coalition to liberate Afghanistan from the communist rule. In the light of the assessment of US policies in and around this part was seen as the culmination of a process of Soviet involvement which began almost

30 years ago, as a reaction, once again, to the US alliance with Pakistan and Iran. Like the every confrontation of the cold war period American policy-makers had defined the crisis in question as a 'test case' of American will and had responded accordingly. Washington concluded that a grave threat to peace existed and that Soviet action had given rise to the most fundamental question pertaining to international stability. At the juncture US used Islamic fundamentalism to counter Soviet communism. To fight Soviet – style atheism, US policy-makers did not hesitate to use religion for political ends – the Catholic Church in Central America and Islam in Afghanistan. In other words, Islam was employed to unite the Muslim world and spur the spirit of Jihad against the Soviet intervention in Afghanistan. The US-led military campaign in Afghanistan was fuelled by succeeding American administration. The Reagan Doctrine of arming anti-communist freedom fighters in places such as Afghanistan, Angola, Combodia and Nicaragua sanctified the doctrine of low-intensity conflict.[36] This apart, the United States of America was also largely responsible for blocking peaceful transition of power in post-Soviet phase in Afghanistan.

The outbreak of war between the USSR and the Afghans helped the formation of the pattern of supra-ethnic alliance in the name of Islam, uniting Uzbeks and Tajiks against Russia. The alliance was led by the Jama't-i-Islami. In 1981, a Pan-Turkic Islamic Movement was started by Azad Beg's party with Pakistan's support. In the same year he founded in Peshawar with the help of Pakistan government, the Islamic Union of the Northern Provinces of Afghanistan. Its aim was first to unite all the Turkic people of Turk origin in Afghanistan and then use it against both the Soviets and the Kabul regime. Although having initial success the organisation failed because the warlords, in general, did not support Azad Beg. Upon his failure, the Pakistani Inter State Intelligence (ISI) selected the Talibans studying in Pakistani madrassas, gave them military training and sent them across the border into Afghanistan. The Pakistani ISI service was eager to provide a framework to channel Turkic nationalism against Soviet Russia at the instance of USA. The Soviet military intervention in 1979 was depicted as 'Islam in danger'. In the circumstances the interest of the US and Pakistan converged as the former wanted to wage proxy war with Soviet Union via Pakistan. The US arms started flowing into the hands of the Mujahideens. Afghan conflict has militarised Pakistan society.

Terrorism in South Asia is a cocktail of Afghan Mujahideen, Pakistani ISI, Taliban and Al-Qaeda led by Osama bin Laden. They all fought jointly against the Soviet army in Afghanistan and later after Russian withdrawal turned their face to the Indian State of Jammu and Kashmir. Afghan Mujahideens are Afghani refugees who sought sanctuary in Pakistan from Soviet air raids and participated actively in the holy war against the Soviets in Afghanistan. Very soon some foreign aid began coming in officially and more was being surreptitiously pumped in by Saudi Arabia and the CIA agents into the hands of so called Mujahideens.[37] Apart from this there was a massive influx of arms, especially sub-machine guns and automatic rifles as weapons meant for Afghan guerillas. The new factor gave birth to a linkage between the Mujahideen groups and right-wing, religious parties within Pakistan made the whole Afghan issue part of the domestic political conflict. The Soviet intervention in Afghanistan was followed by General Zia's agreement with the US in 1981 for a strategic relationship. Among the Islamic parties of Pakistan Jamiatul-Ulema-i-Islam (JUI) and Jamaat-i-Islami (JI), had been actively involved in Afghanistan, first in the anti Soviet Jihad and later in support of the Taliban.

In fact the intermingling of Pak-Afghan society at various levels led to the formation of the Taliban, a home-grown Pak-militia. It was the product of extreme Deobandi madrassas in Pakistan. Taliban of Afghanistan is the product of Deoband thinking as it evolved in Pakistan after partition. The Wahabis and the Salaifis of Saudi Arabia can be counted as clones of the Talibanised mindset. At the height of Soviet involvement in Afghanistan, the USA had fostered Talibans through the Benazir Bhutto Government of Pakistan to help Mujahideens fight the Soviets. Alignment and realignment of forces took place periodically with a view to marginalising various national movements within Afghanistan until it suited the Pakistan-American coalition interests. Several similar organisations, leaders, Tajik leader Ahmed Shah Masood, Uzbek leader General Rashid Dastum, the Northern Alliance leader Mohammed Fakim Khan and Pushtun chieftain Gulbuddin Hekhmatyar were constantly put at loggerheads with one another to facilitate the prospects of Talibans.[38] The Taliban began as reformers, following a tradition in Muslim history based on the notion of Jihad–holy war against infidels. Jihad, however, does not sanction the killing of fellow Muslims on the basis of ethnicity or sect. Yet the Taliban has used it for just that.[39] Taliban, a force which grew out of Afghan refugee students who got their religious and military training in Pakistani madrassas, gradually established close ties not only with the military but with many sectors of Pakistani society and later formed a government in Afghanistan when Soviet army withdrew at the close of the eighties.

Al-Qaeda, meaning "the base" is a global terror group is the main threat to our open and democratic societies. In its quest to establish the global Kalifat, organisations as Al-Qaeda are seeking to direct a deadly blow to the fundamental set-up of our societies and of the international community as a whole. Osama bin Laden, its supreme leader, was a Saudi fugitive and the Emir General of Al-Qaeda. There is a Majlis called Al-Shura or governing Council with active member-citizens from many countries, who are loyal to Osama. Al-Qaeda does not have specific territorial boundaries. Their borders stretch up to wherever Islam has spread. Osama's greatest success was to make this particular interpretation of radical Islamism globally known. There are other strands of militant thinking and strategy but 20 years of "propaganda by deed" made it the dominant one. A thriving Jihadi subculture has emerged, and it has become, in many ways, a social movement.[40] Its ideology spawned a Pan Islamic thrust. It emphasised that a Muslim's first loyalty was to his creed, not his nation; any means of violence could be employed including weapons of mass destruction to achieve political and other aims; and belonging to one Ummah a Muslim could participate in any struggle world wide where Islam or its believers were being victimised.[41] With this ideology, drawn from scriptures, a Muslim was freed from the need of having any further organisational guidance. The result was that many Muslim groups in many parts of the world, started thinking and acting on identical lines. There was an upsurge in fundamentalism world wide and of terror.

Born in March 1957, Osama bin Muhammad bin Awad bin Laden in Riyadh, Saudi Arabia, was the seventh son among 50 or more siblings. He had united disparate militant groups, from Egypt to Chechnya, from Yemen to the Philippines, under the banner of his Al-Qaeda organisation and his ideal of a borderless brotherhood of radical Islam. Initially for years, when he was not a known face bin Laden had sought to become the principal leader of the Jihadist movement, by developing loose alliances with ideologically affiliated organisations or alliances that were built around personal relationships, and cemented with cash from his coffers.[42] Osama was then a non-entity, going from one ethnic leader to another to seek protection and favour of a fugitive until he settled down with the Taliban leader, Mulla Omar, who had allegedly married his eldest daughter. Marital relations between the families of Osama and Omar fermented their politico-religious alliance to fortitude. Defence of Islam became the common platform of unity. Money got from opium cultivation and narcotic trade cemented the bond between Taliban and Al-Qaeda and over the years both became invincible enemies of democracy.[43] For the first time during 1979-89 bin Laden built reputation helping US-sponsored Mujahideen fight Soviet troops in Afghanistan.

The Soviet takeover in Afghanistan ended in February 1989 marked the end of an era. The supply of US arms which were given to Afghan rebels to fight against the Soviet army and to Pakistan to protect itself from Soviet influences were suddenly came to a halt. The US was not in favour of establishing the kind of government in Kabul that Afghan rebels wanted. The pro-US elements in Kabul also suffered a set back on account of Gulf crisis that prevented them to be famous internationally but, more to Soviet disintegration which marked the end of cold war between the two superpowers and made US least interested in Afghan affairs.[44] In the whole Afghan episode, Pakistan created and nurtured Taliban-Al-Qaeda for transnational terrorism to achieve predominance in the Islamic world. The Pakistan establishment apparently felt that by facilitating the various partners in the Taliban-Al-Qaeda it can obtain their help in pursuing its own foreign policy objectives. The most commonly given rationale for this belief by people like General Hamid Gul, General Durani and General Aslam Beg was that this collective effort succeeded in defeating the Soviet Union in Afghanistan.[45] When a superpower is defeated by this strategy, it will work in other places also, The Taliban's military success in Afghanistan and their missionary zeal has infected Pakistani brethren influencing them with renewed fervour to bring a truly Islamic state.

The terror organisation Al-Qaeda had, at the beginning, a core of just under 200 cadre-120-odd grouped together in a crack unit, and a small number of foot-soldiers handling logistical work and training. By the time a thousand men had graduated from the training camps which ran in Afghanistan, but they were riven by ideological disputation and personal feuds. However, in a decade Osama's Al-Qaeda was linked to its different branches proliferated all over the world and the number of Al-Qaeda training camps rose to 30 in Afghanistan only. Al-Qaeda has always been an organisation that depended as much on local initiative as on top–down direction. Its complex organisational structure is something between a centralised hierarchy and a decentralised flat network. It is a flexible and adaptable organisation that has survived well beyond the lifespan of most other terrorist organisation.[46] But decentralisation remained an integral part of the strategy of Osama. Al-Qaeda was conceived as an umbrella group, channeling and focusing the diverse energies of the various groups active across the Islamic world in the 1990s. This worked for a while but the main regional groups now Al-Qaeda in the Arabian Peninsula (largely the Yemen), Al-Qaeda in the Maghreb (largely Algeria) and Al-Qaeda in Iraq are largely independent of the main leadership. Each is rooted in specific local factors and history.[47] The terrorist organisations spread all over the world made it a wider phenomenon.

Osama bin Laden, the leader of Al-Qaeda, after the 1989 Soviet retreat, returned to Saudi Arabia to be showered with praise but soon during the Gulf conflict he tried to dissuade Saudi government from allowing infidel armies into Saudi Arabia. The Saudi leadership then turned to US for protection. Bin Laden bitterly criticised both–Saudi government and Washington. As a result in 1992 Saudi Arabia freezed Laden's bank account that was followed by his expulsion from the country on known international pressure in 1996. Now he returned to Afghanistan, set up several training camps the same year, and had sought attention of the world by declaring war against the United States of America, a super power. On August 7, 1998 Al-Qaeda bombed US embassies in Kenya and Tanzania which killed 231 people. He gave radical Islam another push by crafting the World Islamic Front in 1998. Interestingly, five extremist organisations of Pakistan including Lashkar-e-Toiba, Harkat-ul-Mujahideen and Hizbul-e-Jihad-e-Islami had joined the Front among others from the Islamic countries and became founder members of the organisation. The Front was mainly meant for Jihad against the Crusaders and the Jews. However, joining of Pakistani extremist organisation and guidance of ISI included Hindu India in the list of enemies and in later years the Front became a tool to fulfil the Islamist ambitions of Pakistan against India in particular.

Today's Islamists, a conglomerate of several groups, want to bring the entire contemporary society under what they call God's sovereignty and laws laid down in the scriptures – as interpreted by them. There are differences in their methods of operations but their focus basically remains on achieving political power by use of force. Terrorism is one manifestation of inordinate use of force for gaining political objectives.[48] Of the terror philosophers the two-Syed Qutb of Egypt (1906-66) and Maulana Abdul A'la Maududi in India (1903-47) and later in Pakistan (1948-79) deserve special mention in this context. Syed Qutb, who belonged to the Muslim Brotherhood of Egypt, interpreted some traditional Islamic norms to mean that use of violent means for achieving power and influence is justified and to fight non-believers was a duty towards God. He preached that any system not based on divine revelation or 'Hadith' is Jahilleye-pagan state of object ignorance that prevailed in pre-Islamic Arabia. Likewise Maududi preached fundamentalist Islam of the Qutb variety. He was the founder of Jama'at-e-Islami in Pakistan which he visualised as a party that must wage Jihad against all infidels and non-conformist Muslim societies.[49] These were the founding fathers of the contemporary fundamentalist movement and Jihad in its present violent form. They wanted to create a religion-based world order in which non-believers have to be converted or destroyed. Thus terrorism poses a threat to globalisation. If terrorism based on religious nationalism is met with nationalism and insularity, the changes for globalism are remote.

Globalisation and Terrorism

In today's world, globalisation, liberalisation and privatisation are gaining growing attention as strategies for survival, competition and growth. True economic globalisation involves a qualitative shift towards a system based on a consolidated global market place for production, distribution and consumption rather than on autonomous national economies.[50] It is an inexorable technology-driven process, which is bringing about an economic impact. The ship, the steam engine, the railroad, civil aviation and the Internet have reduced geographical distances and inspired global economic integration as never before.[51] The compression of time and space triggered by the Third Industrial Revolution–roughly since 1980–has changed our interactions with the international environment. For many, globalisation–the intensified cross border exchange of goods, services, capital, technology, ideas, information, legal systems, and people is both desirable and irreversible. In this age of increasing globalisation and interdependence, the national and international dimension of terrorism in fact, constitutes two facets of the same social phenomenon which infringes upon the interest of all states, not only as an assault against their public order and institutions that protect the liberty and security of their citizens, but also at the same time as a serious danger to peaceful international relations and cooperation, which is clearly understood as encompassing human rights and values as well as the principles of equal rights and self-determination of people. It is, therefore, that the transnational character of contemporary terrorist events has prompted international efforts to suppress them at the global, regional and bilateral levels.

However, the concept and phenomenon of globalisation, in its first phase, dated back between 1840 and 1914 when it reached its height and ended shortly before the World War I. During the height of globalisation, tariff barriers were reduced and prices of goods travelling between continents came down because with bigger ships being used to carry good, transportation costs were lowered. There was also the huge migration of Europeans, about 60 million, for various destinations across the Atlantic. It swelled America's labour force and reduced Ireland's working population leading to a convergence of wage levels across the Atlantic. There was a greater volatility of funds travelling across the continents and those losing out from globalisation triggered a political backlash against it.[52] American wheat imports, for instance, hurt the interests of European farmers who protested and continental Europe closed its agricultural markets and imposed high import tariffs. The United States, too, raised tariffs to protect its infant manufacturing industry and migration was clamped because it threatened American workers' living standards. Other rich countries followed in becoming protectionist and the stage of globalisation came to an end.

In between the years, the world in general made achievements in all the spheres of human life, and in the sixties the concept of global village was given by Marshall Mcluhan which is realising in the current phase of globalisation. There are several things in the concept of global village–an ideal, a destination to be reached and a conceptualisation of the ongoing transformation in the community. The earth in which we live is an integrated, interpenetrated and interconnected unit. The advances of communications and information technology have made the global village a virtual reality and this has paved the way for evolving frameworks of global governance. A major impact of the globalising world is that security can no longer be compartmentalised regionally or nationally and any analysis of the security environment of a region or area has to take into consideration global issues that have a direct or indirect impact on the region.[53] In broader context the genesis of terrorism can be attributed to the development of exclusive instead of inclusive societies. Terrorism draws its strength from one of three sources: militant religious fundamentalism, ethnic intolerance and deprivation. Religion sans frontiers, therefore religious militancy, has to be addressed globally. Ethnic intolerance and deprivation are region specific, with the common thread of economies running through them, and are best dealt with regionally or nationally.

The current position and dark side of globalisation has reminded us the capitalist mode of production which always maintained a global reach whether in the form of colonies or as trading partners across the continents. The inherent logic of capitalist economic system pushes it towards borderless economic transactions and is characterised as 'centralisation-cum-globalisation of finance capital'. This is the epoch of finance capital and of monopolies and we are in a phase of imperialism-led-globalisation. The finance capital operates in the context of unity among the finance exporting leading capitalist countries in which every recipient country of this finance capital operates under a common sword of democles wherein foreign investments can be withdrawn without a moment notice to the recipient of such a finance.[54] It proves the volatility of movement of finance capital and its most disastrous implication is that capital market of any country of the South can be destabilised by the investors who want quick and immediate profits and returns on investments. Joseph Stiglitz, an insider of the World Bank, published a seminal work on Globalisation and its Discontents (2002), in which he warned about the disastrous consequences of the present stage of capitalist globalisation. His brief description clearly indicated that national economy which is controlled and guided by a national state has been replaced and displaced by united globalised capitalism.[55] Even in normal circumstances state systems of the peripheral developing countries are weak while dealing with the centre of capitalism, in the new context of highly mobile and volatile operations of finance capital the nation states have been completely marginalised under the impact of these new trends in global capitalist system. Marginalisation of the state and unity of the capitalist bloc is the reality of present phase of global capitalism.

Under globalisation the movement of people remains tightly restricted. The flow of capital is highly asymmetrical. Over the last two decades, overseas development assistance from the rich to poor countries has totalled $ 50-80 billion per year. In the same period, every year, $ 500-800 billion of illegal funds have been sent from the poor to rich countries. That is, for every one dollar of aid money over the table the West gets back $ 10 under the table.[56] The benefits and costs of linking and delinking are unequally distributed. Industrialised countries are mutually interdependent; developing countries are largely independent in economic relations with one another; and developing countries are highly dependent on industrialised countries. In addition there is also a growing divergence in income levels between countries and peoples, with widening inequality among and within nations. Assets and incomes are more concentrated. Wage shares have fallen. Profit shares have risen. Capital mobility alongside labour immobility has reduced the bargaining power of organised labour.[57] Professor Paul Krugman has admitted in his book, The Return of Depression Economics, that technical change and globalisation have increased the demand for highly skilled workers in the US while reducing the demand for the less skilled.[58] He said that inequality of both wealth and income has increased to levels not seen before since real wages actually declined for many workers.

The emerging implications of the liberalisation process which had begun in the early 1990s, are far more evident in terms of the resultant of new economic policy and change in the historical-ideological orientation of our political economy. Though considerable progress has been achieved in terms of higher growth rate and GDP, the basic needs and the crucial concerns of the core sectors of Indian economy such as agriculture and textiles affected millions of people, pose a challenge to the successive governments.[59] Developed countries erect obstacles to trade in particular, agricultural products and textiles. The West, under the guise of globalisation, pushes the developing countries to open their markets. But they raise barriers of entry into their markets. Globalisation, the way it is practised, encourages an unequal distribution of power and wealth among the countries of the world.[60] The rich agricultural countries fear that agricultural trade liberalisation will be harmful to their highly protected agriculture and the European Union and Japan are reluctant to open up their markets for agricultural products. The US has also retained a protectionist stance regarding its textile industry and has readily used anti-dumping laws. Even the South-East Asian countries which became prosperous through globalisation have also witnessed a strong backlash against the trans-nationalisation and internationalisation of capital because trillions of dollars travel across the globe in seconds.

Like India in many traditional societies agriculture is not considered merely as an occupation but a major source of livelihood and for the vast majority a way of life. The traditional relationship between the people, land and agriculture has emotive overtones and any careless tampering with this delicate subject could unleash waves of violence and social disruption. Its direct result is the increase of insecurity of individuals, groups and nations in various domains – economic, financial, culture, employment, legal, social, health care, ecological, political and personal. And this is why the concept of globalisation is encountering resistance from various interest groups – environmentalists, labour leaders, cultural traditionalists, religious leaders of different persuasions and non-government officers.[61] This apart, the influential international NGOs have been against multinationals and the fast pace of globalisation that they have triggered. They have also come to form an international civil society because national governments no longer have a monopoly on information and because civil society now has access to data on the workings of multinationals and governments around the world.

The new system of capital finance and the ideology of 'roll back the state', which allows market forces and private domestic and global operators to manage the economy in society, has a definite impact on social life of the country. Since every capitalist society is class-divided, a socially disastrous impact of such social divisions is felt very acutely on the majority of peasant and working classes in poor developing countries, especially if economy in such societies is handed over to domestic and external private capitalists. The scholars – James K. Galbraith and John Williamson have also criticised the new global economic policy. Galbraith observed that 'rising inequality after 1980 is the rule' and stated, 'The patterns strongly suggest that forces of globalisation, including high global interest rates, debt crisis, and shock liberalisation are associated with rising inequality in pay structures, John Williamson has also lamented that the 'Washington Consensus' as a policy manifesto of the New Age 'omitted a concern for income distribution'.[62] In the circumstances so long as there exists in the world poverty, strife, injustice and oppression, conditions will exist which terrorists can turn to their advantage. No doubt that the campaign against terrorism is one that must be mounted at various levels, including political, economic and humanitarian.

Even before the Global Financial Crisis (GFC), many developing countries were worried that globalisation would impinge adversely on economic sovereignty, cultural integrity and social stability. "Interdependence" among unequals translates into the dependence of some on international markets that function under the dominance of others. The deepening of poverty and inequality, prosperity for a few countries and people, marginalisation and exclusion for the many, has implications for social and political stability among and within states. The rapid growth of global markets has not seen the parallel development of social and economic institutions to ensure balanced, inclusive and sustainable growth. Labour rights have been less sedulously protected than capital and property rights, and global rules on trade and finance are inequitable. This has asymmetric effects on rich and poor countries.

Recently, globalisation has also let loose the forces of uncivil society and accelerated the transnational flows of terrorism, human and drug trafficking, organised crime, piracy and pandemic diseases. Terrorism continues to be generated by recurrent social crises, arising from the increasing fear of marginalisation of some sections of society caused by the indiscriminate spread of capitalism and the free economy, through much publicised globalisation which may be perceived another dimension of religious fanaticism. Despair caused by social marginalisation, economic deprivation, and political defeat is another cause of this modern phenomenon.[63] When the situation is thus monopolised by global power, when one deals with this formidable condensation of all functions through technocratic machinery and absolute ideological hegemony, what other way is there than a terrorist reversal of the situation. It is the system itself that has created the objective conditions for this brutal distortion. By taking all the cards to itself it forces the other to change the rules of the game. And the new rules are ferocious, because the stakes are the same. The terrorist groups are not ordinary civilians or some misguided youth but the paramilitary organs of militant extremism such as LeT, Naxalites, and the like who believe in the culture of extreme violence and whose objective is destruction of the established social system and structures, that is, the whole way of life of free societies. This virus does not take long to infect homegrown products and soon enough local criminal gangs get drawn into the terrorist's web.

Globalisation also cast a dark shadow on the governing pattern and civil society of the nation state system. The growth in transnational flows has not been matched by an equivalent growth in global governance mechanisms to regulate them. And yet the very nature of the structure of globalised network, which intertwine global actors and interests, ensures that no single power is able to maintain its position within the newly emerging global disorder without making compromises with other global players. The transfer of state functions to supra-national forms of regional governance could enhance the capacity of individual states to combat uncivil society. The sharing of expertise, institutions, policy tools, personnel and other resources can go a long way in stemming the tide of unwanted activities. In this context justice is one of the strongest pillars for the parliamentary democracy. Justice is truth in practice. Rule of law provides citizens a sense of protection and self-confidence. We should not forget that denial of justice breeds terrorism.[64] It is not terrorist or terrorism who divided Ireland nor caused Israel-Palestinian problem. Terrorists did not separate India and Pakistan, neither they carved out Bangladesh. As a result of the injustices and inequalities, a different kind of challenge is faced by countries of the world in general, especially by the developing and underdeveloped.

In the circumstances, the outright rejection of globalisation and a retreat into autarky is neither practical nor desirable. Opposing globalisation is like opposing the sun coming up every morning and about as fruitful. A country can not ignore an absolute majority of its population which is poor and dissatisfied. A society can not be peaceful if the majority of its poor population is socially alienated. Even a highly developed modern coercive apparatus of the state will not be able to deal with popular anger and the ruling classes will have to find some answers to meet the challenge of angry and alienated mass of society.[65] Jurgen Habermas, the German Philosopher, clearly brings out the 'Real Assumptions Underlying Globalisation' by mentioning that I. social inequality is a fate, or II. a necessary market outcome; that III. the state is no more than a corporation providing services, and IV. citizens are primarily entrepreneurs and customers. Thus the message of globalisation is loud and clear that the poor should not expect anything from their society and state because market would create its own equilibrium.[66] The Indian Prime Minister Atal Bihari Vajpayee also acknowledged that the experiment that began in 1991 has increased inequalities and his government has decided to give a new pro-poor, pro-village, and pro-employment orientation to the Indian economy.

The big gap which appeared due to globalisation and its offshoot social inequality turned the poor masses look toward the pre-capitalist system of the past for some security and succour. Tribal or caste or religious solidarities of the past attract the vulnerable and helpless poor of the present. In other words, the Western capitalist mode of production has not been able to shake the Asiatic social system based on caste or tribe, or religious loyalties and belief system. Religion is a common binding factor for the whole society in Hindu India, or Buddhist East Asia, or Islam in the Arab world and other Muslim majority countries. Since religion exercises great influence over the whole societies of Asian countries, it plays significant role in the present crisis–ridden social order of these societies. However, at large, terrorism is motivated by a variety of inner drives ranging from financial gains to revenge, from fundamentalism to deprivation, political frustration, regional disparities, marginalisation of subnational groups, extremism, despair, injustice, discrimination, resentment against the existing regime, feeling of insignificance, intervention into personal freedom, weak government, separatism and oppression, inequality etc.

Terror Techniques and Combating

Earlier terrorism was not a widespread phenomenon as it is today in contemporary political system of the world. In the 1960s, national security was perceived as the ability of a nation to protect its internal values from external threats. In the 1990s the notion of national security has been greatly enlarged to mean the capacity to control those domestic and foreign conditions that the public opinion considers necessary for its autonomy, prosperity and well being. It has been interpreted by some to mean any condition which might degrade the quality of life of the inhabitants of a state.[67] In this confused perception of security the terrorists has a ready field to exploit. The relationship between the citizen and the state having snapped, terrorists target the citizens with greater violence and in the least expected places. In response to the terrorists' use of violence the state uses its military apparatus. In the process it alienates the population. The increasing reliance on the military can not and does not stop terrorist activity. It in fact increases the vulnerability of the citizens.

The threats we face from terrorism are constantly changing in all sorts of ways. It is not easy at a time when commercial airlines can be used as flying bombs, and when terrorist strategy is planned by internet, mobile phone, satellite and coded messages on websites. It has now become a global phenomenon with increasing and rather well identifiable links between different terrorist groups and organisations. They use each-other's areas for recruitment and training, exchange of illegal weapons, engage in joint planning and ventures and also provide administrative and other logistic support. This type of terrorist activities show a new dimension due to circumstances characterised by the advancement of science, technology and diverse social, economic, political and historical reasons conditioning it. The development of computer science, satellite and mobile links have also affected the modernisation of terrorist activities. It is also feared that weapons of mass destruction previously controlled by governments can now be purchased on the black market. It is said that not only the weapons but also the scientists with the knowledge of how to make them are available.

Meanwhile, experts in terrorism believe that the next big threat will come from the practitioners of biological terrorism. Dr. Raymond A. Zilinskas, a microbiologist and former UN-SCOM inspector, recently discussed three categories of bio-terrorism. Low technology bio-weapons are delivered in food or water, causing food poisoning. Such acts are extremely difficult to prevent, but rarely have much more than local impact. High technology bio-weapons disperse agents over a larger area, but the use of foggers or sprayers is beset with technical problems. Explosive munitions as dispersal devices kill the agents in the explosion. There is also bioscience-based technology in which bacteria might be genetically engineered to be resistant to all known antibiotics, while viruses may be made more resistant to environmental factors. Dr. Zilinskas warns, 'Nevertheless, we can expect that in the not too distant future, some well-trained molecular biologist will utilise her or his knowledge for military or terrorist purposes.'[68] A 1999 Federal Research Division (FRD) study examined some changes from terrorists of the past, especially the emergence of terrorist acts carried out by individuals and members of small, adhoc groups largely unknown to security organisations.[69] Tactics, as well as sources, had changed, with the greater use of suicide attacks and attacks by women and children. A very significant concern was the possible use, by terrorists, of Weapons of Mass Destruction (WMD). Researchers for a 1999 General Accounting Office had also concluded that this is not a hypothetical fear but it also must be assessed in terms of possible damage, ... except if using toxic industrial chemicals, terrorists would need a relatively high degree of sophistication to successfully and effectively process agents, improvise a device or weapon and disseminate the agents to cause mass casualties ... Effectively disseminating both forms of agent (dry or liquid) can pose technical challenges in which the proper equipment and energy sources are needed.[70]

However, in this context, above all is the fact that terrorists, while having at their disposal all the arms of the system, have also another fatal weapon: their own death. If they limited themselves to fighting the system with its own weapons, they would be immediately eliminated. If they did not oppose the system with their own death, they would disappear as quickly as a useless sacrifice: this has almost always been the fate of terrorism until now and the reason why it could not but fail. Everything changed as soon as they allied all available modern means to this highly symbolic weapon. The latter infinitely multiplies their destructive potential. Many terrorist organisations employ attacks in which the death of the attacker is not a risk, but is a certainty if the attack is carried out. Several operations have used trucks loaded with explosives and driven into the target. The driver either manually set off the explosives, causing his own death as well as deaths in the target. For example, the 9/11 attack involved the deaths of both the hijackers that took control of the aircraft, and those that flew it into the target. The suicide attacks have both a psychological and a practical effect. Going back to the World War II. Japanese Kamikaze, who used suicide attacks against purely military targets, said the recipients of the attacks were impressed, and to some extent demoralised, by the determination of the enemy. Current terrorists use the suicide attacker's brain as an equivalent to high technology and obtain psychological benefits as a result. Terrorism is violence for a cause and terrorists always want the world to know about their existence, their causes and the power they wield.[71] When they strike but don't seek publicity then they are working as a proxy.

The terrorists of today have a global network and little firm information is available about the type of data used by network analysts. The experts in general mostly rely on newspaper and other media reports, but it is certain that they maintain a high degree of connectivity and considerable redundancy. The dynamic units are probably small, with high personnel turn over and considerable structural equivalence. The network is not managed in the strict hierarchical sense, but a central leadership appears to plan major moves, to provide training, finance and logistical support but to permit considerable autonomy at the local level. Such structures contrast markedly with typical governmental hierarchies.[72] In fact, to understand networks, one has to interview people; learn about their friends, relations and contacts; describe the relationships; reduplicate so that everyone is represented only once in the network, albeit in multiple roles; describe their movements; determine the processes of fission and fusion that create their particular dynamics; and connect the dots.[73] For the terrorists even nationality matters less than the commitment. The force is composed of a variety of ethnic and national groups, whose belief presumably binds them to the cause, and not necessarily to a given organisation or leader. The breakdown of such a network, whether on the local or global scale, depends obviously on two factors: money and trust.

In combating terrorism three distinct functions are involved. They relate to pre-empting and preventing; containing and managing; and investigating and prosecuting. The fight against terror is larger and more complex than the challenge of dealing with terrorists. The former requires more of statesmanship and good governance. The latter demands legislative and administrative reforms to plug loopholes in criminal law and the criminal justice administration.[74] In addition, timely, accurate intelligence and up-to-date databases on terrorist elements are essential to evolve strategies to counter terrorist activities. This requires multi-agency coordination and time-bound action which only an empowered central body with regional and local field officers with instant connectivity can accomplish. Similarly, a dedicated team of highly motivated, well-trained and fully professionalised officers supported by adequate resources, equipment and authority alone can take timely action to combat terror.[75] In most of the cases of terrorism, regional cooperation can be an effective instrument for the suppression of terrorism. The external support is often found in every operation of terrorist acts in any part of the world whether in the context of interconnection between a group and its rival group, a group and its enemy state, or a state and its unfriendly state.

In the age of global terror, nations targeted by terrorist campaigns find themselves in a difficult situation: they feel tremendous pressure in some way to respond terror attacks, but there is no obvious correct response. Passively absorbing continued attacks on civilian targets is not an attractive policy option, particularly in democracies where public dissatisfaction is a major input into government decision-making; but the alternatives to passive victimhood are often controversial, expensive, and inconvenient and sometimes ineffective as well. Governments in democracies have constantly to balance the citizens' right to live their lives in freedom, with minimum interference with their privacy from the security agencies, against their responsibility to protect their citizens from harm.[76] In the fight against terrorism the strengths of a free society are also its weaknesses. Terrorists use the rights and liberties inherent in a democratic society to operate with comparative freedom and then use the democratic laws to circumvent or evade the consequences.

The countries of South Asia in general are facing the problem of terrorism and insurgency and the both required a different approach in handling. Terrorism needs a top-down approach while insurgency required a bottom-top approach. For an insurgent movement to flourish, it must have support of a segment of the population whereas terrorism can be effective with just a few sympathisers and supporters amongst the population. In tackling an insurgency, it is a fight for the hearts and minds of the people and the people have to be addressed and won over. With terrorism, the leadership or perpetrators of terrorism need to be targeted. Insurgency usually has rural roots while terrorism has an urban bias.[77] The most valuable sources against terrorism are human beings, long-term penetration agents, who will stay in place for a long period and work their way into positions where they can provide key intelligence. Thus human and technical intelligence taken together must be backed up by long-term investigation and assessment, to understand the terrorist organisation, its people, its plans and its methods.

In nutshell, the present thinking on terrorism can be divided into two schools of thought. One school of thought places the terrorist beyond the pale of civilized society and considers him anathema to civilisation and stigmatises him as a plain murderer who needs to be eliminated. The second school of thought encourages an in-depth study of, and a systematic approach to understand and eradicate, the reasons that bring about such upheavals. The rational political, social and economic aspirations of peoples which when frustrated continuously give rise to full blown terrorism of modern day, must be sifted out of the process of terroristic actions and looked at separately. Those political aspirations must be addressed honestly and seriously.[78]

A State sponsoring terrorism or instigating violence in another country has long term strategic or political agendas, and state-sponsored terrorism when used as a foreign policy tool translates into an unconventional war. Generally no-solid evidence can be mustered against a state that is sponsoring terrorism as they use proxies and mercenaries instead of employing its own army or Special Forces. Determining the threat posed by international terrorism whether state-sponsored or otherwise is a difficult and complex task. This kind of terrorism has attained dangerous dimensions both in South and Central Asia. It constitutes a serious threat to regional and international stability. Therefore, terrorism is a phenomenon which must be condemned, fought, resisted, controlled and, eventually, eliminated at all levels – national, regional and international. Conditions necessary for wiping out terrorism must, accordingly, be cultivated and strengthened nationally, regionally and internationally, and unilaterally, bilaterally or multilaterally as well. Terrorist acts confronted by a state can not be eliminated by the affected states alone because of the international linkages of the terrorist groups. It is, therefore, clear that all the nations must form a common front to fight terrorism. If the much needed spirit of international cooperation in the required degree is not properly established, the world would become a dangerous place to live.

References

1. D.R. Goyal, 'International Terrorism: Challenge and Response', in Mahavir Singh (ed.), *International Terrorism and Religious Extremism–Challenges to Central and South Asia* (New Delhi: Anamika Publishers, 2004), p. 1.
2. Jessica Stern, *The Ultimate Terrorist* (Massachusetts: Harvard University Press, 1999), pp. 11-12.
3. C. Uday Bhaskar, 'New Rules for the New War', *The Hindustan Times*, 7 October, 2001.
4. Suman Singh, 'Terrorism in South Asia', *South Asia Politics*, Vol. 9, No. 2, June 2010 (New Delhi), p. 50.
5. Jagdish Prasad Verma, 'If You Wish for Peace, Understand Terrorism', in *Ibid.*, Vol. 9, No. 7, November 2010 (New Delhi : 2010), p. 49.
6. Suman Singh, 'Terrorism in South Asia'.
7. Jagdish Prasad Verma, 'If You Wish for Peace, Understand Terrorism'.
8. Jean Baudrillard, 'The Spirit of Terrorism', 2 November, 2001.

9. Ajit Doval, 'Outsourcing Terror,' *The Times of India*, 18 July, 2011.
10. Jagdish Prasad Verma, 'If You Wish for Peace, Understand Terrorism,' in *ibid*.
11. Gwynne Dyer, 'The Slow Decline of Terror', *The Hindustan Times*, 24 August, 1998.
12. R.A. Seligman (ed.), *Encyclopaedia of the Social Sciences*, Vols. 13-14 (Newyork : The Macmillan Company, 1954), p. 575.
13. *Ibid*., p. 576.
14. *Ibid*., p. 578.
15. Jagdish Pradad Verma, 'If You Wish for Peace, Understand Terrorism', p. 49.
16. Rajkumar Singh, *Past, Present and Future of Kashmir* (New Delhi: Gyan Publishing House, 2008), p. 47.
17. Prakash Singh, 'Militancy from Kashmir to Coimbatore,' *The Hindustan Times*, 23 February, 1998.
18. B. Sheik Ali, *Islam: A Cultural Orientation* (Delhi: 1981), p. 14.
19. *The Quran*, English Translation, Abdullah Yusuf Ali (Leicester), 5:35.
20. *Ibid*.
21. Afsir Karim, 'Challenges of Terrorism and Religious Extremism in Central and South Asia' in Mahavir Singh (ed.), *International Terrorism and Religious Extremism-Challenges to Central and South Asia*, pp. 69-70.
22. Rajkumar Singh, *Past, Present and Future of Kashmir*, pp. 51-52.
23. Nandy, 'The Sociology of Sati', *The Indian Express*, 5 October, 1989.
24. Chandrika Bandaranaike Kumaratunga, 'Original Sins', *The Hindustan Times*, 29 April, 2002.
25. B. Sheik Ali, *Islam: A Cultural Orientation*, pp. 137-38.
26. A.K. Verma, 'Radical Islam and Terror', *South Asia Politics*, Vol. 7, No. 8, December 2008 (New Delhi : 2008), p. 16.
27. Abbas Rashid, 'Pakistan : The Ideological Dimensions in Mohammad Asghar Khan (ed.), *Islam, Politics and the State: The Pakistan Experience* (London: Zed Press, 1985), p. 75.
28. K.R. Malkani, 'Inside the Muslim Mind', *The Hindustan Times*, 13 October, 2001.
29. Paul Kennedy, *Preparing for the Twenty-first Century*, p. 224.
30. Samuel Huntington, 'The Clash of Civilizations', *Foreign Affairs* (Summer, 1993), pp. 22-49.
31. John Mueller, 'Nine Propositions About the Historical Impact of Nuclear Weapons', in Jorn Gjelstad and Olav Njolstad (eds.), *Nuclear Rivalry and International Order* (London: 1996), pp. 56-57.

32. Rajkumar Singh, *India and Pakistan–Social, Political and Military Perspectives* (New Delhi: Regal Publications, 2009), p. 236.
33. Majid Tehranian, 'Khomeini's Doctrine of Legitimacy', in Anthony J. Parel and Ronald C. Keith (eds.), *Comparative Political Philosophy* (New Delhi: 1992), p. 220.
34. Verghese Koithara, *Society, State and Security: The Indian Experience* (New Delhi: Sage Publications, 1999), p. 186.
35. Satish Kumar, 'Militant Islam: The Nemesis of Pakistan', *Strategic Digest*, Vol. XXX, No. 8 (August 2000), p. 1075.
36. Rajkumar Singh, *India and Pakistan–Social, Political and Military Perspectives*, pp. 251-52.
37. Benazir Bhutto, *Pakistan: The Gathering Storm* (New Delhi: 1983), pp. 63-64.
38. P.L. Dash, 'Afghanistan: The Epicentre of Terror,' in Mahavir Singh (ed.), *International Terrorism and Religious Extremism–Challenges to Central and South Asia*, p. 141.
39. Ahmed Rashid, 'The Taliban Exporting Extremism', *Foreign Affairs*, Vol. LXXVIII, No. 6 (November-December 1999), p. 118.
40. *The Hindu*, 3 May, 2011.
41. A.K. Verma, 'Radical Islam and Terror', pp. 16-17.
42. Praveen Swami, 'Osama's Death a Gift to Resurgent Al-Qaeda', *The Hindu*, 3 May, 2011.
43. P.L. Dash, 'Afghanistan: The Epicentre of Terror', p. 141.
44. Rajkumar Singh, *Contemporary India with Controversial Neighbours* (New Delhi: Gyan Publishing House, 2011), p. 129.
45. Veena Kukreja, *Contemporary Pakistan–Political Processes, Conflicts and Crises* (New Delhi: Sage Publications, 2003), pp. 180-81.
46. Matthew C. Waxman, 'The Structure of Terrorism, Threats and the Laws of War', *Duke Journal of Comparative and International Law*, Vol. 20, May 2010, p. 108.
47. *The Hindu*, 3 May, 2011.
48. Afsir Karim, 'Challenges of Terrorism and Religious Extremism in Central and South Asia', p. 70.
49. *Ibid.*
50. J.C. Mohanty, 'WTO and Implications for Indian Agriculture', in Ramesh K. Arora (ed.), *Administrative Change*, Vol. XXX, No. 1 & Vol. XXXI, No. 2, January-December 2002 (Jaipur), p. 67.
51. Rahul Mukherji, 'Noose Tightens Over Global Order', *The Hindustan Times*, 30 June, 2003.
52. B. Ramesh Babu, 'The Liberal Capitalist West as the New Global State', *International Studies*, Vol. 43, No. 3, July-September 2006 (New Delhi: Sage Publications, 2006), p. 291.

53. A.S. Kalkat, 'Ensuring Security in the Age of Global Terror', *The Hindu*, 13 September, 2006.
54. Prabhat Patnaik (Introduction), V.I. Lenin, *Imperialism: The Highest Stage of Capitalism* (New Delhi: Leftword, 2000), p. 24.
55. C.P. Bhambhri, 'Globalisation and Neo–Primordialism', in Mahavir Singh (ed.), *International Terrorism and Religious Extremism–Challenges to Central and South Asia*, pp. 11-14.
56. Jorge Heine & Ramesh Thakur, 'The Dark Side of Globalisation', *The Hindu*, 10 January, 2011.
57. *Ibid.*
58. Jayshree Sengupta, 'Threats to Globalisation', *The Hindustan Times*, 4 February, 2000.
59. Rajkumar Singh, *Contemporary India with Controversial Neighbours*, p. 76.
60. C. Sheela Reddy, 'Globalisation–A Human Rights Perspective, *South Asia Politics*, Vol. 5, No. 2, March 2007 (New Delhi), pp. 39-40.
61. James K. Galbraith, 'Rising Inequality After 1980 is the Rule', *Foreign Affairs*, July-August 2002 (Newyork), p. 179.
62. John Williamson, 'The Washington Consensus and Beyond', *Economic and Political Weekly* Vol. XXXVIII, No. 15, 12-18 April, 2003 (Mumbai), pp. 1475-1481.
63. Sheikh Saleem Ahmed, 'Dimensions of Terrorism and Religious Extremism: Two Sides of the Same Coin', in Mahavir Singh (ed.), *International Terrorism and Religious Extremism–Challenges to Central and South Asia*, p. 38.
64. *Ibid.*, pp. 38-39.
65. C.P. Bhambhri, 'Globalisation and Neo-Primordialism', p. 22.
66. As quoted in *Ibid.*
67. V.R. Raghavan, 'Response to Terror', *The Hindustan Times*, 6 January, 1999.
68. N.C. Menon, 'Terrorism as an Epidemic', in *Ibid.*, 18 August, 1998.
69. Hudson Rex A., 'The Sociology and Psychology of Terrorism: Who Becomes a Terrorist and Why?', *Federal Research Division*, Library of Congress, September 1999.
70. *General Accounting Office*, Combating Terrorism: Need for Comprehensive Threat and Risk Assessments of Chemical and Biological Attacks, September 1999.
71. Ajit Doval, 'Outsourcing Terror'.
72. Richard Rothenberg, 'From Whole Cloth: Making up the Terrorist Network', *Atlanta*, USA, 2 November, 2001, p. 36.
73. *Ibid.*

74. N.R. Madhava Menon, 'Combating Terrorism, and Some Management Issues', *The Hindu*, 12 January, 2009.
75. *Ibid.*
76. Stella Rimington, 'Terrorism Did Not Begin On 9/11', *The Hindustan Times*, 8 September, 2002.
77. A.S. Kalkat, 'Ensuring Security in the Age of Global Terror'.
78. Chandrika Bandaranaike Kumaratunga, 'The Original Sins'.

3

US Strategy and Terror Response in South Asia

The US interest in the region South Asia began explicitly in the initial years of cold war in post-World War II phase. At the time its global rivalry was with the former USSR and the two superpowers had their areas of influence clearly divided in world politics. They both were vitally conscious towards their global strategy and acted upon them strictly. In their global competition the Soviet intervention in Afghanistan in December 1979 and creation of anti-Soviet forces by the US with help of Pakistan and other western powers brought the ugly face of terrorism to South Asia's doorstep. After Soviets' withdrawal from Afghanistan the leader of Al-Qaeda, Osama bin Laden became anti-America and anti-West who masterminded the attacks of 11 September 2001. In post-9/11 the US launched a global war against terrorism but particularly in Afghanistan and near Af-Pak borders where the outfit cadres and its leaders had taken refuge. However, Osama bin Laden, the most wanted face of terrorism, had been killed by the US forces at Abbottabad in Pakistan, in early May 2011, the outfit's affiliates with different names and changed faces along with the same motto continued to be violently active in the region for the same cause and target.

Terrorism in South Asia and USA

Following the World War II an explosive situation between then two superpowers drove many countries recently decolonised and willing under their umbrella. India's position on non-alignment goaded the Cold War warriors in Washington under John Foster Dulles to put India in the Soviet camp and the Pakistani Generals took full advantage of a sort of McCarthyism in the US foreign policy and strengthened Pakistan's security alignment with the US through SEATO, CENTO and other arrangements. Earlier in 1947 George Keenan wrote an article, 'The sources of Soviet conduct'. in which he prescribed for containing and then destroying democratic despotism through implacable opposition to its continuance. The brilliance of George Keenan lay in his prescient understanding of the fact that the excesses of police apparatus had fanned the potential opposition to the regime into something for greater and more dangerous than it could have been before those excesses began. Since the US could not expect in the foreseeable future to enjoy political intimacy with the Soviet regime, Keenan argued, it must continue to regard the Soviet Union as a rival in the political arena and adopt a policy of firm containment, designed to confront the Russians with unalterable counter force at every point. Consequently at various stages of the cold war, as theorised by George Keenan, the US sometimes by assisting despots presiding over failed states countered Soviet moves taking a long term, patient but firm and vigilant policy to contain Russia's expansive tendencies.

The United States of America in pursuance of the policy of containment of the Soviet expansionism, created NATO in Europe, got involved in Vietnam War and promoted military dictatorships in Latin America, Africa and Asia including several military governments in Pakistan. As states do not dissolve by themselves many despotic rulers continued to exercise control over captive population often supported and assisted by the erstwhile super powers due to the logic dictated by the Cold War.[1] The german philosopher and social theorist Jurgen Habermas had also observed that if the political community is fragmented into opposed religious, ethnic, racial, and ideological groups, more familiarly known as identity polities, then democratic structure is threatened. Meanwhile, source of threat to global stability has moved from nuclear war to regional rogue states to transnational or non-state actors. Effectively American definition of the threat has de-escalated from 'evil empire' to 'axis of evil' to 'evil actors'.[2] The international community, therefore, demands that democracy should be not only an international norm but a domestic norm as well. If a state were to disenfranchise entire or part of its population then democratic states may justify foreign intervention to enfranchise the people of the non-democratic states; they may intervene to install a democratic government through internationally supervised elections. In early years with a view to policy of containing communism, it placed higher priorities on West Asia, where a Soviet military threat to Iran and Turkey was perceived, and to South-east Asia where the Chinese were suspected of long-term expansionist ambitions. In the process the West while insisting that democracy be practised in their own countries willed to accept some of the developing countries as 'Antarctica of democratic values, where liberal values were kept frozen for getting short-term security benefits by the dictators.

In the case of Pakistan finding religion as insufficient basis for nationhood the Generals in collusion with the landed aristocracy and economic elite achieved dominance in 'a nation without clear definition or cohesion'. Stephen Cohen, perhaps the greatest expert the US has on South Asian Affairs, called this compact, 'moderate oligarchy... an informal system that tied together senior ranks of the military, the civil service, the key members of the judiciary and other elites.'[3] Cohen held various US administrations responsible for the ascendancy of the army in Pakistan and encouraging Pakistan's nuclear ambition. Analysing the state of sectarianism in Pakistan Brussels based International Crisis Group remarked that sectarian conflict in Pakistan was the direct consequence of state policies of Islamisation and marginalisation of secular democratic forces. Cooperation and patronage of religious parties by successive military governments have brought Pakistan to a point where religious extremism threatens to erode the foundation of the state and society.[4] The choice that Pakistan faces, the crisis group warns, is not between genuine democracy and a military mullah that is responsible for producing and sustaining religious extremism.

Especially Zia-ul-Haq used Islam as a legitimisation strategy for the consolidation of his autocratic military rule in an unprecedented manner and therefore cultivated and strengthened Islamist elements most vigorously.[5] Zia's laws and policies resulted in making vast sections of the population extremely vulnerable to the Islamic militancy by replacing a tolerant and liberal civil society with an intolerant and retrogressive one. He did not employ Islam with the intention of inculcating positive values, such as peace, and honesty, imbibed by Islam. His uses of religion was limited to aggregating power with an authoritarian state, through the police, army and bureaucracy; exercising arbitrary control; and the denial of human rights to the Pakistani citizenry. A survey of laws and policies instituted by Zia reveals that Islam was invariably employed where rights were to be curtailed and not for the expansion thereof.[6] As a result of the policies pursued by Zia Pakistani generation has been brought up with hatred in their hearts for Jews, India and the West, notably America. In the forefront are the Pakistan Army and its Inter Services Intelligence (ISI) offshoot. No informed person can entertain any doubt about the Pak military's abiding commitment in concert with Saudi Arabia to spread the Wahabi brand of Islam in Afghanistan, the Indian subcontinent, Central Asia and elsewhere.[7] In other words Zia misused religion to prolong his despotic rule. Political workers were awarded harsher punishments including lashes for speaking against the government.

Thus, at the height of Islamic fundamentalism in Pakistan, the Soviet intervention in Afghanistan took place at the close of seventies (December 1979). Zia's significant objective of Islamisation was concurrent with the Soviet military intervention in Afghanistan and the event was depicted as 'Islam in danger'. Further it converged the interest of the US and Pakistan as the former wanted to wage proxy war with Soviet Union via Pakistan. According to Eqbal Ahmed during the 1980s, there was trend towards the growth of fundamentalists neo-totalitarian Muslim movements which is contrary to the political culture and historical traditions of the Muslim majority.[8] The fundamentalists such as Muslim Brotherhood in the Arab world, the Jamaat-i-Islami in Pakistan, the Sharekat Islam in Indonesia, and the Islamic government of post-revolution Iran seek to restore the past in its idealised form. But none of these movements succeeded in attracting the majority of workers, peasants and intelligentsia.[9] In sum, as a result of Zia's cynical exploitation of Islam, the Islamists appetite grew. It opened the floodgate for religious schools, mosques, and mullah inspired criminal gangs which enjoy official protection and are often used to settle political scores.

At the juncture, more ominous was the role of the United States of America who compounded the Soviet intervention of Afghanistan. It used Islamic fundamentalism to counter Soviet communism. To fight Soviet–style atheism, US policy-makers did not hesitate to use religion for political ends – the Catholic Church in Central America and Islam in Afghanistan. In other words, Islam was employed to unite the Muslim world and spur the spirit of Jihad against the Soviet intervention in Afghanistan. The US–led military campaign in Afghanistan was fuelled by succeeding American administration. The Reagan Doctrine of arming anti-communist freedom fighter in places such as Afghanistan, Angola,

Combodia and Nicaragua sanctified the doctrine of low-intensity conflict. By funnelling billions of dollars, worth of arms through conduit states and their agencies, Washington allowed the conduits to bring into play their own interests, biases and rivalries.[10] The Soviet intervention in Afghanistan was followed by General Zia's agreement with the US in 1981 for a strategic relationship. As it was concluded in the background of Afghan crisis, it made Islamabad a major recipient of US economic and military assistance. After a gap of over a decade, the Pakistani military was able to support an ambitious modernisation programme involving the introduction of some of the latest weapon system into the forces and the acquisition of advanced military technology.

With the eruption of crisis in Afghanistan, thousands of refugees sought sanctuary in Pakistan from Soviet air raids. The Government of Pakistan had every reason to be worried about the Afghan refugees. They began to create troubles. The use of Pakistan as a base by several Afghan guerilla organisations and the arrival of millions of Afghan refugees have helped aggravate internal strife. Western nations have funneled hundreds of millions of dollars worth of sophisticated weapons through Pakistan to the Afghan rebels, but the large quantities of the supplies have found their way into underground Pakistani arms markets. Elements in the Pakistani army police and the refugee administration are still operating scams to sell weapons and relief supplies for personal gains.[11] In that covert US war against the Soviet Union and a series of Soviet-backed regimes in Afghanistan, the USA chose Afghan religious extremists as their allies. Hand picked by Pakistan's Inter Services Intelligence agency from among Pakistan-based Afghan dissidents and refugees, trained by the Pakistani military and the US Central Intelligence Agency (CIA) and given generous US military assistance, the Mujahideen (Holy Warriors) waged a Jihad against the government in Kabul and its Soviet allies.[12] During this period, the CIA also recruited thousands of volunteers from states in the Middle East and North Africa including Algeria, Egypt, Saudi Arabia, the United Arab Emirates and Yemen to join the Mujahideen. Motivated by religious zeal and the sight of fellow Muslims fighting against the mighty Red Army, these volunteers eagerly underwent military training and joined the Jihad.

The Islamic Jihad, like any other multinational is now a global entity. Thanks to these men, and to the heroism of the Mujahideen and the Afghan people and also to the Stingers, Western and Muslim money, the Red Army, the most powerful military force on Earth, was stopped and turned back. Followed by the death of General Zia in August 1988 in an air crash, the Soviet take over in Kabul formally ended in February 1989. The Afghans won the war but lost the peace. Jealously, tribalism and the lust for power very soon replaced by the holy war. It was a demoralising spectacle; humankind at its lowest ebb; politics as usual. At the other end, the Soviet withdrawal marked the end of an era.

In the post–Afghan period, though Pentagon helped during 1992-95, with the movement of thousands of Mujahideen and other Islamic elements from Central Asia, even some Turks, in Europe to fight alongside Bosnian Muslims against the Serbs, a large number of Afghan Mujahideens became irrelevant to the US. Once the Afghan Jihad was over, the Generals did not know what to do with the fighters being turned out by the madrassas. But the United States of America was largely responsible for blocking peaceful transition of power in post–Soviet phase in Afghanistan. Its weapons and other aid created a pro-US element that had come to haunt regional and international security. These elements were fattened by the ISI at the expense of US tax-payers. Further it was a White House ceremony attended by some bearded and turbaned Afghan guerillas in the mid 1980s that Reagan proclaimed Mujahideen such as Osama bin Laden as the 'moral equivalent of the Founding Fathers' of the United States.[13] When Soviet tanks started rolling out of Afghanistan, the Americans too pulled out without installing their nominee in Kabul. The chaos and bloodshed that followed only helped Pakistan to make Afghanistan its colony.

In the period of US-led war against the Soviet Union in Afghanistan and thereafter Islamabad knew it well that the United States interest in Pakistan stemmed less from a concern for the security of this area and more from its own global strategy. This interest would wax or wane with changes in Washington's perception of Moscow's designs in the region. Hence, should either the Russians withdraw from Afghanistan or the two superpowers agree to a détente in Europe or there be a change of heart between Washington and New Delhi, the American interest in Pakistan would decline. In fact, Pakistan used its participation in the covert US operation not so much to rout the Soviet forces in Afghanistan as to strengthen its military position against India and to favour Afghan guerilla groups based in Peshawar. Islamabad easily pushed its agenda because the United States had accepted its condition that the ISI would control the weapons flow and select the arms recipients.[14] Before Pakistan one option was to turn them into private militias and to use them to terrorise Pakistan's minorities. The other, more attractive alternative, was to export them to Kashmir to try and repeat the so-called Afghan Jihad.

On the other there was no doubt in the fact that the Islamic victory in Afghanistan ignited the new Intifada. Muslims across the world were elated, emboldened and made proud by the victory over Soviet Union in Afghanistan by Islamic faith and ardour, many Muslim reasoned, they could just as well liberate themselves from oppressive regimes, the Israeli occupation of Southern Lebanon, Indian misrule in Kashmir, Catholic oppression in the Philippines, or Russia's brutal repression of the Caucasus.[15] Disgusted by the bloody mess in Afghanistan, many Mujahideen turned their attention outside Afghanistan. A year after the Soviets withdrew from Afghanistan, rebellion erupted in India-held Kashmir. As the Afghan war veterans took their war outside Afghanistan, the security of the United States, several Muslim states, the Philippines, China and Russia came under pressure. But many thought the greatest impact of the movement of these men was felt in South Asia. India particularly began to identify itself as bearing the burnt of the terrorist acts perpetrated by Islamic militants. Indeed Pakistan has been identified by many as 'waging a war by proxy in India-held Kashmir through Islamic militants.[16] Pakistan itself has been wracked by terrorist acts brought about by religious extremism and the drug trade, both a fall-out of the Afghan war.

Pakistan's strategic relations with the United States and the presence of many Arab and other Muslim radicals on its soil have made it a good location for staging terrorist attacks on US and other targets.[17] Despite the traditionally close relations between the United States and Pakistan, there has been an underlying current of anti-US hostility in the Pakistani society. This manifested itself earlier in 1980 when demonstrators burned down the American embassy in Islamabad. The rise of terrorist violence had prompted fortress-like security at the US embassy in Islamabad and also at the embassy in New Delhi. Later in the aftermath of Gulf crisis the promise of Americans as "liberators" had quickly turned into the reality of US troops as "occupiers" in Iraq in the eyes of most Iraqis and that of many countries of the world. Americans are even perplexed and angry over this apparent ingratitude of the Iraqis that they are not appreciative of the immense risk taken by them in causing destabilisation of the international political construct familiar to the people of the world since the second world war.

Even in the long years of cold war the United States of America continued to remain a hot target for many Muslim countries of the world. The Muslim world has the experiences of Israeli occupation of Arab territories which conjures up images of genocidal brutality by Israel meted out to unarmed civilians in the occupied lands. And traditionally among the governments that actively supported terrorist activity were Moammar Gaddafi's Libya, hafez Assad's Syria, Saddam Hussain's Iraq and a fundamentally made-over Iran under Ayatollah Ruhollah Khomeini. Although Gaddafi's Libya had pulled back somewhat from overt association with terrorist activities, Syria and Iran continuously supported the Palestinian Hamas and the Islamic Jihad which have also been included in their repertoire suicide and remote-controlled bombings in crowded malls and market places in Israel. Unlimited oil funds and unbridled megalomania had also induced Saddam Hussain to encourage and employ terrorist organisations to push forward his agenda of eliminating political opponents and unfriendly leaders of neighbouring countries.[17]

Recently the nation that has emerged as the fountainhead of global terrorism is impoverished Sudan, the only African country listed in the US State Department's compilation of seven states sponsoring terrorism. The others are Iraq, Iran, Libya, Syria, Cuba and North Korea. Sudan has been providing paramilitary training, indoctrination, money, travel documents, safe passage and refuge for a wide variety of terrorist groups. Thus, at the close of the nineties terrorism became an incremental epidemic. A new trend towards a decline in state-sponsored terrorism in favour of freewheeling fundamentalist terrorist groups sans any government backing. 'There are many, many groups with no affiliation to a sponsoring state', FBI director Louis Freeh told a Senate panel in 1997, 'I see them proliferating and becoming a more serious threat.[18] It is also the time, as most of us seem, the Clinton Administration and the American people woke up to some hard facts about international terrorism. They do understand the military and political challenges facing America. What they do not comprehend is that the US has become the primary target of terrorists' warfare. They do not appear to understand that without a sound strategic policy on terrorism, the US will not only remain vulnerable, but also become more and more exposed to such heinous assaults.[19]

In fact US governments have traditionally adopted the moral high ground and built a self-image they stand for liberty, democracy, international law and peace. However, the pursuit of real politik has meant adopting policies that are contrary of these ideals. The problem is of too much power on one side and too little on the other, the problem of plenty on one side and nothing on the other. Muslims, especially in West Asia have felt that their land and resources have been misused and misappropriated by outsiders who have been manipulating their leaders. It is a feeling of being at the receiving end of an unfair deal, of being the victims but being portrayed as the perpetrators.[20] The US and Islam represent two major and potent forces in world politics today. The former is politically unified and centralised, economically and militarily dominant, the latter is politically decentralised and weak, has vital economic assets but no control, but is strong in its ideology and sense of hurt and revenge.[21] Islamic radicalism/violent extremism of which Al-Qaeda is a facet is very much a 20th century phenomenon and not a throwback to some medieval stereotype. It is very much the global privatisation of terror. Radical Islam is a reaction of democracy and capitalism as practised by the West.

Among the most dangerous terrorists active with both the will and the wealth to pursue his demented agenda, was the Saudi millionaire Osama bin Laden who fought in the Afghan war and has emerged in recent years as one of the principal sources of funding for Islamic terrorism. Under his guidance and help several terrorist attacks were successfully carried out targeting the USA which had upset the US policy makers and the public as well. At the close of the century militants based in Egypt also bear a deep-rooted animosity towards the United States for incarcerating World Trade Center bomber Ramz Ahmed Yosef as well as their spiritual leader the blind Sheikh Omar Abdel Rahman. In the meantime a terrorist threat against America was issued just prior to the East African embassy bombings by the Egyptian Jihad which vowed to retaliate for Washington's assistance in extraditing indicated Islamic militants from Albania to Cairo. Albania extradited a Muslim extremist sentenced to death in absentia in 1997, along with three members of the Islamic group wanted by Egypt. After the incident Jihadi leader Ayman el-Zawahri told to a Kuwaiti newspaper in July 1998 that 'we inform the Americans of preparations for a response which we hope they read with care, because we will write it, with God's help, in a language they will understand.' He also added, 'if America insists on belittling the

Muslim nation, the only alternative is to declare a Jihad against America and Israel, and the Islamic movement is now in agreement on the need for such a Jihad.' In continuation the Islamic extremists attacked on US embassies in African countries and blew up in October 2000 the American warship, USS Cole, moored at Aden, causing the death of 17 US sailors. Thus, the history of terrorism in the 20th century shows that a war on terrorism can not be won, unless the causes of terrorism are eradicated by making the world a place free of grievances, something that will not happen.

Unfortunately, in the whole context of US campaign against terrorism, from the very beginning, America has displayed a tendency to keep double standards. For instance, Islamic fundamentalism in Iran is totally unacceptable, whereas the Saudi version is winked at. Some American officials and members of Congress even seem to believe that there is a difference between pro-American terrorists and anti-American terrorists, and that they must condone the terrorism of the one and condemn that of the other. Whether it occurs in Africa, the Middle East, China, Pakistan or in India, the US administration must oppose terrorism. condemn it and do its best to stop it with the same vigour.[22] With the passing of time the USA was worried over the issue and struggling hard to find an answer to the growing internalisation of terrorism. In June 2001, CIA Director George Tenet had called terrorism the US's number one enemy. Especially the methods that had been adopted for detecting and foiling terrorists' plans during the Clinton's era, of working with governments, some of them weak and compromised and building intelligence linkages around the world, seemed too slow and uncertain.

Event of 9/11 and Terrorism

The fateful event of 11 September 2001, also called the 'Black Tuesday' has entered the contemporary history of the world as a landmark date. It reminded the prophetic words of George Tenet, the then CIA Director, who told the Congress at the end of January 1999 that Osama bin Laden could strike 'at any time' against symbols of American power. In this devastating attack the terrorists targeted all the symbols of the US power and dominance. The World Trade Center (WTC) represents US economic power; Pentagon its military capabilities and the White House, where target was missed was the symbol of the overall US dominance as a sole superpower in the post-Cold War global power structure.

The twin towers in Newyork city symbolised the magnificence of American capitalism, were reduced to rubble. Brazen and audacious acts of terrorism executed with implacable cruelty exposed the fragility of the world order.[23] Fortress United States, thus far unscathed by the forces of destruction, never imagined that fundamentalist forces could produce demons who, in the name of religion, would seek glory in self-destruction. Michael Cox has described this attack as 'the most devastating terrorist atrocity in the history and the first mainland attack on the USA since the British burnt the White House in 1832.

The twin towers of the WTC in Newyork, symbol of America's greatness and grandeur, had taken seven years to construct at a cost of $ 30 billion. The iconic targets of the Al-Qaeda attacks reduced the magnificant structure to rubble within 90 minutes. CIA, the custodian of America's security with its $ 30 billion annual budget, global reach, mastery over numberous spy satellites and world-wide espionage network of at least 100,000 well trained and fully equipped staff, drew total blank.[24] The failure of the US intelligence was monumental. What a great irony that even a secret office of the CIA was destroyed in the attack, temporarily disturbing normal intelligence operations. It demonstrated further the first major failure of the CIA in half a century since its inception in 1947. Both the CIA and the FBI abruptly failed to tail the movements of Bin Laden's operations. It is estimated that total cost of the lost economic growth around the world might have crossed a trillion dollars where as the Al-Qaeda attack itself would have cost hardly a few hundred millions. A pall of gloom had descended on America in which some six to seven thousand lives are feared lost and citizens of many countries were buried under the molten debris of what once stood as the symbol of America's military and economic pride.[25] The message of the aggressor was loudly heard throughout the world that henceforth the world and America shall not be the same again. No doubt, the attack had global ramifications; it generated unprecedented political trauma, economic downslide, military challenges and ideological vibrations. The whole dynamics of world security underwent a sea-change.

In addition to intelligence failure, the terrorist attacks exposed America's military might, its foreign policy bankruptcy along with its unilateralist postures and expansionist designs which it had continuously nourished since the collapse of the USSR. What a great paradox is contained in the fact that even after the termination of the Cold War, the US kept on continuously spending forty per cent of the world's total military expenditure which accounted for sixteen per cent of US budget. The US defence review holds that it was all set to maintain its dominance in the post-Cold War world.[26] The events of 11 September, 2001 have changed the whole Western approach towards terrorism. Of this there are two specific aspects. One was that for the first time, terrorism attacked the mightiest of the powers, in its otherwise secure home turf, and injected a serious sense of vulnerability in a society that was internally enjoying the supreme sense of security. Secondly, and this is more important that the events were more than a mere act of terrorism. These were a challenge to the prevailing hegemonic power structure of the world and a powerful statement that the dominance of the US in this power structure was not acceptable, that it could be challenged through the use of force and violence.[27] In the circumstances, what was most unacceptable to the US was the challenge to its hegemony and dominance. Without massive retaliation the credibility of the hegemony could not have been restored and reinforced.

The incident of 9/11 had evoked resentment in and outside the country, worldwide. The President George Bush, National Security Adviser Condoleezza Rice, Director of Policy Planning in the State Department Richard N. Hass and the national C.E.O. Dick Cheney were important among those who, in the prevailing situation argued to restructure the world order in favour of the US. Apart from complete elimination of Terrorism in future, their statements involved the consolidation of the strategic hierarchy with the US dominance in global power structure. Ms. Rice, for instance, had compared the post 9/11 situation with the one that prevailed during 1945-47 or the formative years of Cold War and pleaded that it is important to try to seize on that and position American interests and institutions before they harden again.[28] Richard N. Hass wanted to evolve a new doctrine of integration that proposed that the US should 'integrate other countries and organisations into arrangements that will sustain a world consistent with US interest and values. The goal in the post 9/11 period, as described by Dick Cheney, is to create the arrangement for the 21st century in order to assure that 'the United States will continue to be the dominant political, economic and military power in the world.

It was in this context the war against global terrorism and the international coalition to fight this war to the finish should be seen and understood. But the attack was not just terror and the resultant agony and a few facts about it stretched beyond human imagination. The incident itself provoked us to serious pondering over the phenomenon of terror, its implications for future inter-state relations and the shape of things to come in international relations. It gave the US and countries of the world a justifiable cause in the name of fighting terrorism. No country can justifiably say that it would not collaborate, in whatever manner possible, in the fight against terrorism or would not support the US war against terrorism. The incident clearly implied that the ugly face of terrorism may fork anywhere, any time, anyway and anyhow. It never came with a warning to America, but it brought loads of loss that humans can not endure any more. This is why cutting across continents, political divide, national and religious boundaries, the world seemed one to fight terrorism to the finish. There is no more the talks about your terrorism, their terrorists or my terrorism. Thus, it is a common, pernicious phenomenon, pervasive everywhere, dangerous to everyone, injurious to the health of every nation and detrimental in every way to the cause of peaceful development.

Terror Combating Strategy of America

For this fateful event the Americans thought Osama bin Laden as the mastermind of terror and his protector the Talibans as the source of terrorism. Talibans and Osama called the American military action a terror, and their fight against this terror a Jihad. Since Osama bin Laden declared war on the United States in 1996 Al-Qaeda and its affiliates have launched repeated attacks that have killed thousands of innocent Americans and hundreds of civilians from other countries. On the other the United States and its coalition partners remain at war against Al-Qaeda and its affiliates, both in Afghanistan and in further operations around the world. The globe–spanning nature of the Al-Qaeda threat has raised the level of complexity and the stakes involved. Even some states forced to act quickly to respond to twenty-first century escalation of attacks and meet emerging threats, have struggled to fit their actions into the international law of armed conflict.[29] Some experts assessed that the primary terrorist threat to the United States would come from Al-Qaeda and other similar terrorist organisations: hierarchical organisations functioning according to some centralised control and with significant operating bases and leadership cores supporting activities abroad.[30] This view is supported by historical accounts of Al-Qaeda's rise to become arguably the most powerful terrorist organisation in history, which emphasises its sophisticated organisation and dependence on territorial safe havens.[31] In that kind of situation the United States in order to protect the nation and its citizens and for the effective conduct of military operations to prevent further terrorist attacks, began to look out for the best possible strategic steps at the earliest.

In combating terrorism the United States of America has a different counter terrorist structure than other close allies, such as Australia, Canada, France, and the United Kingdom. Each has a structure that fits its particular legal system and culture: there is no ideal solution. A continuing issue is whether there needs to be a domestic intelligence service separate from the Federal Bureau of Investigation (FBI) which has had difficulty in breaking away from its law enforcement roots and cooperating with other intelligence services.[32] In past coordinating structures have been created by each President to fit his administrative style and the perceived level of threat. The National Counter Terrorism Center (NCTC) is no longer in the CIA proper, but is in the Office of the Director of National Intelligence (ODNI). However NCTC contains personnel from the CIA, FBI of the Department of Justice and other members of the Intelligence Community. A counter-terrorism center did exist in the CIA before the NCTC was established.

The National Security Act of 1947 had created the CIA but strictly forbade it from having any domestic police authority, however, the CIA still has multiple dimensions. The National Clandestine Service (NCS) of the CIA can infiltrate or otherwise gain human-source intelligence from terrorist organisations, their supporters, or from friendly foreign intelligence service. The NCS has a covert operations capability that, possibly in combination with military units from the United States Special Operations Command (USSOCOM) may take direct action against terrorist groups outside the United States. Above all, the key CIA counter-terror partner is the FBI, which has the domestic operational responsibility for counter-terrorism, both domestic intelligence collection and domestic police work. In the highly decentralised police system of the United States, the FBI also provides liaison and operates cooperatively with state and local police agencies as well as with relevant Federal units. Long before the 9/11 attack the US intelligence community has been dealing with aspects of terrorism. Those aspects included the support of guerillas against Soviets, in South-east Asia, and other places where the guerillas methods may have included terror. In Asia, Latin America and Africa, the US worked with government to suppress terror.

In post-9/11 period the Government of United States felt the need to pass special orders/laws for persons detained by the US authority in connection with terrorist activities. Making the idea more clear Dick Cheney, the Vice President of the country on November 14, 2001 said, 'The basic proposition here is that somebody who comes into the United States of America illegally, who conducts a terrorist operation killing thousands of innocent Americans, men, women and children is not a lawful combatant. They do not deserve to be treated as a prisoner of war. They do not deserve the same guarantees and safeguards that would be used for an American citizen going through the normal judicial process. They will have a fair trial, but it will be under the procedures of a military tribunal'.[33] Although US Congress has not formally declared war against Al-Qaeda, the President has authorise the detention treatment and trial of non-citizens in the Global War on Terrorism under a 'Military Order' derived from the constitutional authority vested in his position as the President and Commander in Chief of the armed forces of the United States. It resulted in the prosecution of the war against terror in the detention by the United States of at least 650 citizens from more than 40 countries at military detention facilities on the US naval base at Guantanamo Bay, Cuba. As per a report prepared by Defense Department lawyer in 2003 Guantanamo Bay was preferred by the Administration because it offers the Administration certain legal advantages as it falls outside the jurisdiction of US courts and hence removes the possibility of detainee's rights to question the detention in US courts. In succeeding year the Guantanamo Bay issue became a controversial one and US Supreme Court as well as a Federal District Court had passed comments in negative and found it a step which undermines the rule of law in the country.

For reasons known to all Osama bin Laden, Al-Qaeda and its various affiliates remained at the top of US research and analysis wings. Thousands of studies were made on the different aspects of Al-Qaeda networks in countries of the world, the US in particular. In this connection some occasional insights were offered in a way that was certainly believable, but without real documentation, it however, described the group a loose organisation of terrorists who may have no idea who the leader is or where the plans come from.[34] Weiser and Golden quote Juliette Kayyem of the Harvard University, Kennedy School of Government: 'Bin Laden is the leader of a movement that does not necessarily need a leader to function and be effective ... This is such a diffuse structure that it can survive without him'. In sum what the reports do describe it is a loose association of two types of persons, planners and doers. The former gather intelligence, pick targets, and provide the materials.[35] the latter are expendable persons whose commitment to the cause, but lack of special training, places them in such a role. Thus, the incomplete picture conjures up a highly dynamic group, with some semblance of leadership structure that may be important for the large efforts, but may not be critical for the maintenance of the terrorist activity. The group is financed by large amounts of money that bin Laden has brought to the process, but has been augmented by significant contributions and, probably, considerable entreneurial activity.

In addition, the event of 9/11 has enhanced the importance of Social Network Analysis (SNA). The basis of social network analysis is that individual nodes, depending on the type of network can be people, event etc, are connected by complex yet understandable relationships that form networks. These networks are ubiquitous, with an underlying order and simple laws. Networks form the structural basis of many natural events, organisations and social processes.[36] Terrorist organisations are well-suited to study using social network analysis, as they consist of networks of individuals, that span countries, continents, and economic status, and form around specific ideology. Terrorist organisations are different from hierarchical, state-sponsored appointments in characteristics such as leadership and organisational structure. At the juncture social network analysis can provide important information on the unique characteristics of terrorist organisations, ranging from issues of network recruitment, network evolution and the diffusion of radical ideas. After the attack social network expert in academia, the government, and even mainstream media including the Washington Post and the Dallas Morning News began to look explicitly at the use of network methodology in understanding and countering terrorism.

It is also to mention here that data collection is difficult for any network analysis because terrorist organisations do not provide information on their members, and the government rarely allows researchers to use their intelligence data. One such social network analysis was published in 2004, namely Understanding Terror Networks by Mare Sageman. Using public sources, Sageman collected biographics of 172 Islamic terrorist operatives affiliated with the global Salafi Jihad, the violent revivalist Islamic movement led by Al-Qaeda. He used social network analysis specifically on

Al-Qaeda operatives since 1998. This analysis yields four large terrorist clusters. The first cluster resides in the Pakistan-Afghan border and consists of the central staff of Al-Qaeda and the global Salafist Jihad movement. The second cluster is a group of operatives located in core Arab states such as Saudi Arabia, Egypt, Yemen, and Kuwait. The third cluster is known as the Maghreb Arabs who, although they come from North African nations, currently reside in France and England. The final cluster is centered in Indonesia and Malaysia and is affiliated with Jemaah Islamiyah.[37] However, for the same work and purpose the federal government had used link analysis which Karl Van Meter describes of two types–the village survey method and traffic analysis.[38] The village survey method is used to understand family and community relationships while traffic analysis emphasises the study of the external characteristics of communication in order to get information about the organisation of the communication system.[39] Thus, the large social network analysis can be used to understand terrorist networks, inform US homeland security policy, and form the basis of a more effective counter-measure to net war.

As the national interests need to clearly take precedence over political partisanship, in America's hour of crisis both the Republicans and the Democrats stood united and speaking in one voice. After September 11, 2001, a new world emerged that was harder, fiercer, less tolerant and more assertive.[40] In that kind of situation a totally different approach to counter terrorism is needed. It was a case of doing what has been done before but doing more of it and doing it more effectively. Now at the heart of countering terrorism is the intelligence and the events of September 11 which have also focussed attention on intelligence work as never before. The US has imposed new border controls along with other anti-terror measures. It began to take the fingerprint of those who come to the country and has given the FBI investigative powers which were previously unacceptable, for example, the power to monitor suspected terrorists without prior evidence of criminal activity and rolling back restrictions imposed decades ago to curb anti-communist hysteria. Now it became more acceptable for the government to take more powers to detain or deport those suspected of plotting terrorism in other countries. Before the incident there was greater concern about the quality of the evidence and the nature of the regime alleging terrorist involvement. But on the other hand it is also necessary, especially in countries like the USA to balance the citizens' right to live their lives in freedom with minimum interference with their privacy from the security agencies, against their responsibility to protect their citizens from harm.

Terror Strategy in Afghanistan via Pakistan

The terrorist attacks of 9/11 were the result of a catastrophic intelligence failure in which different American agencies failed to connect the dots. In response, the George William Bush Administration launched not one but two wars, first in Afghanistan and then in Iraq. The military sledgehammer, produced collateral gains and losses for the US–regime change in Kabul and Bagdad but thousands of body bags too, military bases in the cockpit of Asia but international opposition and even opprobrium as well, a bonanza for its arms and contractor industries but also a fiscal deficit which helped pave the way to a full blown financial crisis.[41] The extraordinary situation in which it was placed forced the US to co-opt Pakistan, the fountain head of terrorist activities,into its crusade against global terrorism. Pakistan, once again, on account of dictates of geography, became a frontline state against Afghanistan for a second time in the last 10 years. Earlier the American interest in Pakistan somewhat declined after the breakdown of the Soviet and cessation of the cold war. But the event of 9/11 had regenerated the US interest in Pakistan because it was at the centre of the world's worst Islamist terrorist network. The Bush Administration lifted all the sanctions imposed in post-nuclear explosion period, and it became an essential partner in global war on terror.[42] The US in its war against terror had, without hesitation strengthened General Pervez Musharraf, the then military ruler of Pakistan, who was not a democrat. Musharraf seized power in a coup, overthrowing a legally elected government of Nawaz Sharif. In addition his closest neighbour, the largest democracy accuses him of fomenting violence and sponsoring terrorism.[43] The key feature of this strategy was that the US worked through the government of Pakistan and not in disregard of it. It strengthened Musharraf's capabilities, instead of weakening them.

However, the US support of Pakistan had pushed the military regime in the biggest dilemma the country has ever faced. On the one side, the world's most powerful nation, wounded and angry, was bluntly telling the General that if he did not act as a friend now he would be considered as the enemy. On the other were the Taliban leaders of the most brutish police state in the world and their hordes who threatened Jihad against the very country that had nurtured them. At the juncture Pakistan with weak economy, a polarised polity, China backing Washington and the Islamic bloc a virtual non-factor, all taking together, made Pakistan to side with the United States of America's global strategy against terrorism. It was apparent that General Musharraf was in a difficult position torn between US demands for cooperation and demands by the Islamic clergy, and terrorist organisations. Ultimately, Musharraf decided to distance himself from the Taliban-ruled Afghanistan and agreed to provide help to Washington in such key areas as intelligence and information exchange, use of Pakistan's air space and logistical support which involved tremendous risks for his regime. In a nutshell, to achieve its goal the US forcibly co-opted Pakistan and, through economic inducements, coupled with public praise and private admonition, made Musharraf turn on Pakistan's protégés, the Taliban and the Al-Qaeda in Afghanistan. Once again the United States war against terror had changed Pakistan's destiny. Islamabad's profile in the eyes of the West, and particularly the Americans, had changed completely. General Musharraf had been courted and flattered by world leaders as the defender of the faith of the civilised world.

In post-9/11 period the first anti-terror war that the US had fought was in Afghanistan where ultimately a pro-terror regime was dethroned. By the time of the event in the USA terrorism has become a system with its wings in nearly sixty countries of the world and it was not wisely for the Washington to antagonise them all at one time. In Afghanistan alone there were 30 camps[44] and the world was united to fight this international network of terrorism under the leadership of the United States. In addition, the terror networks in Afghanistan change their colours and mutate their names too fast and adapt to adverse and inclement conditions swiftly. The all Jihadis were united in and around Pak-Afghan border territory with different names, such as, Zamaut-ul-Islam, Harkat-ul-Ansar, Al Faran, Harkat-ul-Mujahideen, Laskar-e-Toiba, Jaish-e-Mohammad, Sipahi Sabah and many others of their local branches. These all terror organisations had bases and branches in the Taliban-controlled Afghanistan, Pakistan and Pak-occupied Kashmir.[45] Their involvement in subversive activities across the border of many countries and beyond makes terrorism a cross-country problem to be addressed and tackled collectively.

The 'Operation Enduring Freedom' of the United States of America in Afghanistan began on 7 October, 2001 with the night bombing of Kabul, Kandahar and Jalalabad at 9 p.m. and all the NATO allies stood by the side of America. On the occasion President George Bush had claimed that 40 countries had pledged support to the US to stamp out terrorism from the face of earth, others have extended logistic support; still others have made encouraging gestures. But from the beginning there was a discernible difference between what the USA tried to protect and what the Taliban regime in alliance with Al-Qaeda sought to preserve. While the former wanted to restore democracy and preserve human rights in a country ravaged by over two decades of continuing war, the latter sought to defend their misrule and mal-administration under the guise of Islam.[46] Despite the paradox, the US decision to co-opt Pakistan to fight Taliban was certainly a tactical move, strategic in nature.

The US anti-terror operation in Afghanistan lasted just two months. It is said to be masterful in both design and execution. The USA dropped more smart bombs on Afghanistan that the NATO dropped on Serbia in 1999. The Taliban forces, estimated at 50,000 to 60,000 strong and a few thousand Al-Qaeda fighters were crushed by the US troops numbering around 60,000 and the allied forces numbering approximately 15,000. War-ships of Japan, Italy, Britain and the Netherlands were deployed in the Arabian Sea. The bombers of the US armed forces operated out of Diego Garcia. Land-based aircrafts flew from Oman and planes from the American aircraft carriers, based in Arabian Sea provided the rest of the combat punch. The cost of the Afghanistan War reached $ 3.8 billion, whereas the military cost of the Homeland Security efforts in the USA was $ 2.6 billion.[47] The US forces, which have claimed to have staged impressive feat of quickest possible military action, lost about only 30 personnel whereas 8,000 to 12,000 Taliban troops are believed to have died.

As the war against terrorism in Afghanistan progressed, it became clear that Musharraf was not prepared to forsake the Taliban entirely. In fact Pakistan was playing a double game-helping the US offensive while trying to ensure that their old Taliban allies have a prominent role in post-war government. General Musharraf had opposed US support to the Northern Alliance (NA). Sections of the US media felt that Pakistan was not a reliable ally. The CIA had accused the ISI of playing a double-game of pretending to help yet allowing the flow of weapons into Afghanistan.[48] On the other hand even after destroying all the suspected hideouts of Taliban-Al-Qaeda, the leadership of neither of the two organisations were to be seen anywhere. They were neither captured nor killed. Further, in the post-Taliban scenario, one finds that the evidence of close ties Islamabad has had with the Taliban, Osama bin Laden and Al-Qaeda, and these three had with terrorist militias like the LeT, JeM and HuM directly and through Pakistan's ISI, had destroyed its credibility with the US and other Western countries. Hence, Pakistan was under intense pressure to clamp down on these and reform the country into a moderate Islamic state. It was because despite the success of the United States-led coalition in the Afghan war, terrorism is alive and well.

Earlier the military action of United States of America in October 2001 was justified on the grounds that the then Afghan regime was harbouring people responsible for the terrorist atrocities of September 9/11, it however, was not supported by other analysts who propose that on the same grounds Britain could have bombed Boston or Newyork in the 1970s and 1980s as these cities certainly harboured and helped finance IRA terrorists, Cuba could attack Florida now, and at various times India could have claimed justification for an all-out assault on Pakistan. The second execuse on the issue was complaints by the US and British officials that the insurgents are hiding themselves among the populace, using civilians as "human shields" betray the dangerous logic characteristic of military intervention of this type.[49] But above all, was the fact that the US intervention in the wake of 9/11 was primarily motivated by a petty concern for the US reputation as a country that knows how to get its way in the world. It endorsed a war on terror whose aims were frightening open-ended, whose methods were in essence lawless and disproportionate, and whose targets were to be defined as the convenience of the world most powerful nation.[50] The US military intervention in Afghanistan had certainly eroded international support for America in its fight against terror. At the time it had also failed to capture Osama bin Laden 'dead or alive' as its President promised.

Even the second military operation of the US in Afghanistan launched on June 15, 2006 involved a massive force of 11,000 soldiers of whom 6000 were Afghans and the rest were Americans, British and Canadians. In this phase the centre of operation was the mountains of four southern provinces–Kandahar, Zabul, Uruzgan and Helmand. All the four provinces have harboured insurgents right from the time the Taliban were forced to flee to Pakistan in the wake of the fierce coalition attacks in late 2001.

Sporadic and limited operations to clean them up throughout the last four years and more having miserably failed and the Taliban having made a definite comeback, the operation of June 2006 two had turned into a long-drawn war with the Taliban. Likewise the US blatant illegality of Iraq war and the use of naked force without global consent had put many in the world in a quandary. The US wars in Afghanistan and Iraq had eroded its image as a reasonable superpower in world politics. The US unilateral actions left a strong sense of loss of dignity, hurt and anger in the Muslim world that will take generations to heal.

Earlier alike, in pre- and post- 9/11 phase the double speak, double standard, and double-edged foreign policy of the United States of America continued for a long time to come. In devising a strategy to prevent 9/11 type terrorist attacks in future, following the incident within a year George William Bush, the then President of USA, had withdrawn from involvement with the Khatami regime in Iran on the grounds that it was not moving fast enough on the steps that the US wanted it to take and issued a call to all democratic Iranians to work towards a regime change in country. It had supported the ouster of Arafat in Palestine and less directly, of Crown Prince Abdullah from the Saudi line of succession because of his firm opposition to the use of American bases in his country to attack Iraq.[51] In addition, the US had a long list of countries, at least 14 where it felt there is scope for potential anti-terrorist action. According to General Peter Pace of the American Marine Corps and vice-chairman of the joint chiefs of staff, who disclosed that the US might have to intervene directly to pre-empt a terrorist threat in Iran, Iraq, Yemen, Somalia, Sudan, Lebanon, Syria, Libya, Georgia, Colombia, and significantly Malaysia, Indonesia, the Philippines and North Korea. But to utter surprise the US list did not include Afghanistan and Pakistan where the Americans were present with the support of the local government and where things could turn sour in a flash. It was also not clear why the US list had not included Egypt, Algeria and Turkey, where strong Islamic movements exist or Saudi Arabia, which in US defence department presentation had been dubbed as the source and key financier of Islamist terrorism in the world.

Thus, the US policy regarding combating terrorism remained under severe attacks. Most of the analysts were of the view that any military intervention in the name of change of regime or otherwise would worsen the situation by making the state system itself weak and any pick and choose in this regard would work against the spirit of counter-terrorism. The fatal flaw in the present strategy of the US was that it in its search for a solution that was both quick and secure it had proposed a cure that will be harmful for both the parties concerned. Military intervention in any country normally comes head-on against the powerful sentiment of nationalism and align it with the terrorists. Pressures upon the states to tolerate or shelter terrorists will increase instead of decreasing. Their capacity to cooperate in the international coalition against terrorism will weaken.[52] Even a newly installed government will be less capable of attacking the terrorists in its midst and will have to be replaced by other. However, the proper way to strengthen a nation is to provide it with both the motive and the capacity to keep terrorists away from establishing bases upon its soil.

In the spheres of war in Afghanistan and Iraq and distinction among states on no rational ground has earned a bad reputation for the United States of America in and outside the country. Arguing that the war on Afghanistan constituted a greater terrorist act than the September 11 attacks on the US, Professor Noam Chomsky denounced state terrorism in all forms. The terrorist mentality of the US neo-conservative establishment was exemplified by a response to the killings of civilians in Afghanistan by a Pentagon official who said, "The people there are dead because we wanted them dead."[53] In fact, there has been failure to deliver on the promises made to Afghans because the premises of the invasion of their country were from the outset, profoundly flawed. Meanwhile millions of Afghans face starvation in terms of the then situation and the development and democracy promised by western leaders has yet to materialise.

The criticisms made in the country and at the global level were bound to make on the US a deep impact. In this context on September 5-6, 2002, the US State Department hosted a high-powered conference on anti-Americanism, an unusual step indicating the depth of American concern about this increasingly globalised phenomenon. Anti-Americanism can be mere shallow name-calling. Criticising the US image world over, The Guardian described the Americans as having "a bug up their collective arse the size of Manhattan," and suggested that American is a type of personality which is intense, humourless, partial to psychobabble and utterly convinced of its own importance.[54] Especially the Bush Administration had made a string of foreign policy miscalculations. In fact after the brief flirtation with consensus-building during the

Afghan operation, the US's brazen return to unilateralism had angered even its natural allies and on the issue of military intervention in Iraq which took place in the year 2003. James Baker, the Republican grandee, had warned Bush not to go it alone, at least in the little matter of effecting a regime change in Iraq. The State Department's anti-Americanism was aimed to support the Powell line and undermine the positions of the hawks to whom Bush listened closely.

In this connection there were several concrete evidences that showed the United States', self-serving, opportunist and immoral actions in international politics that marred its credibility as a super power, particularly in Muslim world. The seriousness of the matter was felt at the authoritative level and Charlotte Beers, former Under Secretary of State for Public Affairs and Public Diplomacy, in one of the Senate Foreign Relations Committee's hearings spoke of the "frightening wide" gap between how America sees itself and how the rest of the world sees America. Regarding the Muslim world he told the committee that "Millions of ordinary people have gravely distorted but carefully cultivated images of US-images so negative, so weird, so hostile that I can assure you a young generation of terrorists are being created".[55] Although President Bush considered it the failure of the American public diplomacy in trying to do a better job of telling our story and stylistic difference but his claims did not carry sufficient weight and in many cases this part of US foreign policy appears right even today.

However, despite much hue and cry over the US policy in Afghanistan via Pakistan, its policy with the latter remained smooth and cordial as ever and Islamabad was considered to be the main instrument in the fight against the terrorism in foreseeable future. The Af-Pak strategy made a strong case for providing military assistance to Pakistan to help its government root out terrorists now settled along the tribal belt of the state along its western borders. The US strategy, although mentioned that such assistance will not be unconditional and will be contingent on Pakistan demonstrating its willingness and commitment to take action against terrorists thriving and operating from within its territorial boundaries. In addition, it called for providing financial assistance to Pakistan to build up its basic infrastructure and public service capabilities-measures the US believes will enable strengthening of Pakistan's democratic institutions and in turn, prevent more people, especially the youth, from turning to the Taliban and other extremist groups. Such an isolation of Al-Qaeda from the Pakistani people, it is hoped, will help stem the growing anti-American sentiment in the region and the increasing alienation of the people from the Pakistani state.[56] Finally the strategy was significant in that it envisioned a role for regional stakeholders such as India, China, Russia, the Gulf, Iran and the Central Asian Republics in devising solutions to usher in peace, security and development into the war–torn state by supporting the upcoming Afghan elections, training Afghan security forces and a greater civilian commitment to the Afghan people.

The US strategy on terrorism and its liberal attitude was exploited by Pervez Musharraf, the then military ruler of Pakistan, as now the latter could not support the Taliban and Al-Qaeda in previous way. In a calculated move Pakistan made a tactical withdrawal and decided to cooperate with the West to the extent it was necessary to protect Pakistan's strategic interests. In a dangerously calibrated response it made queer deals and counter-deals with both the sides. Pakistan is an ally of the US in the war against terrorism and Musharraf had agreed publicly in his 12 January, 2002 speech to wage the war domestically and make the choice which the US and the democratic world wants him to make. After his speech of 12 January the whole world seemed to be in a mood to give the General a standing ovation for his bold and visionary approach to tackle terrorism.[57] On the other hand, in a televised address to the nation Musharraf tried to portray his US friendly act as a strategic decision that was designed to prevent a proactive India from isolating Pakistan on the international scene in the aftermath of Pentagon episode. He also expressed country's concern for cooperation with the US on Pakistan's integrity, the state of economy, the sustainability of its strategic assets of nuclear weapons and missiles, besides the Kashmir issue.[58] In a nutshell the image of Pakistan had improved considerably in the West, but mainly in the eyes of the US who assessed Islamabad as an important bulwark in the anti-terror fight. Especially the US has made it clear that it will stay in Pakistan till it is cleansed of terrorism. It will support Musharraf as long as he plays the role Washington wants.[59] Thus the overall situation in world politics became in favour of Pakistan and the latter again focussed its attention on Kashmir issue to be settled in its favour.

Particularly in post–Taliban period, General Musharraf had only the Kashmir issue to build domestic support in his favour and divert attention from the foreign policy failures. Accordingly a well-planned, carefully crafted terrorist attack by the JeM was made on the Indian Parliament, located at the heart of the capital's high security zone, on 13 December, 2001. The incident clearly gave India the message that despite the success of the United States–led coalition in the Afghan war, terrorism is alive and active. The attack was also a proof that the Musharraf regime had not sold out to the US and its alliance with the latter was meant to safeguard Pakistan's nuclear arsenal and prevent the US from including its cross-border terrorism against India in its anti-terrorist agenda. Pakistan's policy of different strokes for different folks bracketed the terrorists in three broad categories–those targetting the West, those responsible for domestic violence and those hitting at India. And Pakistan countinues to be soft on the groups operating against India. Their top leaders live and move around in Pakistan freely, travel on Pakistani passports and run businesses with impunity. The training camps and other terrorist facilities have also not been rolled back, though greater discretion is exercised.[60] The General on number of occasions reiterated his usual formula on the issue and said that Kashmir is a part of every Pakistani's blood.

However, the US administration of late has become frustrated as Pakistan had not been able to wipe off the terrorist hideouts from the country. Not only that the Al-Qaeda was controlling the terrorist activities from their base in Pakistan. They have also reconstituted their positions on the Pak–Afghan borders. In previous years, General Musharraf had played that 'I am your final line of defence against the Jihadists taking over in this nuclear–armed country' card to win grace, favour, money and arms from the US. The $ 5 billion was provided through a programme known as Coalition Support Fund, which reimbursed Pakistan for conducting military operations to fight terrorism under a separate programme, Pakistan received $ 300 million per year in traditional military financing that pays for equipment and training.[61] Despite this immense help in Islamabad Washington military officers of the Bush Administration had said that they believed much of the American money was not making its way to front line Pakistani units. They concluded that money had been diverted to help finance weapons system designated to counter India and not the Al-Qaeda or the Taliban.

In December 2007, for the first time after six years the Pentagon had completed a review that produced a classified plan to help the Pakistani military build an effective counter-insurgency force. The US leadership, particularly in the Congress had expressed doubts in the intentions of Pakistan on controlling terrorist activities. The misuse of US funds in Pakistan had also reached to People's court and now the American citizen has started asking about the intelligent use of its money, particularly when they use the dollar becoming more productive and yielding higher returns in India. A kind of rethinking on the issue was felt by the American government who favoured the restoration of a democratic set up. 'It is true that Pakistan's government needs greater popular legitimacy won through the ballot box in order to advance both long and short-term counter-terrorist goals.[62]

From the year 2007 turbulence in Pakistan's national life started when Pervez Musharraf's five years extended term as President expired. The fast moving events and actions of Pakistan had made the US options difficult to operate. The reasons are two. First, the USA has become a hated word in Pakistan and any leader who acquires power with the visible or even invisible support of America may not be acceptable to masses in the country. Second, the army in Pakistan is too embedded in the political hierarchy and social fabrics. Markey, a famous scholar of the US, believes, 'Any attempt to crack down on Pakistan will exacerbate distrust resulting in increased Pakistani support for Jihadists; coercive threats will undermine confidence without producing better results.[63] Even for the present mess in the Pak polity West is more responsible than the Pakistan itself. Sixty years of pampering of the military dictatorships has brought about a strong military system that controls not only the political system but also the economy. In a nutshell, the US has become a deciding factor in Pakistan whether civil or military. 'Washington can win the confidence of Pakistan's military establishment without accepting its exclusive political authority, and it can help empower civilian leadership without jeopardising the army's core interests.

Terrorism and George William Bush

The terrorist attacks on the World Trade Centre in Newyork and the Pentagon had on the one hand exploded the myth of American invincibility and on the other thrown up the prospect of a possible war. The incident had changed the perception of the entire security scenario throughout the world. People in general all over the world began to think that if terrorists could strike at the WTC, a symbol of US economic supremacy and the Pentagon, the seat of the US defence establishments, they could strike anywhere.[64] According to America, September 11 was the day that changed the world. Nothing was ever the same. The only possible parallel in its historical significance was the attack on Pearl Harbor the so-called day of infamy when the US also faced death and destruction from the skies. But there are reasons for America's preoccupation with the WTC attacks. The US has always fought its wars in other people's countries. Even the Pearl Harbor raid did not touch the mainland. So any attack on the continental US or America's financial capital was the event of unprecedented significance for US citizens.[65] The shocked world fully knew the consequences of the attack and it was a matter of time before the Americans retaliate and send clear signals to perpetrators that the war against terrorism has only begun and would end with its elimination. No one had even thought, least of all the Americans themselves, that impregnable US security could be subverted.

Things changed dramatically after the terrorist attack of September 11, 2001, and it gave the whole Western world a new approach towards terrorism. In addition to the world-wide condemnation of the attack George William Bush, the then US President and Dick Cheney, the Vice President had responded to the attack with all the eloquence of a yokel and there was enough in the statements that came out of Washington. Colin Powell, too, promised a continuous and concerted war against terror. The first lesson of September 11, as Bush told, was revenge. Speaking about Osama bin Laden, he declared, 'There is a poster in the Old West that says, 'Wanted: Dead or Alive.'[66] The second lesson followed from the first: you did not bother about proof, you followed your own instinct. The US had no evidence that Al-Qaeda was behind the WTC attacks. But it had intelligence leads that suggested a bin Laden connection. The third lesson was that anybody who associated with or harboured a terrorist suspect was to be treated on par with the terrorist. The fourth lesson was that the concept of national sovereignty and of international borders was irrelevant in the fight against terror. Today's terrorists recognise no nations and respect no borders. Bin Laden, an Arab, was based in Afghanistan and headed a force that included Sudanese, Jordanians, Egyptians, etc. If you were fighting international terrorists then you had to adopt their rules. If they did not respect borders, then you had to do the same.

Thus, in the light of lessons learnt, the first principle emerged that the Americans have told the world that any country that is attacked by terrorists has the right to retaliate. In the situation if the terrorists are taking shelter in another country and the government of that country does not agree to hand over the terrorists, then war is an acceptable option. It was under this principled policy that the US had invaded on Afghanistan in 2001 and made an attack on Iraq in the year 2003. No doubt the US-led war against terrorism was supported by most of the countries of the world, it, however, in afterwards, failed to make a distinction between terrorism and Islam. As both terms are not interchangeable as long as it was confined to terrorism, it was in the right direction, but when it went in the other directions it became a part of US agenda of global restructuring. When the coalition launched its campaign against Al-Qaeda and Taliban in Afghanistan in 2001, Denmark fully supported the legal conclusion that a state may engage in an armed conflict with an international terrorist network such as Al-Qaeda. In the beginning of 2002 the coalition joined the fighting in Afghanistan. Back then, most agreed that we were engaged in an international armed conflict in Afghanistan. This conflict in coalition partners' view ended in the summer of 2002.

Likewise, the US attack on Iraq in 2003, as most sensible people accept, was not just or necessary. They argue that Iraq posed a serious threat to the US or its neighbours defy credibility. All she had, at the time of war, was some outdated scuds and crude Al-Samoud-2 missiles lacking guidance system. Nor Iraq at that moment was recklessly expansionist despite its despotic and repressive regime.[67] The duality and double-speak of US foreign policy was also clear in case of the treatment of Iraq. Although Bush had rightly accused Saddam Hussain of practising torture, illegal detention, denial of free passage, punishment of families, economic pauperisation, demolition of houses of adversaries etc. Yet, Ariel Sharon did all that and more including extra-judicial assassinations with the full approval of the US. In addition, on the question of Iraq the US interests were in conflict with the interests of its traditional coalition partners like France and Germany, with other major powers like Russia and China and even the international organisations like the UN. The United States of America made the basis for war on Iraq to destroy the so-called Weapons of Mass Destruction (WMD) but when its approach was not endorsed by the major powers, it decided to move alone.[68] The major powers even considered the US policies as undesirable that may pose a threat to the stability of the emerging world order.[69] In a nutshell, two aspects of Bush's approach in this respect deserve attention. One was that it was dominated by military-strategic moves wherein military action, reinforcing and establishing bases, sale of arms, sharing of intelligence and programmes of joint exercises and even joint operations were emphasised. Secondly, it subdued the ideological dimension which was quite prominent during 1990-91.

In Afghanistan and in Iraq the US expectations belied. There was a hope that the Afghan warlords who were purchased would continue to be loyal. They were not. Pakistani popular support to the Taliban, Al-Qaeda and other associated Jihadis had not been unmanageable for Musharraf. Nor had the mainstream political parties been able to challenge the General and his brand of democratisation. In Iraq the US calculations of the Shia enthusiasm for American liberation also went wrong.[70] In both Afghanistan and Iraq, the Americans and Europeans were learning some primary lessons in military craft. A much smaller but better equipped force can overcome the resistance of a much larger but not as well-equipped force. But to keep an inhabited land where the local population is hostile to occupation, the force requirements are much larger. Thus, it was a basic mistake on the part of Pentagon to think that the US would be welcomed as liberators in Afghanistan and Iraq.

Quite naturally the focus of US war against global terrorism was Asia. The US agenda also covered Asia's all major sub-regions, namely the Persian Gulf, West Asia, Central Asia, South Asia and South-East Asia. The first reason for this was that the attack on US installations on September 11 came from within Asia, and there from a group of people who follow a particular ideology of Islamic fundamentalism. Therefore, if Al-Qaeda and the Taliban have to be eliminated, then the war had to be carried out in the Asian theatre, as was done in Afghanistan and the border regions of Afghanistan and pakistan where the terrorists were suspected to have taken refuge as fugitive. The second reason of targeting Asia is that in recent years it has emerged as the most powerful and dynamic regions of the world. Asia also constitutes the largest landmass of the global territorial spread. In terms of military capabilities, Asia houses eight countries that are nuclear-acquired or nuclear-potential powers, and the same number of Asian nations have achieved ballistic missiles having a range of more than 1,000 km. Robert D. Blackwill said that Asia is poised to become the strategic center of gravity in international politics.[71] He also warned the US that regional powers of Asia are developing sufficient capabilities to threaten American vital national interests and those of its friends and allies.

Under its policy and principles the Bush Administration continued its fight against terrorism and in line it attacked on Iraq in 2003. The US and its allies launched the attack to confirm suspicions about the WMD programme but it had a clear energy goal built into it. The US attacks and operations in Iraq were also severally criticised by all including its allies who considered it the US agenda of reinforcing hegemony drawn in the context of making the world safe from terrorism. We have seen the might and power of US military and technology in Afghanistan and Iraq. But US actions were not about shock and awe, they were more about a powerful country acting out of fear. Fear of the unknown; and once fear takes over rationality retreats. American actions in Fallujah, Abu Ghraib, Karbala and Najaf are bound to leave a strong sense of dignity loss, hurt and anger in the Muslim world that will take generations to heal and will only strengthen radical Islam.[72]

In the war against terrorism the US had threatened and undermine multilateral institutions and norms, rules and restraints. These structures including the UN were built painstakingly over two centuries in the face of Westphalian Nation-States' opposition for dilution of absolute sovereignty. The US unilateralism and bullying will undermine the purpose of the UN. Its Charter's very first objective is 'to save succeeding generation from the scourge of war'. In fact there is no territory to be won in a war against terror, and no knowing when the US will finally be able to say that all sleepers in all terrorist organisations have been found and taken care of, we can not ever be able to declare that war against terror has been won. In the situation it can only be fought against targets defined globally, not selectively, not through hard power of military might alone but also with soft power.

Following the event of 9/11 the United States of America launched the anti-terror measures at large scale whose methods and spirit came in conflict with individual rights. In August 2004 the International Commission of Jurists brought together more than 160 international jurists who adopted the Berlin Declaration on Upholding Human Rights and the Rule of Law in Combating Terrorism. The Declaration's 11 principles mediate the relationship between counter-terrorism measures and human rights, and identify a core set of principles that states should adhere to in executing counter-terrorism policies. To further explore this intersection, the ICJ established the Eminent Jurists Panel on Terrorism, Counter-terrorism and Human Rights, whose eight members were tasked with exploring the scope of modern terrorism and the effect of government counter-terrorism efforts on human rights. The Panel conducted hearings and considered submissions from NGOs, lawyers, academics and experts.

On September 6th-8th, 2006, the Panel conducted its hearings at American University, Washington College of Law in Washington D.C. It laid emphasis on three aspects of the issue: I. the political and legal framework of the war on terror; II. the impact of post-9/11 programmes on human rights and the rule of law; and III. the use of military versus criminal approaches to combating terrorism. The testimony and evidence given before the Panel was a proof that the Bush Administration's war on terror has resulted not only in an assault on individual human rights but also more broadly, in an erosion of the rule of law that threatens the continued strength of domestic and international legal system. It was found by the Panel that there were two central propositions underlying the Bush Administration's counter-terrorism policy: the uniqueness of the terrorist threat and the importance of interpretation in defining the reach of human rights, humanitarian, and constitutional law. But emphasis on the uniqueness of the terrorist threat nonetheless remained a fundamental rhetorical device of the Bush Administration in arguments supporting its counter-terrorism policies. The members of the Panel in general, expressed their unhappiness over the inhuman and degrading treatment in detention and formation of a military commission to try designated detainees.

The military commissions are a type of US military tribunal last used in World War II for the trial of spies, saboteurs and war criminals. These commissions are applicable only to non-US citizens and are designed to protect the individual rights of the accused while also safeguarding classified and sensitive information used as evidence in the proceedings. In post-9/11 period the work was conducted under the direction of Vice President Dick Cheney and coordinated by the White House Counsel at that time, Alberto Gonzales, who has since then been elevated to Attorney-General. Although the work commenced little more than a week after 9/11, the legal basis for Bush Administration's approach was laid on 6 November, 2001 in a then-confidential memorandum sent to the Attorney General's office. The memorandum said that the President, as Commander in Chief, has inherent authority to establish military commissions without Congressional authorisation and that the Administration could apply international law selectively. The Administration moved quickly after receiving the

Attorney General's advice and released the Presidential military order on detention, treatment and trial of certain non-citizens in the war against terrorism a week later on 13 November, 2001.

The Presidential order itself and its methods of operation remained a controversial issue nationally and was criticised at various international fora. However, despite the opposition at large the Bush Administration seemed at a fixed as the then State Department Legal Adviser John Bellinger said in 2006, 'There is no principle of international law that limits a state's ability to act in self-defence to a single territory, when the threat comes from areas outside that territory as well ... As a practical matter ... a state must be responsible for preventing terrorists from using its territory as a base for launching attacks. And, as a legal matter, where a state is unwilling or unable to do so, it may be lawful for the targeted state to use military force in self-defence to address that threat.[73] The Panel of Jurists in course of hearings the complains also expressed objectionable remarks about the practice of military commission in the US and highlighted the fact, 'what is more worrisome is that there are several countries that have done similar things in setting up military commissions. In the past we have influenced these countries, and now the US is losing its ability to influence other countries'. And it is clear that the legal framework of the "War on Terror" had resulted in numerous violations of human rights and humanitarian law.

To the surprise of all President Bush's military trials were the exact types of trials that the United States had been openly condemning in the international community. The effect of this apparent double standard is to deny the United States the moral high ground it needs to censure other nations in the future for human rights abuses. Such double standards potentially place the Administration at odds with the values of the American people, thereby creating a fault line that if pressured in the future may degrade the domestic support base for what is going to be a generation-long Global War on Terrorism. Colin Powell held the view that respect for human rights is essential to lasting peace and sustained economic growth, goals which Americans share with people all over the world.[74] Former President Jimmy Carter also deplored the indefinite detention of the suspects at Guantanamo and added, 'I say this because this is a violation of the basic character of my country and it is very disturbing to me'.[75] On completing international hearings the ICJ eminent jurists issued a report in 2007 which reiterated the significance of rights in a democratic society but made no recommendations for how countries should model their counter-terrorism programmes.

In a nutshell the Bush Administration while prosecuting the war against terror had sought to redefine the borders between civil liberties and public safety. The official position of the Administration remained that the detainees at Guantanamo were unlawful combatants and not prisoners of war. In the situation there is a consensus in favour of adjustment which will take its position between the two extremes. The adjustment would be viewed as ensuring a legitimate form of justice in the international community and would do much to reduce the anti-Americanism that is potentially undermining the coalition in the Global War on Terrorism. Such action is needed not just because it is the right thing to do, but because it is in the long-term interests of the United States and the world community to do so. Despite criticisms, even the coalition partners and the democratic countries of the world have acknowledged and respected the fact that the US is using its vast resources to provide protection-not just for itself but for all of us. Terrorism is a threat against all democratic societies, in fact all states.

Terrorism and Barack Obama

Barack Obama succeeded George William Bush as the 44th President of the United States of America on 20 January, 2009. It marked verily a revolution, a culmination of a long fight of the black (Afro-American) population for equality and human rights. Obama expressed his determination to bring about a qualitative change in internal and external policy which has created an atmosphere of hope and optimism all over the world.[76] In his inaugural speech he has eloquently spoken of his ardent desire to unite US bridging different segments of US population and unite humanity transcending national barriers. The US, he said, will be friend of every country in the world. Generally political campaign speeches are bound to conflict with the ground realities when one sits in position of power. As opposed to Bush Administration earlier, Barack Obama has committed himself to base US conduct in global affairs on values which have been beacon light to be emulated by the world, effectively demonstrated over the years and more recently by a change in Eastern Europe after the collapse of the Soviet Union.[77] However, on assuming the office, Obama remained as steadfast as any other leader to relentlessly confront violent extremists who pose a grave threat to security because one rejects the same thing that people of all faiths reject the killing of innocent men, women and children.

Earlier, too, during the Presidentship of George William Bush security of the country and its citizens remained on the top of Bush's agenda. At the close of his regime much of the heat of the war on terrorism was turned on Pakistan after the US identified Federally Administered Tribal Areas (FATA) and North-West Frontier Province (NWFP) as a safe haven for Al-Qaeda and Taliban insurgent. According to the *Newyork Times*, President Bush was believed to have given confidential orders in July 2008 allowing US air strikes and ground operations to be carried out against militant sanctuaries within Pakistan without the prior knowledge or approval of Islamabad. The first of such attempts by US troops to launch a ground attack in September 2008 was met with stiff resistance and reportedly thwarted by Pakistan paramilitary soldiers. These attacks not only caused massive civilian deaths, but were in flagrant violation of Pakistan's territorial sovereignty. A news report in *The News* stated that of the nearly sixty cross-border American drone attacks between January 2006 and April 2009; only 10 managed to hit their actual targets, leading to the death of 14 Al-Qaeda leaders and perishing 687 innocent Pakistani civilians. Despite the visible opposition to their use, drone strikes seemed to be a favourite with the Americans as they claim that these attacks have delivered significant body blows to the Al-Qaeda leadership.[78] Not only that, George William Bush, in his final farewell speech from the White House on 15 January, 2009, defending his administration's eight year long period of war mongering, said that the war on terror, the ideological pivot of his administration, must carry on. The main thrust of his speech was to defend his tenure as president and exhort the new administration to carry forward the global war against terror that his government had launched in the aftermath of the World Trade Centre attacks in 2001.

At the time Barack Obama took over as the President of USA the focus of the war on terror has come to rest firmly on Pakistan which is seen to have become a sanctuary for Al-Qaeda and Taliban terrorists. A major reason for the Taliban's growing strength has been its ability to escape across the Afghanistan–Pakistan border into the safety of the latter's tribal regions and target the US and NATO forces from these areas. In fact Pakistan continues to remain clearly both part of the problem and the solution to the threat of terrorism facing the United States. Indeed, the 9/11

Commission had more or less highlighted Pakistan's deep involvement with international terrorism and recommended a long-term US commitment to provide comprehensive support to Pakistan. A fractured Pakistan that is nuclear-armed is appropriately termed by Western scholars as the "most dangerous place in the world". In the circumstances US officials have begun to acknowledge the importance of Pakistan pursuing more consistent counter-terrorism policies, rather than relying on its past tactics of fighting some terrorists, while supporting others.

On the other hand, the year 2009 also witnessed a surfacing of the debate within the US administration with measures adopted thereof, to undo the assault unleashed on the international human rights framework during George Bush's presidency. As the war on terror entered its eighth year, it is confronted with several challenges. Robert Gates, Secretary of Defence, is reported to have told the Senate Armed Services Committee that civilian casualties caused by US air strikes were during the US enormous harm. 'If Afghans come to see us as part of their problem, not as part of their solution, then we are lost.[79] With anti-American sentiment already on the rise, civilian deaths will only deepen the antagonism. Thus the primary challenge for the US administration was to target Taliban, without causing concomitant civilian casualties. Perhaps it was in this background that President Obama candidly admitted in his Cairo speech that 'we meet at a time of great tension between the United States and the Muslims around the world, but assured the Muslims that he sought a new beginning based on mutual interest and the truth that America and Islam are not exclusive and need not be in competition.[80] In the situation one can easily expect a change in American behaviour/policy during the Barack Obama Administration.

The new President made a significant policy shift in the war against terror. It was in respect of the overwhelming use of military power and war. This was exhibited in full measure in the shock and awe attacks on Afghanistan and Iraq. Perhaps Bush and his close men in policy-making Vice President Dick Cheney and the former Defence Secretary Rummsfield intended to do the same in case of Iran and Syria. But US was so embroiled in Iraq that they had no opportunity to actually implement the threats extended to both these countries.[81] Therefore, Barack Obama distanced himself from using the terms – global war on terror' or 'long war'. Cutting these out from the country's military lexicon, he chose instead to use the phrase "overseas contingency operation". However, use of another term for global war on terrorism does not make Obama's policy for a clean break from that of his predecessor's. In fact America's military engagement in the region only promises to become deeper and wider.[82] Despite his orders to shut Guantanamo Bay and ban torture, Obama categorically denied any plan to close down the Bagram Theater Internment Facility in Afghanistan, seeking instead to invest $60 million to expand the detention facility to accommodate double its present capacity of about 600 inmates. This, skeptics point out, is just one of the several similarities that the Obama Administration shares with its preceding Bush Administration, in that it endorses the continuation of the programme of extraordinary rendition, indefinite detention of terror suspects without trial, and an openness to military commission trials.

In principle, too, the view which extends the boundaries of the conflict to take in Al-Qaeda's operations around the world, has essentially been maintained by the Obama Administration and is a source of tension between the United States and Europe.[83] According to current State Department Legal Advisor Harold Koh, 'whether a particular individual will be targeted in a particular local will depend upon considerations specific to each case, including those related to the imminence of the threat, the sovereignty of the other states involved, and the willingness and ability of those states to suppress the threat the target poses'.[84] The United States believed that its right to use armed force in self-defence in response to 9/11 extends to strikes against Al-Qaeda operatives on Pakistani territory, when Pakistani forces were incapable of reaching terrorists, since it has been conducting predator drone strikes under those very conditions.

In March 2009 in federal court while filing in the detention context, the Obama Administration proposed a flexible standard for the substantive extent of its law of war authority in its armed conflict with Al-Qaeda and its allies.[85] Falling under the asserted detention authority were persons 'who were part of', or 'who provided substantial support' to 'Al-Qaeda or Taliban forces and associated forces' that are engaged in hostilities against the United States or its coalition partners[86] first the administration followed a standard similar to that used by the Bush Administration.[87] In a further statement the State Department's Legal Adviser Koh expained that the United States regards its legal authorities to include 'lethal force, to defend itself, including by targeting persons such as high-level Al-Qaeda leaders who are planning attacks.

Thus, the new administration made no compromise on country's security, it however, felt the need to abide by the Geneva Conventions and stated that America would uphold the highest values and ideals and for the purpose Obama signed an executive order on 22 January, 2009, directing the Central Intelligence Agency (CIA) to close down the Guantanamo Bay detention camp in Cuba within a year.

Keeping in view a variety of factors President Barack Obama in an interview in February 2009, admitted that the US had lost focus of its goals in Afghanistan and therefore, needed a set of clear policy objectives before coming up with a plan to bring American troops home. The new strategy was unveiled on 27 March, 2009, amid growing concerns about a strong and resurgent Taliban and a faltering war on terror. According to the London-based think tank, International Council on Security and Development, at present, the Taliban holds a permanent presence in 72 per cent of Afghanistan, up from 54 per cent until a year ago. The President Obama has described the border region as the most dangerous place in the world; his new strategy identifies as the core goal of the United States–the dismantling, disruption, and defeat of Al-Qaeda in Pakistan and Afghanistan, and prevent their returns to either country in the future. The new strategy has admitted a failure on the part of the US of having diverted vital resources from Afghanistan to the war in Iraq. To counter the situation, the US administration had proposed to deploy an additional 17,000 troops to bolster counter–insurgency operations especially in the south and east of Afghanistan where the Taliban were the strongest.[88] But many officials believed that simply sending in more troops to Afghanistan is likely to achieve little unless there were concomitant attempts to capture the Taliban leadership operating out of Pakistani territory, freeze the group's funding sources and blockade the Taliban's supply routes into Afghanistan.

Earlier, as a part of its new strategy in Afghanistan, the US appointed the former US Ambassador, Richard Holbrooke as its special envoy to Afghanistan and Pakistan to draw up and discuss the implementation of a 'comprehensive strategy' to neutralise militancy and extremism in South Asia through a broader regional engagement. The envoy after a visit to the region, in an interview, described the tour as part of a 'new, intense, engaged diplomacy' aimed at looking at the challenge of Afghanistan and Pakistan within a larger regional context and moving towards an involvement of other countries to 'stabilise an incredibly volatile region.[89] But on war against terror the Obama Administration remained active and assertive. It employed an additional 17,000 troops committed to Afghanistan and greater air strikes against alleged terrorist enclaves in Pakistan, which in turn, will continue to produce further retaliatory attacks in Pakistan. The CIA's predator drone programme was expanded in the new regime which has also decided to reach the war on terror by striking deeper.[90] In addition with a view to larger strategic design an additional 4,000 troops were sent to Afghanistan to train Afghanistan's Army and police force in order that they may be able to gradually take on the responsibility for Afghanistan's security. The US aimed to build up the strength of the Afghan National Army (ANA) to 1,34,000 and that of its police force to 82,000 by 2011.

However, several policy-makers and experts were still doubtful about the attacking capability of terrorist outfit Lashkar-e-Toiba (LeT) and warned the US administration of the menace posed by its rise in Pakistan and the role it could play in threatening the world with terror attacks. The US law makers on 11 March, 2010, urged the Obama Administration to press Pakistan to crush LeT– a Pakistan-based militant group blamed for the 2008 Mumbai attacks and more recently suspected in a deadly attack against Indians in Afghanistan. Gary Ackerman, chairman of the House subcommittee on the Middle East and South Asia said, 'The LeT is a deadly serious group of fanatics. They are well financed, ambitious and, most disturbingly both tolerated by and connected to the Pakistani military'.[91] Apart from this senior Republican law maker, Dan Burton, Ashley Tellis, senior fellow at the Carnegie Endowment, Lisa Curtis of the Heritage Foundation and Martin G. Weinbaum, noted scholar at Washington's Middle East Institute have equally considered the LeT as a growing clout and stressed for its dismantling and elimination.[92] They felt that either the US will have to compel Pakistan to initiate action against LeT or hold Pakistan responsible for the actions of its proxies.

On May 1, 2011, Osama bin Laden, the most wanted face of terrorism, was killed by the US forces in an operation at Abbottabad in Pakistan. He was eliminated by the very nation that once sponsored his cause and on the soil whose ruler was always in doubtful about his whereabout. The place where the terror legend was killed, was a military cantonment town not far from Islamabad. Osama's death came after nearly a decade of the US-led war on terror. President Barack Obama in an address to the nation said, 'For over two decades Bin Laden has been Al-Qaeda's leader and symbol, and has continued to plot attacks against our country and our friends and allies. The death of Osama marked the most significant achievement to date in the US effort to defeat the Al-Qaeda. With caution he added, 'Yet his death does not mark the end of our effort. There is no doubt that the Al-Qaeda will continue to pursue attacks against us. We must and we will remain vigilant at home and abroad.'[93] Obama also took the opportunity to emphasise that his country would never be at war with Islam, and also that Pakistan's counter–terrorism cooperation had been important in the operation. Bin Laden was not a Muslim leader; he was a mass murderer of Muslims. Indeed, the Al-Qaeda had slaughtered scores of Muslims in many countries.

The elimination of Osama bin Laden, the leader of a global terror network, by the US forces was welcomed by all countries of the world. With his death Indian Prime Minister Manmohan Singh hoped that it would strengthen the hands of those forces in Pakistan who want the state to shut the door on militancy, extremism and terrorism once and for all.[94] The Kremlin press service also welcomed "serious success" of the US in the fight against international terrorism and called for stepping up joint coordinated battle against this evil. The Russian Foreign Ministry said the US blow to Al-Qaeda had universal significance showing that terrorism is doomed and retribution strikes terrorist sooner or later.[95] But in the death of Bin Laden Moscow saw a wider US game plan behind the liquidation of Al-Qaeda leader and was deeply concerned about US further strategies in Afghanistan and Central Asia. Russia considered the death of the leader as the result of a deal between American and Pakistan intelligence that would pave the way for a power sharing arrangement with the Taliban and should facilitate US withdrawal from Afghanistan. The Kremlin expressed its worry about US interests in Central Asia. Sergei Chekinov, head of the Centre for Military Strategy Research of the Russian General Staff, said, 'The West seeks wider excess to energy resources in Central Asia and a foothold to advance its interests beyond the region.'[96] He also called for strengthening the Collective Security Treaty Organisation (CSTO). Chekinov apprehended that the killing of Bin Laden may stengthen the hand of a rising interventionist lobby in the White House and Russia viewed it as a dangerous tendency.

In post-Bin Laden period the United States of America got an opportunity to start a new beginning in Afghanistan. From this point onward President Barack Obama needs to rethink the war in Afghanistan. If the ultimate objective is to talk to moderate Taliban in order to negotiate an end to this war, there is no justification for further military operations in that country, and no excuse for delaying the departure of the US and foreign troops. Exactly, the Obama Administration has moved forward in this direction a ground was prepared for talks between the US and the Taliban in June 2011. The Afghan President Hamid Karzai and Robert Gates, the US Defence Secretary, had confirmed that preliminary facts are under way.

As an important step forward in this direction the UN Security Conucil's sanctions list has been divided so as to separate Taliban leaders from those of Al-Qaeda. The US Defence Secretary in a television interview on 19 June, 2011 declared, 'We have said all along that a political outcome is the way most wars end. The question is when and if they (the Taliban) are ready to talk seriously'.[97] He also argued further that US pressure was needed on the Taliban, 'Talks yes, but not yet has long been the Pentagon position. At the juncture Hamid Karzai, the Afghan President, is in difficult situation. Like the Taliban, he wants to end his country's occupation though he is not sure how to do it, given the countervailing pressures from the insurgency and the Americans as well. In fact any long-term bases or talks for withdrawal under the guise of a strategic partnership would not only affect the serious negotiations to end the war but would also undermine the prospect for any regional agreement between Afghanistan and its neighbours.

In the circumstances President Barack Obama's announcement came regarding the drawdown of troops in Afghanistan. Several answers were put forward to the question why he took such a decision. Put simply, his sharp political instincts prevailed. He had a pledge of redeem; he sensed the public mood; he heard "bipartisan" opinion in Capital Hill that the soldiers be brought home; he faces an adverse budgetary environment and he understood that his priority should be to mend the US economy rather than wage wars in foreign lands. Meanwhile Afghan opinion was also turning against foreign occupation and the killing of Osama bin Laden offered a defining moment. On diplomatic front, too, regional allies proved exasperatingly difficult, while European allies got impatient to quit. The regional opinion militates against a long-term US military presence, while the contradictions in intra-regional relationships do not easily lend to negotiations. The Taliban responded to Obama's announcement saying, 'The solution for Afghan crisis lies in the full withdrawal of all foreign troops immediately. Until this happens, our armed struggle will increase from day to day.[98] Unlike his predecessor George William Bush who once said that US would someday consider a Marshall Plan for Afghanistan, Obama pleaded that this is a time of rising debt and hard economic times at home and he needs to concentrate on rebuilding America.

However, from President Obama's declaration it was clear that the US has accepted the Taliban as being a part of the Afghan nation and concluded that it does not threaten America's homeland security. According to Obama's time-line for drawdown 10,000 troops by end-2011, 33,000 by mid-2012 and the bulk of the remaining 70,000 troops at a "steady pace" through 2013-14. With the announcement Obama hoped optimism about the peace process. He estimated that Al-Qaeda is a spent force and any residual war on terror will be by way of exercising vigilance that it does not rear its head again. Besides this, the biggest challenge in Afghanistan is to end 35 years of civil war and no peace deal in Afghanistan will stick unless the era of outside interference by its neighbours comes to an end. Only talks among all the Afghan stakeholders and parties including the Taliban, can do that. The Americans can not control the outcome but they should not impede it either. Therefore, Obama's support for a ceasefire and negotiations on a full withdrawal of US and other foreign troops would be his best contribution to getting the comprehensive settlement that Afghans desperately need and want.

References

1. Kazi Anwarul Masud, 'Terrorism in South Asia and US Foreign Policy', Paper No. 3292, *South Asia Analysis Group*, 5 July, 2009, p. 3.
2. *Ibid.*
3. *Ibid.*, 'Terrorism in South Asia in Global Context,' Paper No. 3215, 26 May, 2009, p. 1.
4. Kazi Anwarul Masud, 'Terrorism in South Asia and US Foreign Policy'.
5. Tariq Ali, *Can Pakistan Survive: The Death of a State* (Harmondsworth: Penguin, 1983), p. 138.
6. Veena Kukreja, *Contemporary Pakistan–Political Processes, Conflicts and Crises* (New Delhi: Sage Publications, 2003), p. 171.
7. Vinod Saighal, 'USA–PAK Potentially More Menacing Than AF–PAK', *South Asia Politics*, Vol. 9, No. 1, May 2010 (New Delhi: 2010), p. 4.

8. Surendra Chopra, 'Islamic Fundamentalism and Pakistan's Foreign Policy', *India Quarterly*, Vol. XLIX, Nos. 1-2 (January–June 1993), pp. 1-36.
9. Eqbal Ahmad, 'Islam and Politics,' in Mohammad Asghar Khan (ed.), *Islam, Politics and the State* (London: Zed Press, 1985), p. 25.
10. Rajkumar Singh, *India and Pakistan–Social Political and Military Perspectives* (New Delhi: Regal Publications, 2009), p. 251.
11. Edward Girardet, 'Corrupt Officials Reap Spoils of Afghan War,' *The Christian Science Monitor*, 7 September, 1988.
12. Samina Ahmed, 'The United States and Terrorism in South Asia: The Lessons of History', *International Security* (2002), p. 78.
13. Brahma Challaney, 'Fighting Frankenstein,' *The Hindustan Times*, 25 November, 2001.
14. *Ibid.*
15. Eric S. Margolis, *War at the Top of the World* (Newyork: 2001), p. 52.
16. Oliver Roy, 'Why the War is Going on in Afghanistan: The Afghan Crisis in Perspective,' *Journal of International Affairs*, Vol. 5, No. 4, December 2000–February 2001, p. 11.
17. United States Department of State, Patterns of Global Terrorism: 1987, *Department of State Publication*, 9661 (August 1987), p. 27.
18. N.C. Menon, 'Terrorism as an Epidemic,' *The Hindustan Times*, 8 August, 1998.
19. *Ibid.*
20. Vikram Sood, 'The War Against Terror,' in *Ibid.*, 1 June, 2004.
21. *Ibid.*
22. *Ibid.*
23. Kapil Sibal, 'Fundamentalism Breeds Terrorism,' in *Ibid.*, 16 September 2001.
24. Thomas Homar-Dixon, 'The Rise of Complex Terrorism,' *Foreign Policy* (Washington: January-February 2002), p. 57.
25. *The Newyork Times*, 2 December, 2001.
26. S.P. Singh, '11 September and America's Balance Sheet in South and Central Asia,' in Mahavir Singh (ed.), *International Terrorism and Religious Extremism–Challenges to Central and South Asia* (New Delhi: Anamika Publishers, 2004), p. 154.
27. S.D.Muni, 'Terrorism: 'Tectonic Plates' and Strategic Equations in Asia,' in *Ibid.*, pp. 27-28
28. *The New Yorker*, 1 April, 2002.
29. Memorandum from George W. Bush on Human Treatment of Taliban and Al–Qaeda Detainees, 7 February, 2002.
30. Mathew C. Waxman, 'The Structure of Terrorism Threats and the Laws of War, *Duke Journal of Comparative and International Law*, Vol. 20, May 2010, p. 105.

31. *Ibid.*
32. Fine, Glenn A., Inspector General of the US Department of Justice, 5 November, 2003.
33. Vice President Dick Cheney remarks made during an address at the US Chamber of Commerce, 14 November, 2001.
34. *The Newyork Times*, 30 September, 2001.
35. *Ibid.*
36. Albert–Lazlo Barabasi, Linked: The New Science of Networks (Newyork: Perseus, 2002) as quoted in Steve Ressler, 'Social Network Analysis as an Approach to Combat Terrorism: Past, Present, and Future Research,' *Homeland Security Affairs*, Vol. 2 No. 2 (July 2006).
37. Marc Sageman, *Understanding Terror Network* (Philadelphia: University of Pennsylvania Press, 2004), as quoted in *Ibid.*
38. Karl M. Van Meter, 'Terrorists/Liberators: Researching and Dealing with Adversary Social Network Connections,' 24, No. 3 (2001), pp. 66-78.
39. *Ibid.*
40. Brahma Chellaney, 'Jehad on Jehadis,' *The Hindustan Times*, 20 September, 2001.
41. Siddarth Varadarajan, 'A Fork in the Road for the US in South Asia,' *The Hindu*, 3 May, 2011.
42. Rajkumar Singh, *India and Pakistan, Social Political and Military Perspectives*, pp. 276-78.
43. Vir Sanghvi, 'US Since 9/11: Lessons and Conundrums', *The Hindustan Times*, 15 September, 2002.
44. John Barry and Michael Hirsh, 'The Real Tip of the Spear', *Newsweek*, 8 October, 2001.
45. P.L. Dash, 'Afghanistan: The Epicentre of Terror', in Mahavir Singh (ed.), *International Terrorism and Religious Extremism–Challenges to Central and South Asia*, p. 142.
46. *Ibid.*
47. Michael E.O. Hanlon, 'A Flawed Masterpiece', *Foreign Affairs*, May-June 2002, pp. 48-50.
48. Veena Kukreja, *Contemporary Pakistan–Political Processes, Conflicts and Crises*, pp. 288-89.
49. Dilip Kumar, 'The Resurgence of the Taliban–Lessons Learned', *South Asia Politics*, Vol. 6, No. 1 (New Delhi: 2007), pp. 48-49.
50. *Ibid.*
51. Prem Shankar Jha, 'Suicidal Move,' *The Hindustan Times*, 13 September, 2002.
52. *Ibid.*
53. Dilip Kumar, 'The Resurgence of the Taliban – Lessons Learned,' p. 49.

54. Salman Rushdie, 'Saddam Impact,' *The Hindustan Times*, 3 September, 2002.
55. Kazi Anwarul Masud, 'Terrorism in South Asia in Global Context'.
56. Sonali Huria, 'War on Terrorism in South Asia–Af-Pak and Beyond,' *Institute of Peace and Conflict Studies*, No. 108 (New Delhi: 2009), p. 1.
57. Veena Kukreja, *Contemporary Pakistan-Political Processes, Conflicts and Crises*, pp. 290-91.
58. Rajkumar Singh, *India and Pakistan–Social, Political and Military Perspectives*, p. 277.
59. K. Subrahmanyam, 'Washington's Waiting–Islamabad's Tokenism will not Work,' *The Times of India*, 11 February, 2002.
60. Ajit Doval, KC, 'Islamic Terrorism in South Asia and India's Strategic Response' (New Delhi: Oxford University Press, 2007).
61. *The Hindu*, 25 December, 2007.
62. Y.C. Halan, 'A Burning Pakistan: Causes and Cures,' *Third Concept*, pp. 15-16.
63. *Ibid.*
64. Pankaj Vohra, 'Prospects of a Full-scale Conflict in India's Backyard Are Real,' *The Hindustan Times*, 17 September, 2001.
65. Vir Sanghvi, 'An American Anniversary,' in *Ibid.*, 8 September 2002.
66. *Ibid.*
67. Praful Bidwai, 'Not in Our Name,' in *Ibid.*, 25 February, 2003.
68. S.D. Muni, 'Terrorism, 'Tectonic Plates' and Strategic Equations in Asia,' p. 30.
69. Stephen G. Brooks and William C. Wohlforth, 'American Primacy in Perspective', *Foreign Affairs*, July–August 2002, pp. 20-33.
70. K. Subrahmanyam, 'Next Move, Next Door', *The Hindustan Times*, 19 July, 2004.
71. The IDSA's 5th Conference on Asian Security held at New Delhi on 27 January 2003.
72. Vikram Sood, 'The War Against Terror', *The Hindustan Times*, 1 June, 2004.
73. John Bellinger's Address Before the London School of Economics, 31 October, 2006.
74. Anton I. Janik, Jr., 'Prosecuting Al-Qaeda: American's Foreign Policy Interests Are Best Served by Trying Terrorists Under International Tribunals,' *Denver Journal of International Law and Policy*, September 2002, p. 132.
75. The Carter Center Conference Report, Human Rights Defenders on the Frontlines of Freedom: Protecting *Human Rights in the Context of the War on Terror*, 11-12 November, 2003.

76. P.R. Dubhashi, 'Obama's US Presidency and India's Foreign Policy', *South Asia Politics*, Vol. 7, No. 11, March 2009 (New Delhi: 2009), pp. 3-4.
77. Kazi Anwarul Masud, 'Terrorism in South Asia and US Foreign Policy,' p. 4.
78. Sonali Huria, 'War on Terrorism in South Asia–Af-Pak and Beyond,' p. 2.
79. *Ibid.*, p. 3.
80. Kazi Anwarul Masud, 'Terrorism in South Asia and US Foreign Policy,' p. 4.
81. P.R. Dubhashi, 'Obama's US Presidency and India's Foreign Policy,' p. 4.
82. Sonali Huria, 'War on Terrorism in South Asia–Af-Pak and Beyond,' p. 4.
83. Anthony Dworkin, 'Beyond the War on Terror: Towards a New Transatlantic Framework for Counterterrorism, 13, *European Council on Foreign Relation*, (2009).
84. See, Harold Hongju Koh's Remarks at the Annual Meeting of the American Society of International Law, Washington, D.C., 25 March, 2010.
85. *Ibid.*
86. *Ibid.*
87. William Glaberson, 'US Won't Label Terror Suspects as Combatants', *The Newyork Times*, 14 March, 2009.
88. Sonali Huria, 'War on Terrorism in South Asia-Af-Pak and Beyond,' p. 1.
89. *Ibid.*, p. 2.
90. Scott Shane, 'CIA to Expand Use of Drones in Pakistan,' *The Newyork Times*, 4 December, 2009.
91. *The Tribune*, 13 March, 2010.
92. *The Pioneer*, 13 March, 2010.
93. *The Hindu*, 3 May, 2011.
94. *Ibid.*, editorial.
95. Vladimir Radyuhin, 'Russia's Tempered Response to Abbottabad,' in *Ibid.*, 13 May, 2011.
96. *Ibid.*
97. Jonathan Steele, 'The Taliban's Wish List,' in *Ibid.*, 22 June, 2011.
98. M.K. Bhadrakumar, 'Taliban's Return and India's Concerns,' in *Ibid.*, 28 June, 2011.

4

Terror Affected Countries of South Asia

As a result of the division of Indian sub-continent Pakistan was created as a sovereign, independent country in August 1947 while its eastern part became independent in December 1971 and formed the independent country called Bangladesh. The three independent countries of South Asia Pakistan, Bangladesh and Afghanistan have a Muslim majority population following Islam actively while India is a Hindu majority country having the followers of different religions.

Although five countries–India, Pakistan, Afghanistan, Bangladesh and Sri Lanka have the tradition of political violence the problem of terrorism erupted in last four decades. It is a region of Jihadi–dominated terrorism which is nowhere near containment and it propagates the pernicious ideology of hate, revenge, and violence. It treats all conflicts with non-Muslims worthy of Jihadi and even considers liberal Islamic regimes, organisations and individuals as non-Islamic.

In most of the countries there are anti-terror laws, but lack of political will to take effective and stern action against the terrorist have made the laws useless or partially useful. Particularly, Pakistan on being defeated by India time and again in declared wars, started cross-border terrorism in India, and after Soviets' withdrawal from Afghanistan, it cleverly used Mujahideen in Jammu and Kashmir and in other parts of India with a view to unstable the socio-political fabric of the country.

While Afghanistan became an epicentre of world terrorism, India is a soft target of terrorists who hail basically from Pakistan and Bangladesh. Thus, Islamic terrorism in India is essentially of an imported variety.

INDIA

Independent India and Tradition of Violence

India is bearing the burnt of the terrorist violence in South Asia which has risen sharply in recent years. It is facing multifarious challenges in the management of its internal security. There is an upsurge of terrorist activities, intensification of cross-border terrorist activities and insurgent groups in different parts of the country. Terrorism has now acquired global dimensions and has become the challenge for the world. The reach and methods adopted by terrorist groups and organisations take the advantage of modern means of communication and technology using high-tech facilities available in the form of communication system, transport, sophisticated arms and various other means. This has enabled them to strike and create terror among people at will. Like every constitution of the world the constitution of India also provides for modifications in law to enable the state to face challenges to its unity and integrity and the security of its citizens. In fact the entire criminal justice system which gives the state the power to use force against its own citizens, going even to the extent of resorting to killing, is designed for the purpose.[1] But in this age of globalisation the heightening levels of political and social consciousness have resulted in higher expectations by the people and consequently states and societies are coming under pressure.[2] The spectre of terrorism haunts us as an omnipotent and omnipresent phenomenon. Living in fear of terrorist attacks is almost becoming today the way of life.

The Indian constitution, born in difficult times after partition, does provide for a legal regime which can accommodate restrictions on liberty, the standards of which can vary depending on the gravity of the challenge and the risks involved for basic rights and constitutional values. It is a secular system with pluralism as its foundation. Here, pluralism must not be confused with secularism. The latter carries overtones of atheism and was born out of twin struggles in the West: of democracy with the Church and monarchy, and of Darwinism with Christianity. Pluralism, by contrast, involves no break with religion and what is more important, with tradition. Instead, it requires acceptance of, and mutual respect between, the many religions in a country. A pluralist state is also secular, but in a different way. For its legal and civil codes seek to accommodate and incorporate particular religious customs and beliefs and not banish them from the public domain.[3] The Indian constitution safeguarded pluralism by creating an ethnic federation on the one hand, and by protecting the marriage, inheritance, educational and cultural practices of the minorities, on the other. The two sets of enactments gave Indians a security of identity that is the secret of modern India's extraordinary stability.[4] Every community wears its identity openly like a badge, because it does not feel threatened. In the absence of threat, no one feels pressured to conform. Historically, every Indian empire, from the Mauryan to the British, flourished because it respected the diversity of identities within India and treated all races and cultures as equal.

As an organising principle of social and political life, the separation of church and state has its origin in the vicious and debilitating 16th century sectarian wars within European Christianity. Ultimately, the only way Western European societies could live with sectarian diversity was via the separation of church and state. Over time, with the rise to prominence of new social groups, long distance trade and industrial capitalism, these ideas were further reinforced. Religion was relegated to the domain of the private.[5] Public or political structures now had to be secular. It is the time when the rest of the world is being evaluated on their ability to imitate this European model, what we do need to recognise is that these ideas of public secularity were the product of a particular history, the result of a certain political, economic and social context. Asia, Africa, or the region we call the Middle East today, had historically developed their own methods of dispute resolution and dealing with diversity. These methods did not necessarily relegate religion to the realm of the personal. As a result, the European colonialism dismissed the methods as primitive or backward.[6] However, in India as elsewhere in the world, we have too many examples of how religious and indigenous ideologies have helped a few oppressed, the many to be able to make a universal case for religion against secularity.

In fact, the plurality and diversity that we found today in Indian society, were existed in pre-1947 era and independent India was born with these contradictions. A dispassionate assessment of history will reveal that the violent outbursts that are tearing apart the fabric of Indian society today are expressions of the same contradictions–religious, class, ethnicity, caste and otherwise that often exploded into violence even during the colonial period. Despite the Indian state's declared profession of adherence to non-violence, in practice the Indian state has repeatedly resorted to the language of violence in trying to resolve these contradictions that plague Indian society.[7] In India's case Independence was brought about through a non-violent mid-wife called 'Gandhism', which is the state's proclaimed ideology. For instance, the Hindu-Muslim communal riots that preceded the partition of the sub- continent and led to the birth of India, are a historical reality which not only knocks the bottom out of the Indian state's official and ideological claim to its non-violent parentage, but also challenges the doctrine of non-violence as propounded by Gandhi as a harbinger of change.

The Indian state acquired a military character almost from its infancy. It started at two levels–external and internal. At the external level, the new born state sent its troops to Kashmir in October 1947 to fight first the Pakistan-aided tribals, and later the regular forces of the Pakistan army, in order to protect a territory which had been acceded hurriedly to the Indian Union by the then Maharaja of Kashmir. The Kashmir adventure of 1947 was followed by four major wars–the 1962 war with China, and the 1965, 1971 and 1999 wars with Pakistan. The internal sources of violence and militarisation can be traced back to the highly centralised model of development adopted by the post-Independence Indian state, which instead of eliminating semi-feudal production relations in large parts of the country opted for investment in selected sectors and regions. As a result, while inequitable distribution of income has sharpened class fragmentation and contradiction, uneven development has led to imbalances in regional growth.[8] The perceived sense of injustice among the people divided them on the lines of caste, ethnic loyalties, language, religious beliefs–which the Indian polity has failed to overcome, despite its commitment to a 'socialist secular democratic republic'.

This apart, in initial years of independence India faced two such situations–the Telengana Movement in 1948 and Naga demand for independence in 1953. The Telengana movement was one of the earliest indications of the Indian state's attitude towards the underprivileged and of its determination to suppress violently any attempt by the rural people to end outmoded social and economic relations. The same treatment was meted out to an ethnic minority group when the state sent its armed forces to Nagaland to suppress the Naga demand for independence. The core of the conflict between these various groups on the one hand, and the Centre on the other, basically concerns how to find an amicable solution to relations between the central authority and different regional communities that inhabit a multi-national state. Keeping in view the dangers ahead the Indian state also augmented throughout the years its repressive apparatus. In 1949, it raised the Central Reserve Police Force (CRPF), modelled on the British government's plan of Crown Representative Police Force.[9] Since then, the number of central paramilitary forces has increased steadily, with the formation of Border Security Force (BSF), the Central Industrial Security Force (CISF), the National Security Guard (NSG) and the commando force called 'Black Cats'.

Gradually, the pattern of state response towards popular grievances followed a common sequence of policy decisions and actions–whether in relation to demands of poor peasants, industrial workers or ethnic minorities. At the initial stage of any demonstration of popular demands, the state then decides to ignore them. When accumulation of the ignored grievances manifests itself in desperate militant agitation, the state decides to treat them as law and order problems and deploy its police to suppress them. Such deployment often helps the state to contain the outbursts temporarily and prevent them from exploding into armed insurgencies. But the same situation and response had a different meaning and depth when the affected area is situated in border states. They witness, normally, better-armed and better-organised insurgencies as the case is in north-west and north-eastern states. However, there is a basic difference between the political character of the Naxalite armed movement and that of the insurgencies in other parts of the country. While the former seeks to base itself on the politics of class conflict, the latter are concerned with more general issues and concerns related to their respective communities, irrespective of class differences that might otherwise divide them.

The region north-east is a compact zone of sub-national states attributing to high levels of ethnic violence. It is comprised by extraordinary ethnic, cultural, religious and linguistic diversity and constituted the seven sisters states of Assam, Arunachal Pradesh, Manipur, Meghalaya, Mizoram, Nagaland and Tripura. The region is inhabited by three distinct groups of people; the hill tribes, the plain tribes and non-tribal population of the plains. Geographically, the north-east of India is located between the two great traditions of the Indic Asia and the Mongoloid Asia. It was only after the British had merged the entire region under the British India administration that the region came to be associated with India.[10] Ethnically, it is diverse and heterogeneous alike the rest of the country.

Historically, immigration from the East-Bengal now Bangladesh, became illegal after the demarcation of international boundary in 1947 between India and Pakistan. But movement of people from East Bengal, later East Pakistan and then Bangladesh into different parts of North-east India continued unabatedly. This has primarily generated a multiple cause for destabilising political, social, economic, ethnic and communal tensions in the region. Large scale and unabated influx of population from the neighbouring countries has resulted in a phenomenon that is visibly reshaping and transforming the demographic, ethnic, religious and linguistic profile of large parts of the region. Consequently the region has opened up to radicalism and to a network of fundamentalist campaigns which have access to arms and easy connections to sanctuaries across the porous international borders which had made difficult for the north-eastern states to comprehend and address.[11] The impact of ethnic-conflict on the security of the region and the nation is enormous and is adding to the problems of the north-eastern people.

In recent years the problem of Naxalism is posing a serious threat to the security of India, democracy and rule of law, particularly in Chhattisgarh, Andhra Pradesh, Orissa, Bihar, Jharkhand, West Bengal and a few other places. It is said that over 230 districts in the country are in the grip of Maoists, Naxalites etc. and the Union Home Minister has declared that countering Naxalism is the biggest challenge.[12] In the areas where the Naxalites have established their influence, they impose taxes mete out quick justice and run administrative bureaucracies, schools and health services. Naxalism unleashed a flow of events which escalated over the years into a political movement that brought about far-reaching changes in India's socio-cultural scene. The fact is that despite the continuing use of the most repressive methods by the police to crush its cadres and inspite of a series of splits that had fissured the movement during the next three or four decades, Naxalism as an ideology has become a force to reckon with in India. Its continuity can be explained by the persistence and exacerbation of the basic causes that gave its birth-feudal exploitation and oppression over the rural poor.

The term 'Naxalism' typifies a particular kind of militant and violent armed struggle by the peasants, tribals, and dalits, led by a leadership drawing a doctrinal support from Marxism-Leninism and strategic inspiration from Mao Zedong. The term itself came from Naxalbari, a small village in West Bengal where a section of

Communist Party of India (Marxist) led by Kanu Sanyal led a violent uprising in 1967. At the sametime Mao launched his Cultural Revolution and in India a group that broke away from the CPM, mobilised about 15,000 peasants in Naxalbari and launched a violent anti-landlord movement, patterned on the Telengana movement two decades earlier.[13] The Naxalites drew heavily upon the iniquitous land tenure system and exploitation of the poor peasants and agricultural labour by landlords in framing their ideological aims.

In 1967, Naxalites organised the All India Coordination Committee of Communist Revolutionaries (AICCCR), which in 1969 gave birth to the most notable Naxalite organisation, the Communist Party of India (Marxist-Leninist) and defined the objective of the Party as 'seizure of power through an agrarian revolution'. The strategy was the elimination of feudal order in the Indian countryside to free the poor from the clutches of the oppressive landlords and replace the world order with an alternative one that would implement land reforms. The tactics to achieve it was through guerilla warfare by the peasants.[14] This way they would eliminate the landlords and build up a resistance against the state's police force. Gradually, they would set up a 'liberated zone' in different parts of the country that would eventually coalesce into a territorial unit under Naxalite hegemony.

Today Naxalism/Maoism has become a significant socio-political force having abiding faith in guerilla warfare and violent means to achieve its objectives. The government figures reveal that the total number of people killed by the Naxalite violence rose by 30% between 2003 and 2005. The number of policemen killed jumped to an astonishing 53% between 2004 and 2005. The annual report of the Ministry of Home Affairs 2005-06 also admitted that the Naxalism is not merely a law and order problem but has deep socio-economic dimensions. Left wing radicalism and extremism is motivated by prevailing socio-economic deprivation.[15] The various groups of Maoists, be they called Naxalites or Peoples War Group (PWG) or otherwise adjective, all have declared very clearly that they have no faith in the constitution of India, in the multi-party democracy and elections. There has to be a strategy by the government to fight the low-intensity war and promote good governance and development. Politically, the liberal democratic state in India needs to be critiqued of the economic policies that have created islands of deprivation, which have over the years emerged as pockets of support for the Maoist movement in the country.

In line the terror attacks and incidents appeared in 1980s in the Indian state, of Punjab and Kashmir. This form of terrorism was different from organised mass movements, or guerilla warfare. Guerilla-based insurrections in China, Vietnam and Latin American countries in the past involved the willing participation of the local people, both in direct and indirect ways, but unlike those forms of armed struggle, the insurgencies in Punjab and Kashmir are dominated by a leadership which aims at harnessing popular nationalistic urges to the objective of establishing theocratic autocracies in these states. The leadership of Punjab and Kashmir appeared to owe allegiance to a form of religious fundamentalism that aims at subjugating members of their respective communities to conservative norms and practices, selectively excerpted from their traditional religious scriptures and systems on the plea of restoring the fundamental purity of their respective religions.[16] Since terrorism without publicity is a weapon that fires only blank, such terrorist actions have had to be directed not only against representatives of the state like policemen, security forces and government officials, but also at gatherings of ordinary innocent citizens. Bomb blasts in crowded places that kill indiscriminately a large number of people invariably become news and give the terrorist maximum publicity.[17] In general, their ideology is intolerant of dissent views, and therefore, they also attack those members of their own community who refuge to accept their fundamentalist religious views.

In real the alienation of the Sikhs began at the time of the reorganisation of states in 1956 when they failed to get a Sikh majority state carved out of the then Hindu majority in Punjab. The relations between the two communities began to sour in 1960s and Punjabi farmers were discontended because they were bound to sell their commodities on prices fixed by the administrators. Rapid industrialisation and shift of the economic power from rural to urban areas also strengthened the feeling that identity of their religion was at stake. In the circumstances there was a perception that native Punjabi enterprise, combined with investment capital from the Sikh diaspora could make 'Khalistan', bloom in a manner that Punjab, mired in India's administrative stodginess, could not hope to. On the other hand, the political needs of the Indian National Congress (INC) played a role in the final lap into insurgency. To undercut the electoral draw of the Sikh political party, the Akali Dal, the INC promoted Bhindranwale, a Sikh preacher even more radical than the Akalis. Initially Bhindranwale campaigned for the INC but soon became first choice of the Congress party in Punjab and was allowed to create an armed fortress in Amritsar's Golden Temple. As a result a two-day major military operation became essential in June 1984 to clear the Golden Temple in which 83 dead and 248 wounded were counted.[18] In Punjab, according to government count, nearly 500 civilians were killed in hit-and-run attacks during the period from 1980 to just before the June 1984. Temporary success in the cleaning up of the Golden Temple in 'Operation Bluestar,' the arrest and killing of few 'terrorist' leaders in Punjab have left a trail of destruction which gave birth to a new generation of insurgents in the state. Many among them–particularly the youth–went underground and joined the insurgency, either for protection or revenge.

Terrorism and insurgency continued in Punjab between 1984 and 1993 and during the period over 12,000 people were killed. The storming of the temple devastated the Sikhs. Indira Gandhi, the then Prime Minister of India, was killed by her Sikh security guards four months later in October 1984 which in turn led to a violent anti-Sikh reaction that cold bloodedly killed about 3,000 Sikhs in the capital Delhi alone. After a one-year-long lull sparked by the rout of the temple militants, a fresh surge of terrorist violence broke out with the assassination of moderate Sikh leader Sant Harchand Singh Longowal shortly after he signed a so-called "Peace accord" with Prime Minister Rajiv Gandhi in July 1985. The intensity and frequency of terrorist attacks had risen sharply since late 1985, with no end in sight to the ever-growing spiral of violence. The extremists had extended their terror campaign to many areas outside Punjab forcing authorities to constantly review and beef up security in a prime terrorist target-New Delhi. The extremists, armed with powerful sophisticated guns had often targeted government and police officers and Hindu and moderate Sikh politicians; but, frequently, they had been engaged in the random mass killing of ordinary Hindu civilians.[19] Several Sikh groups had helped turn the rich farms of Punjab into India's 'killing fields.'[20] They include the Khalistan Commando Force, the Babbar Khalsa, the All-India Sikh Students Federation, the Khalistan Liberation Army, the Dal Khalsa and the Dashmesh Regiment. At least two of these groups, the Babbar Khalsa and the Dashmesh Regiment were believed to be active overseas, particularly in Canada and West Germany.

By the time, organised terrorism in India as elsewhere had been able to acquire newer weapons in an age when sophisticated technology was not contained by national boundaries. At the peak of terrorism in Punjab between 1988 and 1991 there were 5,000 to 6,000 hard core militants enjoying the active support of another 10,000 to 15,000 people. Pakistan supported the insurgency by providing arms, training and sanctuaries. Hand guns were used initially, but by 1987 the terrorists had assault rifles, sniper rifles and rocket launchers. Very soon they were using mortars and sophisticated explosive devices.[21] The terrorist outfits had kept pace with the Indian state in arms race. While the state's armed forces compete with their Pakistani counterparts by bidding for the latest weaponry, bombers and submarines from the West, the terrorists had been buying from the same source armaments that suit their own military tactics. Gradually, the Punjab police built up the members and developed the motivation, confidence and skills needed to prevail. The country including the Sikh community supported the ruthless counter–terror approach that the Punjab police pursued using tactics that noted the fine line between what is legal and what is not.[22] Effective interdiction of Pak border crossings and the weariness of Sikh funders abroad also contributed.

Thus the tradition of violence in independent India has expanded widely and became an integral part of day-to-day life. The language of gun is a decisive force in political discourse in India. It is gradually edging out debates in a democratic framework, and suppressing dissent of the traditional humanitarian variety. India has been troubled by sectarian violence for decades, reflecting a constant conflict between its federal system and ethnic and regional aspirations.[23] But the recent growth and expansion of terrorism across the nation strikes at the very heart of India's constitution and democratic system as a whole.

Anti-Terror Laws and Combating

India's record in anti-terror laws and its combating has been far from satisfaction, to say the least. In general, people feel that we have not given enough thought to improving our methods of dealing with terrorism. Our methods will have to be radically improved. The laws are lax, judicial responsibility is absent, police knowledge of criminals is inadequate, preventive action is almost nil, computerisation of information is not fully developed, the watch on suspicious strangers is negligible, and growth of slums has made it difficult to spot terrorist hiding there. The availability of weapons is almost unchecked because our traps for them are never laid continuously.[24] However, the anti-terror laws, no matter how harsh they are, can not by themselves prevent terrorist attacks, they can help in the successful investigation and prosecution of cases against terrorist and those who aid and abet terrorist acts.[25] Popular criticism against these laws has been based more on the manner in which they are implemented than on any modifications in the laws and procedures. Had the regular criminal justice system performed its task with reasonable results, there would have been no need for special laws or institutions to deal with terrorist acts.

Indian strategic response to terrorism has been a delicate blending of the hard and soft power of the state which at times, invites snide comments like–a democracy that has room even for violence. Besides safeguarding national security interests, Indian response has been conditioned by its democratic polity, need to accommodate communal sensitivities and safety of its citizens. The global and regional settings, complexity of relations with neighbouring countries and international obligations on terrorist front have also influenced the response.[26] Some analysts also say that the anti-terror laws stand in the way of fundamental rights of citizens guaranteed by Part III of the Constitution. The anti-terrorist laws have been enacted before the legislature and upheld by the judiciary though not without reluctance. The intention was to enact these statutes and bring them in force till the situation improves. The intention was not to make these drastic measures a permanent feature of law of the land. But because of continuing terrorist activities, the statutes have been reintroduced with requisite modifications. The problem lies with the implementation of laws and the abuse of powers conferred on the authorities under the special laws.

Terrorism has immensely affected India. The Indian Supreme Court took a note of it in *Kartar Singh vs. State of Punjab* in 1994 and observed that the country has been in the firm grip of spiraling terrorist violence and is caught between deadly pangs of disruptive activities. Apart from many skirmishes in various parts of the country, there were countless serious and horrendous events engulfing many cities with blood-bath, firing, looting, mad killing of women and children and reducing those areas into a graveyard, whose brutal atrocities have rocked and shocked the whole nation. Deplorably, determined youths lured by hard-core criminals and underground extremists attracted by the ideology of terrorism are indulging in committing serious crimes against the humanity.

The reasons for terrorism in India may vary vastly from religious to geographical to caste to history. Islamic terrorism in India is essentially of an imported variety. The manpower weapons, finances, ideological motivation and plans that go in terrorist actions largely has its origin in its neighbourhood. The terror has affected not only Kashmir, Punjab, Mumbai, Delhi but other regions of the country and the North East. We have had insurgency in the North-East for more than 50 years; where the draconian Armed Forces Special Power Act has been in force for the last 50 years. It would seem that the insurgency has hardly waned; despite "tough" military response by the state. Political initiatives to placate the disaffected people have been slightly more successful.[27] Ethnic unrest and rebel violence have been major Indian security concerns since the Chinese-aided Naga and Mizo separatist insurgencies flared in the 1960s.[28] Terrorism covered a large part of Andhra Pradesh, Orissa, Madhya Pradesh, Chhattisgarh and Jharkhand right up to the Nepal border. We had insurgency and terrorism in Tamil Nadu. We lost two of our former prime ministers to this kind of terrorism.

In terms of our sovereignty, unity and integrity and our feeling of nationalism, terrorism strikes at each one of them. This is the enormity of the problem that we are addressing. It is a sad reality that crime in India has become a low risk business. It is a high profit business with a 93% probability that you can commit a hard crime and get away with it. In that kind of situation it becomes necessary in a country like India that if a law regarding terrorism is enacted, it should be made so stringent that the culprit brought to book does not go scot-free just because of the loopholes and lacunaes in the ordinary law, because when our neighbouring nation Pakistan which is the cause of perpetrating terrorism in India can have such stringent laws, why can not have we? Basically, the criminal justice system is not designed to deal with the types of heinous crimes that have appeared in our country in the last 60 years. As a temporary measure, the country needs special laws that empower the government to combat terrorism. Hard crimes and soft justice can not co-exist for long if security is desired.

The Independent India enacted a series of laws to deal with terrorism and terrorist activities. The first law made in this regard was the Unlawful Activities (Prevention) Act 1967. It followed the National Security Act 1980, Terrorist and Disruptive Activities (Prevention) Act 1987 (TADA), the Maharashtra Control of Organised Crime Act (MCOCA) in 1999, Prevention of Terrorist

Act (POTA) 2002, amended Act of the Unlawful Activities (Prevention) Amendment Act, 2004 and the National Investigation Agency (NIA) Act, 2008. The Unlawful Activities (Prevention) Act (UAPA) was designed to deal with associations and activities that questioned the territorial integrity of India. When the Bill was debated in Parliament, leaders, cutting across party affiliation, insisted that its ambit be so limited that the right to association remained unaffected and the executive did not expose political parties to intrusion. So, the ambit of the Act was strictly limited to meeting the challenge to the territorial integrity of India. The Act was a self-contained code of provisions for declaring secessionist associations as unlawful, adjudication of a tribunal, control of funds and places of work of unlawful associations, penalties for their members, etc. The Act has all along been worked holistically as such and is completely within the purview of the central list in the 7th Schedule of the Constitution. It came into force on 30 December, 1967.[29]

The National Security Act of 1980 was enacted to check terrorism in India, while the Terrorist and Disruptive Activities (Prevention) Act, 1987, was the second major act came into force on 3 September, 1987. This act had much more stringent provisions than the UAPA and it was specifically designed to deal with terrorist activities in India. When TADA was enacted it came to be challenged before the apex court of the country as being unconstitutional. The Supreme Court of India upheld its constitutional validity on the assumption that those entrusted with such draconic statutory powers would act in good faith and for the public good. However, there were many instances of misuse of power for collateral purposes. The rigorous provisions contained in the statute came to be misused in the hands of law enforcement officials. Other major anti-terrorist law in India is the Maharashtra Control of Organised Crime Act, 1999 which was enforced on 24th April, 1999. This law was specifically made to deal with rising organised crime in Maharashtra and specially in Mumbai due to the underworld.[30] The MCOCA, in the definition of a terrorist act is far more stretchable than the POTA. For instance, POTA did not take note of organised crime as such while MCOCA not only mentions that but, what is more, includes promotion of insurgency as a terrorist act. Again, the onus to prove a person guilty under POTA lies on the prosecution while under the Maharashtra law a person is presumed guilty unless he is able to prove his innocence.

The constitutional validity of the Prevention of the Terrorist Act, 2002 was challenged in the apex court of the country, and in the case of *People's Union for Civil Liberties vs. Union of India* (2004) the court said that the Parliament possesses power under Article 248 and entry 97 of list I of the Seventh Schedule of the Constitution of India to legislate the Act. Need for the Act is a matter of policy and the court can not go into the same. Once the legislation is passed the government had an obligation to exercise all available options to prevent terrorism within the bounds of the constitution. However, since its making the POTA remained controversial in and outside the judiciary. Finally on 17 September, 2004 the Union Cabinet in keeping with the United Progressive Alliance (UPA) government's Common Minimum Programme, approved ordinances to repeal the POTA and amended the Unlawful Activities (Prevention) Act, 1967. By the promulgation of Ordinance No. I of 2004, it repealed POTA, a law specially designed to deal with the menace of terrorism, with its repeal, the state apparatus combating terrorism has been debilitated.

The Unlawful Activities (Prevention) Amendment Act, 2004 was promulgated by Ordinance No. 2. By this virtually all the penal provisions of POTA concerning terrorist organisations and activities were transferred to the pre-existing milder sounding Unlawful Activities (Prevention) Act, 1967. In the said Ordinance the definition of unlawful association has been expanded to include also any association which has for its object any activity which is punishable under section 153 A of the Indian Penal Code, or which encourages or aids persons to undertake any such activity or of which the members undertake any such activity. Section 153 A is about promoting enmity between different groups on grounds of religion, race, place of birth, residence, language, etc. Among the special provisions dropped are those restricting release on bail and allowing longer periods of police remand for the accused. Now suspected terrorists may roam free under the bail a rule, jail an exception dictum, but all terrorist organisations banned under POTA would continue to remain banned, under the Unlawful Activities Act, after the repeal of the Act.

The Amendment Act of 2004, as reported by *The Indian Express,* UAPA is more draconian than POTA when it comes to the admissibility in evidence of telephone and e-mail intercepts. The police can now produce intercepts in the court without abiding by any of the elaborate safeguards provided by the repealed law. Thus, if the police can not anymore extract a confession in custody, they have been given more scope than before to plant evidence in the form of interception.[31] In nutshell, the new law has retained all the operational teeth of POTA or it has made only cosmetic change. The difference between POTA and UAPA is substantial even as a lot of provisions are in common. In addition, the new act has also defined the word terrorist act, 'whoever' with intention to threaten the unity, integrity, security or sovereignty of India or to strike terror in the people or any section of the people in India or in any foreign country, does any act by using bombs, dynamite, other explosive substances or inflammable substances or firearms or other lethal weapons or poisons or noxious gases or other chemicals or many other substances of hazardous nature, in such a manner to cause, or likely to cause, death of, injuries to any person or persons or loss of, or damage to, or destruction of any property or equipment used or intended to be used for the defence of India, or in connection with any other purposes of the Government of India, any State Government or any of their agencies, or detains any person and threatens to kill or injure such person in order to compel the Government in India or the Government of a foreign country or any other person to do or abstain from doing any act, commits a terrorist act, as Section 15 of the new law. Likewise provisions regarding death or imprisonment for life, and offences, punishment have also been incorporated in it.

But gradually, as terror attacks went on rise in different parts of the country it was felt that timely, accurate intelligence and up-to-date databases on terrorist elements are essential to evolve strategies to counter terrorist activities. In the direction the most important change brought about recently is in respect of streamlining the investigation and prosecution of terrorist offences at the Central level. Under an Act of 2008, the National Investigation Agency (NIA) was established for effective handling of terrorism-related offences. Parliament passed the law with near unanimity, which indicated the willingness of different political parties ruling the States to enable the Centre to act on the issue. Combating terrorism is a joint responsibility of Central, State and local governments.[32] The NIA Act envisages Centre-State partnership in the investigation of terrorist cases but includes the offences against the state and offences relating to currency and bank notes in the scheduled offences for NIA responsibility.

At the sametime, the second piece of legislation–the Unlawful Activities (Prevention) Amendment Act, 2008 was also passed that makes a number of substantive and procedural changes to empower the NIA to act effectively and decisively on terrorism-related activities. Under the passed law the power of the police to arrest and search have been tightened. Sections 43 A to 43 F have been substituted with provisions that enlarge the power to search any premises and arrest any person about whom such an officer knows or who the officer has reason to believe as a design to commit an offence covered under the Act. The provision of anticipatory bail (Section 438) does not apply to offences under the Act. In addition, the new law is more significant for the procedural modifications brought about than for any substantive changes that are attempted. Section 43 E introduces the principle of presumption of guilt in respect of a terrorist act when arms, explosives or other substances specified in section 15 are recovered from the possession of the accused and there is reason to believe that substances of a similar nature were used in the commission of the offence. Similarly, presumption is raised when finger prints or any other suggestive evidence involving the accused is found at the site of an offence.[33] Finally, the Act empowers the Central government to freeze, seize or attach the financial assets of those engaged in or suspected to be engaged in terrorism. These are strong measures if imaginatively and responsively employed in combating terrorism. Legitimate power is to be given because this is an extraordinary situation. Extraordinary situations require extraordinary remedies.

With each passing day the issue of terrorism is becoming the biggest existentialist challenge for the countries of the world. As a general rule the external support is often found in every operation of terrorist acts in any part of the globe whether in the context of interconnection between a group and its rival group, a group and its enemy state, or a state and its unfriendly state. Combating terrorism at regional level is becoming effective and popular.[34] In the spirit of regional cooperation every state is supposed to refrain from organising, instigating, assisting or participating in acts of civil strife on terrorist acts in another state or involved in organised activities within its territory directed towards the commission of such acts as well as prosecuting and punishing the perpetrators of terrorist acts.

The vexed issue of combating terrorism through effective regional cooperation was raised at the 4th meeting of South Asian Association for Regional Cooperation (SAARC) Interior/Home Ministers held in Thimpu (Bhutan) on 23rd July, 2011. Addressing the gathering P. Chidambaram, India's Minister of Home, without naming Pakistan, said, 'As long as the territory of a country is used by non-state actors to prepare for terror attacks, that country owes a legal and moral responsibility to its neighbours and to the world to suppress those non-state actors and bring them to justice. We have no alternative but to deploy the best instruments and resources at our disposal in our fight against terrorism.[35] In the meeting he emphasised the need for examining the existing mechanisms for countering terrorism, drug trafficking, trafficking in human beings, arms smuggling and counterfeiting, including organised production and distribution of fake Indian currency notes. He termed the terrorism as the most significant existential challenge to peace and security in South Asia and said that it was the single largest hindrance to socio-economic development in the region. He added further that the threat of terrorism, which was a common challenge in the region, could be tackled only with the fullest cooperation amongst the member-nations of the SAARC.[36] The 3rd Conference of the Home Ministers of SAARC countries was held in Islamabad in June 2010 where, too, the member nations agreed on the broad contours of cooperation to combat terrorism. As early in 1987 the South Asian countries recognised the importance of combating terrorism at regional level and consequently, signed a Convention titled the "Convention on Suppression of Terrorism, 1987" and ratified it.

As one of the world's major victims of terrorism, India needs to be in the vanguard, not in the margin of combating the menace. In this context to analyse the best strategy to mitigate the risk of terror strikes we would look at the past success and failure of anti-terror measures. Success is when the state has managed to degrade the capacity of the concerned terrorists in terms of weapons, strike capability, viciousness, anger, desperation etc. over the years. While failure is defined by a steady and unrelenting upgradation of the capacity of the terrorists in terms of weapons, strike capability, viciousness, anger, desperation etc. over the years. In India when we look at success, is the Khalistani terror of the 1980s and the Naxalite terror in West Bengal and Kerala of the 1960s, which no longer pose a great threat to the security of the country. At best the twin policy of the time led to these success which included;

(i) Tough action against violence, helped with strong intelligence;

(ii) Deliberate efforts not to demonize any group of people; and

(iii) Helped by measures to identify and address root grievances.[37]

On the other hand there are regions and places in India from where the terror has refused to go away,even if this is temporarily subdued from time to time. In those areas there is still constant and continuing threat of terror strikes,with the result that the anti-terror apparatus and infra-structure can not be sealed down, where the terrorists have become more sophisticated and organised over the years. This happened today when, apart from dozens of designated custodians of national security, such as Prime Minister, Home Minister, Director of the Intelligence Bureau and Chief of the Research and Analysis Wing (RAW), we have had any number of well-meaning, intelligent, dedicated and committed men in various security outfits who must have had the occasion and opportunity to introduce new ideas in dealing with threats from professional terror-vendors.[38] It is a sad state of affairs that even today we are far from having a national strategy that would mobilise our collective resources and energy to protect ourselves.

In the final analysis, what is crucial in any anti-terrorist strategy or measure is proportion, discrimination, balance and efficacy. The Indian political system, established following the independence of the country, has failed in introducing conditions, habits and thinking to equip ourselves to deal effectively with the trouble makers.[39] On the issue of combating terrorism the divided political leadership in India is unable to infuse a sense of purpose in security agencies to move beyond their routine bureaucratic turf battles. They are also not prepared to recognise the imperative of pooling in a meaningful way the vast resources at national and state level, in a centralised force dedicated to fighting terror. The time for argument is over.

Major Terror Attacks in India

Security and independence for the nation-state have become a complex mosaic in the uneasy post-cold war years. In this phase the ability to inflict mass destruction is no longer the sole purview of the state, and the non-state actor and fringe group zealot has emerged as a new challenge to state security and stability. The insidious proxy war, often supported and abetted by external agencies has the potential to pose a strategic challenge not merely to India but to the region and globe as well.[40] A heady infusion of religious fervour and the proliferation of lethal small arms–the prefix being a complete contrast to the massive destruction possible have enhanced the profile of the practitioners of this proxy war. It is not uncommon to find terrorist/militant /proxy war waging groups on the Indian periphery now having at their disposal fire power capability including artillery pieces and anticraft missiles that would normally be associated with a regular army brigade.[41] For India stakes are high since what is threatened by this proxy war is not mere territoriality but a concerted attempt to hack at the roots of the often taken-for-granted Indian independence and nationhood based on democratic principles and abiding secularism.

In this context India, even today, continues to look at the military dimension of the security aspect long after the rest of the world has understood it to include other important elements. The use of the state's armed apparatus to maintain order, without regard to the political and socio-economic factors of dissent, has been the basic approach of successive Indian governments. The militarisation of political and social discourse by the use of arms in urban and rural areas has grown over the years.[42] This has happened as a consequence of an armed response by the government. Ever more frequently, and in the states, the normal response to an outbreak of violence is of rushing to raise more battalions of armed police and other paramilitary forces. Hardly any effort goes into addressing the political and other non-military issues which are at the root of the problem. National security has therefore been given a distorted perspective over the years. The roles of the citizen and the state have also been wrongly viewed in regard to the security.

In reality India has been at the receiving end of cross-border terrorism in Kashmir and surrounded areas. With the Soviet withdrawal from Afghanistan in the year 1989, the US interests in Afghan affairs declined and the pro-American elements in Kabul suffered a set back on account of Gulf crisis that prevented them to be famous internationally. At the juncture the Government of Pakistan exploited the changing situation in its favour to a large extent and tactfully turned the face of Afghan rebels and others towards Kashmir.[43] According to an estimate during 1988-94, over 50,000 Kashmiri youth have been trained in Pakistan. Terrorist incidents went up from 400 in 1988 to 5,000 in 1993, and deaths from 30 to 2,600. Mujahideens freed from Afghan conflict were sent to Kashmir and their numbers peaked at about 1,600 in 1994.[44] Gradually and knowingly the entire social spectrum was converted to the point where violence and terror began to be considered a justified means of communication.[45] The overall environment and even state institutions sustained terror in which collection of funds, settings up of training camps, free movement of arms and drug trafficking was not uncommon. The entire Kashmir problem as it exists now is because of Pakistan's extraordinary interest in our internal affairs and also due to the fact that most militants operating in India enjoy support from the ISI as well as the Jihadi groups based in Pakistan and Afghanistan.

In the decade nineties and thereafter it has been clearly established that riding the wave of success in Afghanistan, the Pak-Army-ISI combined had decided to replicate the Jihad in Kashmir by diverting the surplus of the Mujahideen on the Valley. With its new-found leverage with the Americans, Pakistan had in fact launched a new proxy war against India using the groups like HuM and Lashkar-e-Toiba that were totally under the thumb of its Army and extended the scope of its attacks beyond Jammu and Kashmir to targets in the rest of India.[46] This is how foreign Mujahideen started making their appearance in Kashmir for the first time in the early nineties and terrorist attacks also started occurring in Delhi, Mumbai and other centres. These Pak-sponsored outfits had no quarrel with the West–historically, politically and ideologically, which made it easier for Pakistan to get the US to easily accept its denial in the acts of cross-border terrorism.[47] The other notable groups participating in the terrorist attacks on India were Jaish-e-Mohammad and the Harkat-ul-Jehad Islami (HuJI) and these two were under the clutches of the ISI.

As a result, scores of innocent civilians continued to be gunned down at all with almost frequent intervals, and bomb explosions kill and maim hapless victims in buses and trains as well as in the market places. From the arms captured from terrorists and from the statements of those apprehended, it has been abundantly clear that the ISI, Pakistan's intelligence wing, has its fingerprints all over the terrorist intrusions into Kashmir.[48] The bomb blasts have outraged every patriotic Indian. No civilized nation can allow this kind of barbaric inhumanity to be partly or fully supported or sponsored by any neighbour or domestic insurgents. The only way we can combat it is to minimize, if not eliminate such occurrences.

In an important development of Indian politics the Babri Masjid was demolished on 7 December, 1992. It hurt the religious sentiments largely in India and all Muslim countries of the world, the Pakistan in particular. Although the destruction of Babri Masjid was condemned by virtually all segments of opinion in the country, it raised the communal temperature and gave comfort to all the forces of intolerance and irrationality. In reaction the extremists in Pakistan had a field day, arousing the emotions of religious bigotry and fanaticism, much to the delight of their Indian counterparts, some of whom had gleefully participated in the destruction of the Mosque's structure.[49] Its net result was the Bombay blast of 1993 in which more than 300 lives were lost with the niddle of suspicion pointing to Pakistan's involvement. Although this was a serial blast of 13-bombs across the city which was hotly denied by Pakistan but in time Indian suspicions were confirmed. India believed that the prime suspects had fled to Dubai and from there to Karachi. India warned Pakistan of "serious consequences" if Islamabad did not hand over to the Indian authorities six members of the Menon family who were the main suspects in the explosions.[50] Another disturbing fact about the blast was that in this incident many of the new terrorists were from the middle-class, well educated, not terribly religious, with no previous criminal records.[51] This means more and more middle class Muslims will be subjected to surveillance, search and interrogation.

To probe the overall issue of communal riots in Mumbai during December 1992-January 1993 and March 1993 serial 'last' the government appointed justice B.N. Srikrishna Commission. The Commission in its report attributed the immediate causes to I. the demolition of the Babri masjid, II. the aggravation of Muslim sentiments by the Hindus with their celebration rallies and III. the insensitive and harsh approach of the police while handling the protesting mobs which initially were not violent.[52] On the serial bomb blasts, the Commission says, "There was a large amorphous body of angry, frustrated and desperate Muslims keen to seek revenge for the perceived injustice done to and atrocities perpetrated on them or to others of their community and it is this sense of revenge which spawned the conspiracy of the serial blast".[53] Whenever blasts occur, we blame the police and the Intelligence Bureau (IB). Instead of indulging in blame game which will lead us nowhere, we should try to cleanse the socio-cultural ambience from which this cold-blooded inhumanity spawns.

On its page 18 fifth chapter the Commission strongly recommended strict action against the police personnel who were found actively participating in riots, communal incidents and incidents of looting, arson and so on. The recommendations of the commission aim at strengthening the secular fabric of our society. It says that religious observances in open public places must be strictly discouraged. The Commission hoped that the calamitous events of December 1992, January 1993 and March 1993 would serve as eye-openers and lead to introspection and that all concerned attain the maturity to accept constructive criticism and mend their ways.[54] However, it was frank enough to add that the deep-rooted polarisation that took place in our country after the Babri Masjid demolition in 1992 is growing at the vitals of the nation. We should find sincere ways to stop it. At the moment, if we stand together as Indians, irrespective of our religions, blasts and attacks will cease to occur in our cities.

Attacks, both major and minor, and other related terrorist activities continued unabated in different parts of the country and in line the Indian Airlines IC-814 was hijacked in December 1999 by Pakistan–based elements and took it to Kandahar (Afghanistan) via Kathmandu from where they put their initial demands through the Taliban.[55] Simultaneously, the incident also questioned the security lapses at Kathmandu airport where the hijackers were able to board the aircraft with weapons and grenades. For most of this decade, Indian security agencies have been warning that Kathmandu has become the terror capital of South Asia. Virtually every militant group from the LTTE to the Taliban is allowed free access through Nepal.[56] After the hijacking the Government of India, initially seemed unable to make up its mind about the necessary steps. In fact, considerable risk was involved in dealing with the kind of terrorists who had taken over the Indian Airlines plane. Driven by religious frenzy, they were seemingly capable of any desperate action that may be justified by their fanatical adherence to their faith.[57] As such any move to approach them had to be undertaken with great care.

Right from the time when the news of hijacking became known, both the government and the airline authorities had given the impression of being overwhelmed by the event. Attacking the citizen is the means by which the population is terrorised. This makes the government look helpless and incompetent. The citizens' pressure built up in due course, the government capitulate and sought to come to terms with the terrorists. The legitimacy of the government was then questioned by the citizens. The political cost of not being able to protect the citizens on the one hand, and the failure to tackle the terrorist threat on the other, is quite heavy.[58] In response to hijackers' demand the Government of India, ultimately agreed to release their terrorist colleagues from Indian jails and in this way the mighty authority of the state was undermined. The three terrorists who were released in exchange, were hardcore militants of the outfit. After the release Masood Azhar became a public figure in Pakistan and Omar Sheikh later kidnapped journalist Daniel Pearl. The hijackers numbering half a dozen, wielding knives and pistols, obtained what they wanted and got away. More than the release of their colleagues, the terrorists showed up the security vulnerabilities of the Indian state. Through one incident they lowered the confidence of the citizens in the government's ability to protect lives.[59] The hijackers had energised others who had sought ways of making the Indian state respond to their perceived grievances. Now it became a hot issue of debate whose security matters more–the state's or the citizen's.

In continuation two devastating attacks were made in the year 2001. On 1 October, 2001 a brutal suicide squad of JeM was made on the Kashmir Assembly complex followed by a terrorist attack on the Indian Parliament, located at the heart of the capital's high security zone on 13 December, the same year. The car bomb explosion at the State Assembly building in Srinagar that killed many innocent bystanders came just three weeks after the appalling attacks on the twin towers of the World Trade Centre. Complicity with the insertion of militants who carry out any heinous act means complicity with the act itself. Much was riding on the understanding of this linkage by Pakistan's new military hierarchy.[60] This attack had a direct linkage with Pakistan's volatile situation emanating from Jihadi violent demonstrations against Pakistan's decision to make common cause with US against the Taliban. Having joined the US in its fight against terrorism, General Musharraf needed as rarely before to pacify the Jihadis and demonstrate its commitment to Kashmir.[61] Terrorism has several consequences that have to be faced in the context of a growing threat to the country.

The Jammu and Kashmir Chief Minister broke down in public at the daring terrorist attack on State Assembly complex in Srinagar and the gruesome deaths that ensued on that fateful day. The Indian official reaction to this attack was terse, it noted that, 'there is a limit to India's patience'. On the other hand, the global community had reacted cautiously to Srinagar since the focus of this constituency was on September 11 and the possibility of an imminent military strike by the US-led coalition against the Taliban regime. In addition, the event of 1 October, 2001 symbolised the significance of the target, the seat of democratic rule in the state and not just any government building.[62] The timing of the attack was no less relevant. It occurred on the eve of Gandhi jayanti and the tenets of non-violence were placed in the sharp contrast to the blood and gore that was strewn in Srinagar.

On 13 December 2001 the JeM made a well-planned, carefully crafted attack on the Indian Parliament which was timed with precise intelligence inputs. The Indian Prime Minister Atal Bihari Vajpayee, promptly laid the blame for this "stab at the heart of Indian democracy" on two Kashmiri militant groups, Lashkar-e-Toiba (the Army of the Pure) and Jaish-e-Muhammad (the Army of Muhammad).[63] He said that the terrorist attack on Indian Parliament had shown beyond a shadow of doubt that the anti-India forces in Pakistan are prepared to wreak any havoc on our soil. It was an attack on our sovereignty, on our national self respect, and it was a challenge to our democratic system. He took the opportunity to reiterate that India has been a victim of cross-border terrorism for the past decades and has lost tens of thousands of innocent men and women and security forces.[64] Pakistan would be solely responsible for the consequences of encouraging terrorism against India and when expedient, turning a blind eye to terrorist groups with trans-national linkages operating from its soil.

The terrorist attack on Indian Parliament was aimed, on the part of Pakistan, to convey two strident messages. The first was that despite the success of the United States–led coalition in the Afghan war, terrorism is alive and well. It had become imperative to send it to raise the morale of terrorists in India and Pakistan which had sunk to their boots following the collapse of the Taliban regime. Secondly, the attack was a proof of the fact that the Musharraf had not sold out to the US, and its alliance with the latter was meant to safeguard Pakistan's nuclear arsenal and prevent the US from including its cross-border terrorism against India in its anti-terrorist agenda.[65] At the juncture, quite clearly, there was a crying need to fight the menace of terrorism unitedly. Partisanship of any sort in dealing with the ISI-sponsored terror attacks in India should be abandoned forthwith. Today terrorism has reached the heart of India in New Delhi's Parliament House. And to suggest that preventive detention laws without any safeguards whatsoever against their misuse were required in the seventies and eighties but are not required now.

In the post-Taliban scenario General Musharraf had only the Kashmir issue to build domestic support in his favour and divert attention from the failure of the foreign policy. In the situation one easily finds the evidence of Pakistan's close ties with the Taliban, Osama bin Laden and the Al-Qaeda, and these three had with terrorist militias like the LeT, JeM and HuM directly and through Pakistan's ISI. Its genesis lies in post-9/11 predicament of the Inter-Services Intelligence (ISI) when the agency realised that in the changed global environment it needed a tactical shift in its strategy of using terrorism as an instrument of state policy.[66] The run up to 9/11 was laid in Afghanistan after the US took a leading hand in ousting the Taliban that had assumed power there in 1996. Left to itself Pakistan had no problems with the Taliban; it was Benazir Bhutto who had dispatched the Taliban to that country in 1993 to clear the mess created by the tribal warlords in the post-Soviet scenario and established a friendly rule in Afghanistan to give 'strategic depth' to Pakistan against India.

In continuation Indian big cities/places remained number one target of the Pakistani terrorists. However terror's first preference was Mumbai in Maharashtra where they exploded bombs on short intervals. On 6 December 2002, 27 January, 23 March and 28 July, 2003, 11 July, 2006, several serial blasts were undertaken by the terrorists of LeT, JeM and HuM in which hundreds were killed and thousands injured. The bomb blasts on local trains at various places killed 209 and injured over 700 innocent people. The number of blasts in Mumbai since 1993 is more than sufficient for anyone intending to do an analysis to get the root of the problem. It just can not happen that the few individuals who placed the blast devices did so without support or assistance from the local population.[67] It becomes all the more pronounced as Mumbai has a total floating population which surpasses the resident population of the city. If only our local police are a little more alert, the chances of such schemes getting leaked can not be ruled out. At least, the previous incident that happened must have alerted us to get ourselves ready for any eventuality.

In the ever-worst terror attack in India, a devastating event took place on 26 November, 2008 in which Mumbai, the financial capital of India, was the target. On this saddest day Mumbai faced a terror attack by ten professionally trained men of Pakistani origin which represented the gravest provocation to the Indian states in decades. The terror attack was made at Hotel Taj, Nariman House, Hotel Trident Oberoi and other places in the city. It took about two hundred precious lives, and left over 300 people severally injured. The casualties included Indians, foreigners, police personnel, NSGs and others. It lasted for about 60 hours in which nine terrorists were gunned down and one was caught alive. In the operation against the terrorists 20 policemen and 2 NSG Commandos were killed. Among the dead 23 were of foreign nationals.[68] The 26/11 attack on Mumbai was in several respects very different from those in the past. It was a bold, brave frontal, ferocious attack in which terrorists were well prepared. Once again the attack demonstrated how incapable India is as a nation to prepare itself to fight against terrorism. It not only shocked the nation, but also gave us an impression that we can only boast of preparedness, but the reality is alltogether different.[69] Our intelligence agencies are not as alert and fast as the terrorists are. Now after six decades, the state can not even perform its basic function of protecting its citizens, never mind giving them a better life.

The terror attack in Mumbai at different places in the city had furthered India-Pakistan relations in all spheres near collapse and created a war-like situation between the two countries. For a long Islamabad refused the truth that the attackers were Pakistani nationals, it however, lastly accepted the fact that they were our citizens and attack's plan was prepared on Pakistani soil. But to India's dismay, the US establishment-obviously driven by its own, national interests, refused to see the Pakistani's hand in 26/11. The US policy makers desperately wanted to bail out Pak army from the well founded charge of complicity in the Mumbai terrorist attack. Their primary concern was somehow not to let this grave provocation cause an escalation of Indo-Pak tension that would give Pakistan a ruse for not concentrating on its task on the western front.[70] US responses might have been guided by the American national interests but they were unhelpful for India never-the-less.

About the same time several attacks were made by the terror groups at different places in New Delhi, the capital of India. Earlier the repeal of POTA in 2002 had emboldned the Students Islamic Movement of India (SIMI) and put the law enforcing agencies on the back foot. Especially after the 9/11 the SIMI and the Indian Mujahideen have been a frontal to mislead the security agencies and simultaneously organising themselves aggressively. In a meeting after the 13 September, 2008 attacks in Delhi, the SIMI leadership decided that the organisation should take advantage of the favourable environment to recruit for Jihad. They also decided to refrain from sporadic acts of terror till they strengthened themselves enough to make big strikes.[71] While they strengthened their relations with Pakistan through the LeT and the underworld, their role was by and large confined to assisting the Pakistan-based terrorists.

The SIMI/IM is only a motley growth of youth recruited and motivated by Pakistan for indigenisation of terror in India. It has negligible support among the Indian Muslims and all Muslim outfits have denounced their ideology and activities. In post-9/11 the big and famous terror outfits along with the ISI made SIMI their front organisation. Using Dawood Ibrahim, CAM Bashir, a SIMI leader from Mumbai was called to Dubai in 2001 and the process of converting a radical Islamic youth organisation into Pakistan-controlled terrorist outfit started. With re-organisation of the outfit, its mentors hoped to use the groups for direct actions rather than the support role they were playing. The Students Islamic Movement of India (SIMI) is being accessed, financed and controlled through locations in West Asia and the underworld is being primed to enhance its striking capabilities. The group is also emerging as a coverging point for the ISI, crime syndicates, radicalised local youth to bleed India. If Pakistan and the radical forces supported by it succeed in their nefarious designs of indigenising terror, it could lead to violent communal conflict, a long cherished objective of Pakistan.[72] The new strength of SIMI and IM, good ground knowledge and local contacts are worrying. India's inadequate laws, ill-equipped police force and the absence of political will to deal with the threat have only increased the problem.

Even in the years 2010 and 2011 several terror attacks were made in different parts of the country,at New Delhi and Mumbai in particular. In 2010 the Jama Masjid firing on 19 September and the Sheetla Ghat bomb blast on 6 December took place in which many precious lives lost and hundreds injured. Later it became clear that the rapid e-mails sent by the terrorist group Indian Mujahideen after the Jama Masjid and Sheetla Ghat incidents were uploaded from Mumbai through the Opera Mini platform using servers in Norway. The recent bomb blast before the Delhi High Court is also in line. The chain of events poses serious questions about our capability to root out terror in the country. The answer, perhaps, lies in radically over-hauling our counter-terror strategy. Broadly speaking, enhancement of our capabilities to neutralise terror threats outside our land and sea borders should be our first priority.

Another and the latest terror attack took place in Mumbai on 13 July, 2011. On that day the terrorists exploded three blasts at Opera House, Zaveri Bazar and Dadar West in which 26 persons were killed and over 130 injured. As a custom the incident will be remembered again, when the next blasts occur, to compare statistics on the number of persons killed and injured and the names of the groups responsible for the ghastly attacks. The chain of terror incidents with links to Mumbai indicate that terror modules in Maharashtra have regrouped and they have dedicated-and-tested lines of communication and logistics.[73] For any counter-terror strategy to succeed, these lines need to be disrupted on a regular basis. The investigations in the Mumbai 13/7 bombings are stuck partly because we do not have information to either dismiss or confirm theories about the involvement of the ISI or any terror outfit. The line of defence should be to unearth and uproot terror modules within our country so that terrorists don't get time to regroup and launch attack. This is the task of the local police and dedicated anti-terror squads as the logic is that a terrorist on the run can't plan and, thus, can't strike.

In fact we follow a hit-and-miss strategy to tackle terrorism. The last firewall in our fight against terrorism should be a proper and scientific investigation after the strike. It's a matter of concern that important clues at terror spots get trampled upon by an intrusive media and curious onlookers or they get hosted out by over-eager civic agencies. The next set of problems emanate from the fact that our counter-terrorist doctrines, structures and systems have evolved around the threats from foreign terrorists. Apprehending domestic problems, the government has always denied that there could be local participation. But this reality should be accepted so that the intelligence agencies can include domestic players in their coverage. This acceptance will also increase the role and responsibility of the district and local-level intelligence units of the states that are in the state of neglect.

In the emerging scenario, the government must increase their contacts with the religious, social and civil society, Muslim leaders and deny any space to foreign-inspired subversive elements. It is important that while taking firm actions against anti-national elements, the innocents are protected and collateral damages are avoided. The same logic applies to living in cities. There is no fun blaming every person on this earth but we can start our own surveillance and protection wings in each area. There is need for the police to conduct area-wise, local get-togethers and attend to problems. We have many things in our favour and the nation is capable of meeting the threats. But to do this, the political parties must start looking at the problem from a national, and not an electoral perspective.

PAKISTAN

Promotion of Religious Fundamentalism

The word 'Pakistan' was first coined by Rahmat Ali when he published a 4-page pamphlet at Cambridge in January 1933, almost seven years ago of the period (23 March, 1940) Mohammad Ali Jinnah, the *Quaid-i-Azam* of the country, asserted his demand for a separate nation at the Lahore session of the Muslim League. The creation of Pakistan was not the work of clerics and religious divines: it was the result of the efforts of a liberal Westernised leadership that successfully articulated the aspiration of the Muslims in different parts of India for substantially improved material conditions and an absence of Hindu economic and cultural domination.[74] Actually, the then Muslim intelligentsia wanted to break the psychological yoke of Hindu domination and consequent extermination. Hence they encouraged the paroxysms of the ordinary Muslims who were cohabiting with their Hindu counterparts for centuries in a 'more-or-less' conducive socio-political atmosphere.[75] There is no doubt in the fact that the leaders of Muslim League including Jinnah and earlier Sir Syed Ahmad and Mohammad Iqbal had thought sincerely about the application of Islamic principles, but they certainly did not regard the movement for Pakistan as an effort to recreate some kind of a 'golden age' in Islam. In the minds of most, whatever the other inducements underlying the demand for Pakistan, the project certainly had an idealist element involving the issue of identity and Islam.[76] But since religion had played an important role in the creation of Pakistan, the role of religion in the context of post-independence developments assumed significance.

Religion, as a faith, is supreme, but as a basis of nationhood does not carry much weight because it can not unite areas which are different: socially, economically, geographically, linguistically and culturally. History has proved that after the first few decades or at the most after the first century, Islam was not able to unite all the Muslim countries on the basis of Islam.[77] Among the three stalwarts–Sir Syed Ahmad, Mohammad Iqbal and Jinnah, the first sought a rational exposition of Islam that represented a qualitative change from the past into the modern era. He held the Quran to determine our understanding of Islam and brought out its relevance to the new society of his day and rejected the canonical traditions and the authority. Mohammad Iqbal took a step further in this regard and rejected the static traditionalist interpretation of Islam and asserted that the Quran provides an essentially dynamic world-view for Muslims.[78] Even after the independence of Pakistan on 14 August, 1947, Jinnah regarded the religion as a personal matter, not a state matter. His ultimate commitment to Islam remained intact and while formulating the broad principles he held the view, 'Islam is not only a set of rituals, traditions and spiritual doctrines, Islam is a code for every Muslim which regulates his life and his conduct in all aspects, social, political economic, etc. It is based on the highest principle of honour, integrity, fairplay and justice for all. One God, equality and unity are the fundamental principles of Islam.[79] Jinnah's view on religion was treated for a long time as the 'Magna Carta' of minority safeguards in Pakistan.

The new state called Pakistan was a creation of the Muslim League that was founded in 1906 to oppose the Indian National Congress (INC) and therefore, the former had hardly any members who had fought for the independence of the country. The result was that the power came into the hands of either to retired officials or men who had been brought into public life under British patronage. It created a wide gap between the ruler and the ruled in the newly formed nation while the public or society of it was a bewilderingly patchy. There are classes within class, castes within caste, social groups, ethnic groups, linguistic groups, urban modern educated elite, rural, feudal benighted masses, opulent industrialists, rich feudal lords and the seedy hangers on the fundamentalists with the arch conservative and orthodox outlook, and the secular, democratic enlightened and liberal sections of society with the modernist view of man and society. In 1947, all Sikhs and nearly all high-caste Hindus left Pakistan. Cities and villages became totally Muslim. The resultant confessional homogeneity in Pakistan created favourable environment for Islamic folk culture. The situation of that time was also characterised by the low level of religious education.

The perception of "Fundamentalism" has come to imply a dogmatic adherence to tradition, orthodoxy, in flexibility and a rejection of modern society, intellectual innovations, and attempts to recreate a golden era. Essentially the term suggests going back to the basic texts and reproducing as closely as possible the laws and institutions found in its domain. Apart from its more ominous aspects, it also suggests bypassing the clergy and going back to the original sources for guidance. In the confusion engendered by modernisation, it means authenticity and rootedness which gives it strength and resilience. That all of this is not enough for it to grapple with contemporary reality, to respond to that challenge or even to release the full potential of its adherents is another matter altogether.[80] However, the term 'Fundamentalism' has been used in Western discourse to designate the moribund and hostile 'other'. The assessment is frequently made about Third World Muslim societies which in general lacks appreciation of the dynamic populist movement.

It is in the name of Islam that the country has created an image of being the most potent source of religious terrorism, which poses a threat to peace and stability in large parts of the globe. This conception of a Pakistani ideology and Pakistani identity based on Islam was put forward by the religious circles rather than the founding fathers of the nation. At the time of independence even the secular ideologists were also looking at Islam as the key symbol which consolidates the newly born and somewhat anomalous nation.[81] The motive force for Pakistan came largely from the middle class Muslims of North India, many of whom had been educated at Aligarh. At some level, they identified with the ideas of Syed Ahmad Khan and Mohammad Iqbal along with the leaders of Muslim League including Mohammad Ali Jinnah. They all thought sincerely about the application of Islamic principles, but they certainly did not regard the movement for Pakistan as an effort to re-create some kind of a 'golden age' in Islam or to re-establish Wahabiism. The large number of Muslims who opted for somewhat secular leadership of the Muslim League accepted the Islamic values but denied the belief that the *Ulemas* derive their authority from within the Quran and Sunnah. According to them there is in Islam no Church or priestly class, counterposed to the state enjoying a kind of divine sanction.

This situation of Islam in new-born nation disappointed a large number of people mostly *Ulemas* who had migrated there to establish themselves and as a result from the start they challenged the leadership on the Islamic nature of the Pakistani state. The *Ulema* were in favour of Islam playing a dominant role in Pakistan. However, they were never clear and unanimous about what the role should be. In contrast to this view, the modernist, Western-educated political leaders and intellectuals sought the Pakistani state to be based on the Western parliamentary model with Islam playing a role only in the personal lives of the people.

The new nation, starting with this position allowed the debate on the kind of state but soon Pakistan shifted significantly in favour of the Islamist lobby. The pro-Islam Objective Resolution was introduced in the Constituent Assembly in 1949 which with some modifications became the preamble to the Constitution and eventually was made a substantive part of the Constitution. The Objective Resolution affirmed that 'sovereignty over the entire universe belongs to God Almighty alone', that therefore the people of Pakistan were to exercise power only 'within the limits prescribed by Him' and that Muslims would be enabled to order their lives' in the individual and the collective spheres in accord with the teachings and requirements of Islam as set out in the Holy Quran and Sunnah.[82] In the circumstances the leadership that had assumed control of the new state, though committed to Islam in broader terms, was largely Westernised and secular in outlook, it however, faced a widespread disturbances in the Punjab in 1953 which showed a remarkable strength of the Islamists on the one hand and weaknesses of the government on the other. From there onwards the Islamist parties of the time became keenly aware of the potential for agitational politics under the cover of sensitive religious issues. As a result successive civilian governments sought the short-cut of adopting an Islamic formalism to assuage what they saw as potentially disruptive forces in society. At various points of time in Pakistan's history, religion has been exploited by the ruling elite to gain popularity and legitimacy and fight political opponents. Even the modernisaion of Islam by Ayub Khan and later by Z.A. Bhutto failed to outplay the conservative Islamist circles which did not trust them and their policies.

A major step forward was taken to promote religious fundamentalism in Pakistan from the mid-1970s especially when on 5 July, 1977, a military takeover under Zia-ul-Haq, the Chief of Army Staff, assumed power in the country. Zia-ul-Haq, the new ruler, was everything–judge, jury and executioner, Head of State, Chief of Martial Law Administrator, Commander-in-Chief and honorary mullah. Though like Ayub and Yahya he did not wage any war with India but prepared the society of Pakistan for a long-proxy war, first in Afghanistan against the Soviet Union, and then in Kashmir against India.[83] With a view to legitimise his rule Zia began to be working towards creating structures for an Islamic state and society within Pakistan. He started with a series of 'reforms' designed to bring law in various areas of activity in conformity with the tenets of Islam. The radical Islamisation of Pakistan began under Zia when he drafted the *Ulema* or mullahs to legitimise and extend his unconstitutional rule. In the process several controversial Islamic provisions were inducted in the constitution, which later proved to be so damaging to the constitution and the rights of the people. It is widely held that they changed the very complexion of an otherwise non-violent Pakistani society. The shameful Hudood laws curbing the rights of the women, redefining law of evidence, amending the blasphemy law, establishing Federal Shariat Court and revising religious laws to create rifts among various sects were some of the more obscurantist changes.[84] Zia exploited the religion to the hilt. He misused religion to prolong his despotic rule.

At independence Pakistan had five major ethnic groups– Bengalis, Punjabis, Sindhis, Pathans and Baluchis; since independence, one ethnic group (Punjabis) has dominated the rest. This was possible perhaps for two reasons. The Punjabis had been the backbone of the British Indian army, and became so also of the Pakistan army. The political leadership's concern with Pakistan's territorial security catapulted the military to political prominence, which created a permanent role of the military high command in national politics. This apart was the fact that the Punjabis comprised 56 per cent of West Pakistan's population at the time, also led to Punjabi domination of the affairs of the state.[85] In the then ethnic distribution except Punjabis, Sindhis constitute 22 per cent, Pathans 13 per cent, Baluchis 4 per cent and rest 5 per cent.

The coming of Zia-ul-Haq as the new ruler of Pakistan was responsible for the ethnic disturbances in the country. Some sectarian groups – Sipah-i-Sahaba and Tehrik-i-Jafena surfaced and flourished under Zia's patronage. Ethnic parties especially Muttahida Quami Movement, formerly Muhajir Quami Movement (MQM) and its rival group Haqiqi were also said to be creation of the martial law administration. He started a calculated move to part between Sindhi and non-Sindhi, Sindhi and Mohajir. The hanging of Z.A. Bhutto in 1979 had further widened the gap not only between the Sindhi in rural areas and the military regime but also with the people of Pakistan in general. The new incident had created an overt hostility between the military and the Sindhi population. The power of the central government became identified with a particular ethnic group.[86] In order to undermine the political support of Pakistan Peoples' Party (PPP) in Sindh Zia encouraged the Mohajirs who constitute about 20 per cent to come together under one political platform, and it was for the first time that an All Pakistan Mohajir Student's Organisation (APMSO) was formed in 1978. In nutshell, General Zia was responsible overtly and covertly for the confrontation in both rural and urban region of the province. In targeting the Sindhis Zia succeeded in assimilating discontended Pathans into Pakistan national politics.

The regime of General Zia witnessed the growing importance of Islamic militants in the political system. The two main Islamic parties of Pakistan, Jamiatul-ulema-i-Islam (JUI) and Jamaat-i-Islamic (JI) had been actively involved in Afghanistan, first in the anti-Soviet Jehad and later in support of the Taliban. The Jamaat-i-Islami had organised itself as armed cadre of workers, particularly among students. The external arms and money linkages were developed by Islamist forces. What mattered here was the existence of these militant organisations, their initial training in Pakistani Madrassas, their operations in Afghanistan, their links with political parties, the ISI and the army. As a fallout from Afghan turmoil, guns, drugs and state sponsored terrorism have proliferated; a mafia-like culture prevailed in parts of Pakistan, further straining its weak institutional framework and thereby creating a threat to internal security and stability.[87] Thus, Zia's laws and policies resulted in making vast sections of the population extremely vulnerable to the Islamic militancy by replacing a tolerant and liberal civil society with an intolerant and retrogressive one. Zia-ul-Haq used Islam to perpetuate his autocratic rule but left behind a legacy of division, disruption, contradiction and conflicts.

The Islamisation drive of Zia-ul-Haq brought to the surface all sorts of contradictions among Muslim trends and sects. The difference between different religious trends produced alienation among the Muslims and pushed them in open antagonism, enmity and bloodshed. The Deobandi school is extremely intolerant of all Islamic trends, its radical part looks at the Shi'ites as infidels. The enmity between them in central and southern Punjab developed into a blood feud typical of the local folk culture and a string of terrorist acts that were going on for many years. By the late eighties detachment of militants had been strengthened with the people who fought in Afghanistan. The Jihad against the Soviet troops was felt in Punjab and other provinces. The geopolitical sickle of Islamic extremism stretched from Afghanistan and Kashmir in the north and reached Pakistan its middle part. This situation survived throughout the last decade of the twentieth century and the beginning of the new century and was even strengthened with the sickle of radical Islamism.

Further in the regimes of Benazir Bhutto and Nawaz Sharif, despite restoration of democracy, orthodoxy nexus of Zia's period remained unchanged. After the death of Zia-ul-Haq in a air crash in August 1988, Benazir Bhutto became the Prime Minister of Pakistan. Though the PPP did show an inclination to roll back the Ziaist Islamisation but it was not in a position to make much headway. In her period the military maintained a decisive authority but under overall civilian supremacy. Her government became soft to military power to deal with the near anarchic situation in the province. Nawaz Sharif in the year 1990 succeeded Benazir Bhutto and the former, too, was known as working on behalf of the old power cocktail. In his second term he gave a new diplomatic twist to Pakistan's Kashmir policy asserting that Islamabad would extend 'moral, political and diplomatic support to the Kashmiri people on the Indian side of the Line of Control LoC'.[88] In this phase Nawaz Sharif also declared Shariat or the social system of Islam through the 15th Constitutional Amendment (1998), and like his predecessors used the Islamic card for his political survival in the face of imminent economic collapse and growing sectarianism in the country. The amendment to the constitution aimed to change the complexion of state from democracy to theocratic and of the leader from elected representative to absolute monarch.[89] As expected in post-Kargil humiliation, the democratic government of Nawaz Sharif was overthrown in a military coup by General Pervez Musharraf on October 12, 1999.

General Pervez Musharraf inherited the ethnic tension and a more acute and formidable 'Islamisation Programme' in the then Pakistan. The post-Zia regimes headed by Benazir Bhutto and Nawaz Sharif continued with more or less the same sort of highly centralised, repressive and negative approach as adopted by their predecessors to deal with the regional tensions. The already complicated scene in the Sindh province was wrecked by violence. Thousands of innocent people had fallen victim to the sectarian fanaticism of armed militia. The polarisation of Muttahida Quami Movement (MQM), Pakistan Muslim League (PML), Awami National Party (ANP) and other factions of Pakistan sharpened when the Sharif government unveiled its plan to introduce a constitutional amendment to amass more powers.

At the time Pervez Musharraf tookover, the Islamist hardliners, who were on the defensive in the initial days, had started to make a comeback with their characteristic assertiveness. After the regime's retreat on the issue of rationalising the blasphemy law, the Islamist political forces had even found the courage to challenge the military establishment. Alike to Zia-ul-Haq Musharraf began to tell the world that Jihad in its true understanding delineates war cultures and shuns terrorism and therefore, the two should not be confused. The implied meaning of his statement was that his military regime has no control over the Mujahideen whom he called freedom fighters and that their actions are purely voluntary. Hence, Pakistan is following Jihad, not terrorism.[90] In a hurridly convened press conference in Karachi Lieutenant General Tareeq Wasin Ghazi, the Corps Commander of the Sindh province made it clear that no official campaign was going on against the Jihadi organisations to stop them from collecting funds.

In fact Pervez Musharraf never initiated a crackdown on Jihadi, its organisations and producing factory–madrassas in order to appease the religious support for his rule. As part of the alleged 'deal' the military government, not withstanding its public statements, turned a blind eye to the Jihadi activities. The ordinance promulgated to regulate the functions of madrassas on 19 August, 2001 remained a piece of paper and madrassas remained factories for the mass production of zealots ready to die for Jihad all over the world. Madrassas are the labour suppliers, producing the raw material on which Jihad is driven. The wheels of which are well oiled by the wealthy Pakistani diaspora who pour in money along with Wahabis of Saudi Arabia. Besides, Pakistan's government has encouraged the establishment of such a large number of Islamic militant organisations and groups–Taliban, Harkat-ul-Mujahideen, Lashkar-e-Toiba, Hizb-ul-Mujahideen, Hizb-e-Wahadat, Sipah-e-Sabaha Pakistan, Lashkar-e-Jhougvi, Spipah-e-Mohammad Pakistan and Jaish-e-Mohammad in the last 10 to 15 years.[91] The most typical of these organisations, and the one with the largest manpower and resources is the Lashkar-e-Toiba. The Lashkar was formed after the Afghan Jihad against Soviet occupation was nearly over and it is primarily meant to train recruits to fight battle in Kashmir.

In a dramatic development the general elections in Pakistan were held for the National Assembly in February 2008 and restoration of democracy in the country was welcomed by all. As a result of the victory a coalition of PPP and Pakistan Muslim League (Nawaz Sharif), an elected government took over the administration with Yousuf Raza Gilani as the new Prime Minister of Pakistan in March 2008. But the restoration of democracy had hardly made any difference on the promotion of religious fundamentalism. In the name of Islam it has created an image of being the most potent source of religious terrorism, which poses a threat to peace and stability in large parts of the globe. It has become the biggest source of most of its internal conflicts in recent years.

Terror Laws and Related Activities

Today Pakistan is unable to contain the forces of anarchy it has unleashed. The struggle to establish a parliamentary democracy in a federal setting has been handicapped by inter-ethnic strife, social strains, fragmented elite, praetorian rule, and the influences of external power– both regional and global. Since independence, 'the men on horseback' have four times administrated governments by martial law, seeking to gain legitimacy through the so called 'civilianisation and democratisation of the military regimes'. The present day Pakistan is a land where the problem rests on the belief of those that sustain terror through the employment of state institutions. The problem resides in the precincts of power in Islamabad—Rawalpindi that justify the covert and overt employment of violence and terror as a tool of diplomacy.[92] The use of Jihad and gun culture as tools of state policy to acquire strategic depth has boomeranged on Pakistan. Madrassas as 'schools of hate' that were created to wage the proxy war in Afghanistan and later in Kashmir have served, no doubt, Pakistan's short-term interests. But in the long-term they have created fanatical fundamentalists who are ultimately likely to wreck and ruin Pakistan.[93] Drugs, weapons and terrorism, originally meant for export, are now threatening to destroy Pakistan's own society and polity. In Pakistan, non-state actors possess money power, weapons and a certain mindset that is threatening society and has gone beyond the control of government to dictate how, when and where these would be used and against whom.[94] There were serious gaps in Pakistan promised and what it delivered.

It was in that kind of situation prevailing in the country that Pakistan thought of making some new terror laws to control the terrorist organisations in a more effective way. Recently Pakistan passed the 1997 Anti-Terrorism Act. Under Section 5 (2) (1) of the Act the right to shoot to kill was provided under which an officer of the police, armed forces and civil armed forces may after giving prior warning use such for as may be deemed necessary or appropriate, bearing in mind all the facts and circumstances of the situation, against any person who is committing, or in all probability is likely to commit a terrorist act or a scheduled offence, and it shall be lawful for any such officer, or any superior officer, to fire or order the firing upon any person or persons against whom he is authorised to use force in terms hereof. However, this provision of the Act was criticised and it is said that the enactment of broad provisions empowering summary execution is not the way a modern civilized state ought to act. Rather the government should set strict limits to the circumstances in which firearms could be used to prevent an arbitrary killing by the security forces. The broad powers given to the police and consequently, to the military and civil armed forces contravene major international standards, human rights.

Several immunities were given to security forces in Section 39 of the act while section 26 embodied the laws regarding admission of the confession. To quote section 39 of the act, 'No suit, prosecution or other legal proceedings shall lie against any person in respect of anything which is in good faith done or intended to be done under this act'. This is tantamount to providing impunity to the security forces for abuses, including extra-judicial killings. To explicitly place any acts of police or other law enforcement personnel, including possibly random resort to lethal force, outside scrutiny and accountability may give law enforcement personnel the impression that they may commit such acts with impunity if only they can claim to have done them in good faith. The said provision breaches a basic requirement of the rule of law, namely its equal and exceptionless application to everyone. While section 26 says, 'The special court may, for admission of the confession in evidence, require the police officer to produce a video tape together with the device used for recording the confession. Article 14 (2) of the Constitution of Pakistan prohibits the use of torture, though only in the limited context of extraction of confession. 'No person shall be subjected to torture for the purpose of extracting evidence'. However, Pakistani law enforcement officials, to extract confessions from the accused, routinely use torture. Lending greater legal weight to confessions and putting pressure on police to speedily resolve crime may indirectly contribute to the continued and perhaps increased use of torture.

Another sections 15, 31 and 22 of 1997 Anti-Terrorism Act defined the right to be tried in a public place without prejudice to the defendant, right to appeal and death penalty respectively. Under section 15 of the Act the government may direct that for the trial of a particular case the court shall sit at such place including the place of occurrence as it may specify. As explained, this is intended to expose the defendant to public expressions of outrage, anger or even violence for his deeds to humiliate him and to deter others by the specter of public exposure, it does not appear to serve the purpose of helping the judiciary establish the truth and do justice in a detached circumspect manner and in calm circumstances. The right to be presumed innocent, the Act lays down that only special courts may grant bail to people tried for offences under the act but they may not release a defendant on bail if there are reasonable grounds for believing that he has been guilty of the offence with which he has been charged and unless the prosecution has been given an opportunity to show cause why he should not be released. This gives the prosecution the right to veto to deny bail.

Likewise section 31 reads, 'A judgement or order passed or sentence awarded by a special court, subject to the result of an appeal under this act shall be final and shall not be called in question in any court'. By this provision the possibility of the defendant to appeal to a court in the regular judicial system, either to the provincial court or the Supreme Court of Pakistan is therefore excluded. People convicted and sentenced by the special courts are clearly disadvantaged in so far as their legal remedies are restricted: they have only one possibility of appeal, whereas people convicted by regular courts may also appeal to the Supreme Court. This provision violates the principle of equality before law laid down in the Constitution of Pakistan. It is also the fundamental principles of international human rights law. Moreover, the right to appeal is restricted in so far as it is subject to severe limitations. The defendant may not in seven days be able to present an adequate appeal while the prosecution has 15 days for the appeal. Moreover, the right to appeal of those facing the death penalty also appears to be seriously infringed under the act. Under section 7 (1) of the 1999 Amended Anti-Terrorism Act, for terrorist act resulting in death, courts have to mandatory impose the death penalty. This does not give any discretion to the judiciary. According to section 22 of the 1997 Anti-Terrorism Act the government may specify the manner, mode and place of execution of any sentence passed under this act, having regard to the deterrent effect with such execution is likely to have. The section 22 opens the possibility for public executions of death penalty.

However, soon the Government of Pakistan felt the need of a more effective measure to combat terror activities and in 2002 it issued an ordinance to include the military officers in the panel of judges to try terror offences. This not only determines the independence of the judiciary, but makes the anti terror law in the country even more draconian. Described as necessary that appropriate administrative and judicial measures be adopted to fight a spate of terrorist activities and heinous offences in Pakistan these anti-terrorism laws opened the door to grave violations of human rights including the right to be safe, the prohibition of torture, the right to liberty and security and the right to fair trial. Inter alia they provide for the creation of anti-terrorist courts and give wide powers of arrest and interrogation to the police and army. Amnesty International, in its report, had criticized the legislation and held the view that the existing legal and judicial system is already equipped to deal with offences referred to in the act. The problem then seems to be a lack of implementation, not a lack of laws. In an attempt to hide this inefficiency, Pakistan adopted the anti-terrorist acts which provide speedy trial without necessary guarantees for the accused, unfair trials and license to kill, etc.

Traditionally, the state of Pakistan has an potential enmity with India by birth and a long-term border difference and ethnic tension with Afghanistan. After independence it has fought four declared wars with India without any success. The policy of Islamisation pursued by the regime of Zia-ul-Haq and later governments proceeded from the Sunni Hanafi legal interpretation which predominated in Pakistan. With the strengthening of religious fundamentalism and opening of countless Madrassas in the country, Pakistan's social composition and nature of the polity began to change in terror direction. The social and economic conditions also played their role: sectarianism, the phenomenon akin to communalism, sprang out of enmity between religious-political groups. The clashes between Shi'ites and Sunnis started in the early eighties first in small towns of central and southern Punjab, one of the most backward and poorest parts of the country.[95] Independent Pakistan inherited a border dispute on account of a boundary sketched in 1893 by Sir Mortimer Durand, Foreign Secretary for the British Empire in India. It is now called the Durand Line and runs right through areas inhabited by Pashtuns, splitting them in half. The Afghanistan government does not recognise the line and at the time of partition of India, it had demanded the redrawing of the line. It suggested to make the Indus river as the new border but it was ignored. From then onwards, it has been a constant source of bitterness between Pakistan and Afghanistan.

With Russia's invasion in Afghanistan on 27 December, 1979 Kabul became a battleground for the cold war between the United States and the Soviet Union. America and the Soviet Union brought two other neighbours into that cold war fight: Pakistan and India. New Delhi stood by the Soviet Union as it quietly did in many other areas. Pakistan and its intelligence service became the middlemen between the United States and the Mujahideen. It acquired the status of a frontline state in the US-Soviet cold war.[96] Pakistan's army was used by the US to organise resistance to the pro-Soviet regime in Afghanistan. During the late 1970s and early 1980s, Pakistan's patronage to hard-line Islamists within the country, the massive recruitment for military and ideological training, and the spread of weapons provided by North Atlantic Treaty Organisation (NATO) countries, created a fertile ground in both Pakistan and Afghanistan for Islamic insurgency in the region.[97] At the time of invasion India called for a withdrawal of Soviet troops, it also expressed its apprehensions about United States military commitments to Pakistan. New Delhi feared that newly acquired United States arms could be used against India, rather than to secure the Afghan border, and such fear certainly had a strong base, as in the forthcoming years, these weapons were used by various violent groups to destabilise Punjab, Kashmir and India's political and social stability.

As a result of crisis in Afghanistan thousands of refugees sought sanctuary in Pakistan from Soviet air raids. Naturally Pakistan became worried as it created troubles for the country in various parts and upset the population balance. The use of Pakistan's soil by Afghan guerilla organisations and millions of refugees created a law and order problem for the administration. The easy availability of advanced weapons, including rockets, grenades and automatic rifles had helped increase criminal and terrorist activity in Pakistani society. The years between 1977 and 1987 saw a steady inflow of Afghan refugees into Pakistan and the use of Pakistan as a conduit for arms for the Afghan war. In 1987, 17 per cent of the 832 incidents of international terrorism recorded in the world occurred in Pakistan alone; if Pakistan is excluded, the level of international terrorism actually declined by almost 10 per cent from the level of 1986.[98] The US government blamed Soviet-trained agents of the Afghan intelligence service for carrying out 127 of the 138 international terrorism strikes in Pakistan, leaving 234 people dead and 1,200 wounded. Several terrorist strikes by Iranian and Palestinian agents in Pakistan were reported. True to the proliferation of terrorism it is said that the growth of international terrorist movements should be linked to the willingness of some nations to directly or indirectly sponsor campaigns of terror, often through proxies and other means.[99] State sponsorship of groups has strained relations between India and Pakistan, Pakistan and Afghanistan, and Sri Lanka and India.

Throughout the period of Soviet occupation in Afghanistan, Pakistan in collusion with the anti-Soviet forces of US, worked with full power and strength. Over the years Afghanistan has been serving as breeding ground for Jehadi groups. The western regions of Pakistan and the southern regions had became vast network of training camps for highly motivated militant youth. The nexus against the Soviet forces in Afghanistan was also reported to have involved in drug trade.[100] The drug money helped in the growth of the ISI from its modest origins to become an extensive intelligence network with global operations in less than a decade's time. The US deliberately ignored the problem of narco-terrorism in this region. In fact, the US encouraged drug trafficking to raise funds for the Mujahideen fighting against the Soviets. The CIA was in full command of the region and purposedly allowed the illegal trade to flourish. It was disclosed later in September 1994 by Nawaz Sharif, the former Prime Minister of Pakistan, in an interview to *The Washington Post*. The premier said that 'Pakistan's Army Chief General Aslam Beg and its Central Intelligence Chief, Durrani had sought in approval in 1991 for a detailed blue print to sell heroin to pay for covert military operations'.[101] Consequently Pakistan emerged on the international narcotics scene in the late 1970s and in the span of 10 years became one of the major sources and routes of heroin supply to the western world. However, even after the Soviet withdrawal from the Afghanistan in 1989 and the terror attack on Pentagon on 11 September 2001, the Pakistani interest in Afghan affairs did not come to an end. It continued its terror activities in Afghan through Al-Qaeda and other militant groups to gain a strong foothold in country's society and politics.

In fact the end of Soviet takeover in Kabul in 1989 was the beginning of the first phase of terrorism and proxy war in Kashmir. Pakistan having failed to wrest Kashmir from India by means of direct armed conflicts in 1947-48, 1965 and 1971, now opted for a low cost proxy war against India, by sponsoring terrorism in Jammu and Kashmir. Pakistan's involvement in creating and supporting terrorism has been established long ago as India has experienced more terrorist violence than any other country. It was evident from the US House Republican Research Committee which, in its report titled The New Islamist International dated 1 February, 1993, quoted, 'In 1986, with growing experience in training, organising and running the Afghan Mujahideen, and with military supplies available through US, Saudi and other foreign assistance, Pakistan began expanding its operation to sponsor and promote separatism and terrorism, primarily in Kashmir, as a strategic long-term programme'.[102] Initially, the emphasis on this programme was on using the Afghan support infrastructure in Pakistan to support Kashmiri militants. Indeed, during the main escalation of Islamist violence in Indian Kashmir in mid-1988, Pakistan provided assistance in the training and arming of Kashmiri terrorists, as well as sanctuaries to Kashmiri insurgents across the border.

Cross-border terrorism has been on the rise in the valley over the years. The porous border, free flowing information and modern means of communication, all have made cross border terrorism an easy game. Under a well- thought policy thousands of Islamist terrorists have been pushed inside Kashmir and to facilitate the infiltration of Islamist mercenaries, Pakistani forces resort to firing at Indian pickets along the LoC, to divert attention and to provide cover to the armed intruders. The Islamist mercenaries have extended their operation from Kashmir to Poonch, Mendhar, Rajouri, Doda, Kishtwar and even made forays into Chamba in Himachal Pradesh. It also seeks to acquire control over the strategic and high altitude areas in Jammu and Kashmir for carrying out its future offensive against the Indian forces. The end result of this was the Kargil aggression of Summer 1999. Even the coming of General Pervez Musharraf to power in October 1999 has not helped matters to any significant extent. One of his first goals after seizing power was to reverse the Talibanisation of Pakistan by clipping the wings of the then flourishing Jihadi organisations. In 1999 and 2000, he tried to make their members stop carrying arms in public, tried to move them out of mainland Pakistan into 'Azad Kashmir'.[103] Musharraf feared that any change in his country's Kashmir policy may cost him the very authority he is exercising due to vocal supports, some of these groups have in Pakistan.

The continuum of history and geography on one hand, and the prevailing politico-military ambiance between India and Pakistan on the other that had nurtured this phenomena can not be compared with any other experience in the world.[104] The event of 11 September, 2001 suicidal attacks in the United States brought a rapprochement between Pakistan and the West. Pakistan agreed to co-operate with the US's campaign against Osama bin Laden's Al-Qaeda network and the Taliban rulers of Afghanistan. The US response to the attacks confronted the political leaderships of both Pakistan and India with unique challenges and opportunities. Pakistan had to quickly choose whether it would become an adversary of the US and risk the expected consequences, or side with it, and confronts its own Islamic-fundamentalist allies in Pakistan and Afghanistan. It chose to side with the US invasion of Afghanistan. On the other hand, for the first time New Delhi found the opportunity to categorise all Islamist resistance to Indian armed forces in Kashmir as terrorism, and it wanted endorsement for its efforts to crush them and the US did declare multiple Islamist groups to be terrorist organisations.

In post-9/11 General Pervez Musharraf delivered a policy speech on 12 January, 2002 in which he had committed himself to pushing Pakistan towards Islamic moderation and agreed to stop cross-border terrorism. His bold and visionary address was mainly for the people in the West, particularly the United States, his own country and India. Musharraf had two messages for the West but the decade-old message for India that contained nothing new. For the US the first message was that Pakistan was breaking with Islamic fundamentalism and charting a new path towards becoming a modern, dynamic, Islamic welfare state. The second message was that his country had enough of terrorism which had played havoc with its life, killing thousands of people in sectarian violence filling it with hatred and intolerance, destroying the sanctity of its holy places, and projecting it as a retrogressive, non-performing state.[105] However, all this was aimed to please the western countries, particularly the United States, which are now deeply concerned over the rise of Islamic fundamentalism in Pakistan and its emergence as a world-wide exporter of terrorism.

Unfortunately, for India, there was no working message. Earlier by joining the war on the Taliban, Musharraf had angered not only the religious parties but also vast majority of the Pashtuns, who dominate the North-West Frontier Provinces (NWFP) and are a decisive force in Baluchistan. His haunt for Al-Qaeda had put him on a collision course with the die-hard Islamic Jihadis in Pakistan. A section of the army was also annoyed with him and Musharraf was able to persuade the forces that he had no choice on Afghanistan but the implicit bargain he had to have been that he would make no such concessions on Kashmir. On the other India had asserted that Pakistan should dismantle its terrorist infrastructure and stop cross-border terrorism. It stressed that if the US wants to overcome terrorism, it must realise that the focus should be on Pakistan and not on Jammu and Kashmir and that the military fundamentalist character of states like Pakistan must change.[106] Indian President, A.P.J. Abdul Kalam had also emphasised that cross-border terrorism and insurgency had emerged as a global threat to peace and harmony of human kind as they were not restricted to one country or region. He urged the world community to stall the financial channels of terrorist outfits.

General Musharraf's message to India was different to the West and the US. There was hardly anything different for India in the speech. He has not changed even a comma in the policy Pakistan has been following towards India for the last fifty years. He employs the same phrase- 'We shall continue to give Kashmir moral and diplomatic help'- which one of his illustrious military predecessor, Zia-ul-Haq used, to camouflage cross-border terrorism.[107] Since taking over the helm of the country, General Musharraf had actively used the country's religious establishment to promote Pakistan's agenda vis-à-vis India, particularly furthering the strategic depth in Afghanistan and giving impetus to terrorism in Jammu and Kashmir.

The problem in Jammu and Kashmir and other parts of India is cross-border terrorism and is externally driven. India must realise that these foreign mercenaries do not owe allegiance to India but to the foreign power and can strike against the very people who have been instrumental in their release. Each country has to see what suits its national interests the best. We must evolve our own policy. We must clamp down the cross-border terrorism and choke their money and arms supply with army vigilance at the LoC as well as on the international border. It is the state's duty to provide security and an atmosphere of peace for growth and development to its citizens. The state that can not do so loses the right to rule.

TERRORISM IN AFGHANISTAN

Modern Afghanistan emerged during the nineteenth century as a buffer state squeezed between the Russian and British empire. From the beginning it was a pawn in the battles between world powers. It had to accommodate different ruling regimes of diverse character in her state structure through coups, counter coups, strife, invasions, etc. entailing into a permanent war-like culture especially from the early 1970s.[108] As a matter of fact, decades of conflict had shattered government and social structures in Afghanistan, the world's fifth poorest country with a life expectancy of 43. According to the UN report more than seven million people are chronically hungry, and 53 per cent live on less than a dollar a day. One in four children do not survive beyond the age of five. Seventy per cent of the population suffers severe malnutrition. Less than a quarter has access to safe drinking water, only 12 per cent to adequate sanitation and 10 per cent of electricity.[109] The life expectancy of 45 is 20 years lower than in neighbouring countries. In some provinces, the maternal mortality rates are the worst ever recorded, anywhere.

The history of Afghanistan in recent past has provided us with many significant revelations. In 1973, King Zahir Shah was overthrown from power in a Soviet supported coup led by Mohammad Daud Khan. Since then, Afghanistan's role as a buffer state among superpowers began to change obviously, and the geo-political balance was broken up. Now the Soviet influence became dominant which disturbed the US. The US policy in Afghanistan was in tune with its overall policy towards the oil producing countries, especially in the Middle East. In addition to geopolitical factors, access to sources of energy has been a great concern for the US. It knows that world oil reserves are depleting faster than few discoveries of the fuel. The impending depletion of the world's oil has been motivating the West in pinning its faith on the Caspian region.[110] In the days of Soviet domination the relatively radical social reforms practised by Daud threatened the status of traditional tribes and religious powers, and their interests as well, many kinds of confrontations, including armed revolt had been building up. The intensification of social conflicts made Daud regime which had not strong and firm foundation fall into predicament and caused domestic conflicts and clashes to escalate continuously. In April 1978, a communist-led 'Saur Revolution' eventually brought out the collapse of Daud Khan. He was replaced by a pro-Soviet Noor Mohammad Tarakki, he however, was killed due to inter-factional conflict in the ruling party, leading to Soviet military intervention on 27 December, 1979. Thus Afghanistan lost its role as a buffer state completely and became the front land of the Soviet Union's southward expansion.

The Leftist coup in Afghanistan installed Babrak Karmal, a leader of Moscow's choice, in the place of Hafizullah Amin as the new ruler of Kabul. The coup in Afghanistan and its possible fallout for the two neighbouring countries, Iran and Pakistan was noticeable. It had upset the precarious balance gained in bilateral fields, particularly, with Pakistan during Daud. Before the Soviet intervention in Afghanistan, the fall of Shah's regime in Iran and the emergence of Khomeini in his place marked a new revival of Islamic tenets.[111] In late 1970s it got an emphasised meaning in Libya and Iran. Further it caused a new surge of revivalism in Pakistan which was manifest in Bhutto's latter years and was culminated in General Zia's programmes of Islamic reforms. The new rising tendency, at least, in general was the result of the failure of the secular ideologies. The increasing hegemony of the two world political and economic systems–as represented by the military, technological and economic domination of the United States and the former Soviet had left little room for the autonomy of the liberal/nationalist or Marxist/nationalist movements. They made the course of development a difficult one in Muslim countries.

In the changed circumstances the region became a valuable area for the global narcotic trade. Two areas of the world–the 'Golden Crescent' of South-West Asia consisting of Afghanistan, Iran and Pakistan and the 'Golden Triangle' of Thailand, Myanmar and Laos are traditionally known for narco cultivation in the world and provides for 60 per cent of heroin reaching America and 80 per cent for Europe.[112] Opium cultivation and use has been continuing in this region for the last few centuries. Under the British rule opium production was licensed. In the eighteenth and nineteenth centuries, the British used to import opium from India to China for reducing the balance of payments' deficits caused by large tea purchases. Drug money has changed the economic and social scene in the country. Although a small and powerful group of narco barons has reaped the major profits, members of the law-enforcing agencies, bureaucrats and hangers have also benefited from the trickle. The conflict following the 1979 Soviet intervention in Afghanistan facilitated increased opium production. It also provided a source of funding for the anti-Soviet war efforts and allowed traffickers to exploit the support to the Mujahideen by Iran and Pakistan, by using those countries as transit routes.[113] The drug problem became even more serious with the civil war and political anarchy reigning in Afghanistan.

When the Soviet Union invaded Afghanistan in December 1979 it had to confront directly with two kinds of powers. The first was the domestic opposition parties, including national, tribal, and religious powers, as well as part of the social forces that approved of democracy and modern reforms. All these compose a loose union under the banner of anti-Soviet. The second was the Western countries headed by America and Pakistan. In the later period of Daud's regime, the US began to interfere into Afghanistan's affairs and opposed the Soviet Union's presence and expansion in Afghanistan. After the Soviet invasion into Afghanistan, the US immediately strengthened its support to the opposition parties in Afghanistan. Taking Pakistan as a base, the US supplied with abundant financial, military and staff assistance as a guarantee for the final military success of Afghanistan's opposition powers.[114] It was during this period that the religions of the Gulf Bay, mainly the Wahabi, entered Afghanistan with the slogan of 'Jihad'. Osama bin Laden was the most active participant and organiser. He also set up a fund named 'Volunteers' home' enrolling volunteers from Saudi Arabia and other Arabic countries to go into Afghanistan for Jihad.

To flush out the Soviets, Islamic zealots were brought from all parts of the Islamic world to Pakistan and Afghanistan forging a unity among those who shared nothing in common but willingness to die for a cause they considered Islamic. This convergence, enabled by Western powers, not only made a superpower to retreat and eventually fall apart but made Islamists aware of the potential of Jihad and force multiplication effect of networking. Its aftermath saw ascendancy of Taliban-recruited, trained, weaponised and militarily backed up by Pakistan, an ally of the West. More sinisterly, Taliban under the patronage of Pakistan, converted Afghanistan into a breeding ground for Islamic terrorists with training bases and infrastructural support to extremists from Turkey to Indonesia, Chechnya to China and Europe to Africa. It became the home of Al-Qaeda and gave Islamists a geographical space to pursue their global agenda with impunity.[115] The situation aggravated in Afghanistan when Jihad was launched by the Mujahideens sponsored by the US and Saudi Arabia through ISI of Pakistan against Soviet occupation. The fact is that the motivations of those who finance and train them are hardly religious per se. From Al-Qaeda to Tehrik-e-Taliban Pakistan (TTP) terrorist organisations misuse the faith of Islam to justify terrorism in its name, even though their principal terrorist motivation is political. For the next ten years after intervention there was a continuous conflict between the Soviet troops and the Mujahideen and the US actively supported the latter throughout the period.

By 1989, mounting casualties, dissatisfaction among the troops and international pressure led to the withdrawal of Soviet troops from Afghanistan. Further the power vacuum in Central Asia prevailed with the disintegration of Soviet Union and feuding among the ruling Mujahideen in Afghanistan. In the situation the United States of America was lured by the prospects of controlling the oil and natural gas resources of Central Asia as well as being right next to the underbelly of Russia and China. Now the US oil giants were pushed by the US government for humouring the Taliban to access the Central Asian oil and gas through pipelines that would touch the Indian Ocean through Afghanistan and Pakistan. Lures of financial gains and strategic needs combined to make the whole region very important for outside powers. Central Asian leaders became obsessed with projected pipelines, potential routes and the geopolitics that surrounded them, which led some of them like Turkmenistan to deal even with the Taliban regime.[116] The new US game started in the early 1990s especially after the collapse of the Soviet Union.

The energy and other resources of Central Asia attracted major regional and international powers. During the cold war days the US had been romancing religious Jihadi groups in Pakistan and Afghanistan. These were important to position US multinationals favourably, to control the considerable resources of the region and to complete the encirclement of the world's major energy resources in the area. After the Soviet collapse, the United States sought to harness these groups to serve US geopolitical interests in energy-rich Central Asia. In between 1994-96, the CIA-ISI nexus and its arms pipeline marginalised more traditional tribal-based parties and moderated leadership in Afghanistan and catapulted the radical Islamists into the forefront of Afghan civil war.[117] The US was not reluctant to forceful intervention, if deemed appropriate to achieve its interests.[118] The region, although could not compare with West Asia in terms of reserves, it was attractive to exploration and production (E&P). For instance, Turkmenistan, which borders the north-west of Afghanistan, holds the world's third largest gas reserves and have an estimated six billion barrels of oil reserves. Enough, experts say, to meet American energy needs for the next thirty years.

In mid-1990s, in particular, America showed keen interest in the Caspian Sea region of Central Asia, which was estimated to have 200 billion barrels of untapped oil. The American oil giants–Enron and Unocal had been known for their interest in Caspian

Sea region projects and were negotiating with the Taliban for permission to construct an oil pipeline through Afghanistan to Pakistan and out to the Arabian Sea. Enron had carried out a feasibility study for pipeline from Kazakhstan, through Afghanistan and Pakistan to the border of Malta for bringing this oil to the market.[119] In December 1997, a delegation of Taliban mullahs travelled to America and even met US State Department officials. George William Bush and Dick Cheney have both worked with oil business and have close ties with major corporations in the oil sector. Consumer countries in Europe, the US and Japan are already dependent on the Saudi-dominated Middle East Oil Producing European Countries (OPEC) suppliers for 40 per cent of the world demand for crude oil. The dependence on a single region will be dangerous for the US and her allies in the years to come. Thus, tapping in to the reserves in the Caspian Sea region was viewed as a strategic goal to meet the growing energy demand and to reduce the US dependence on oil from the Middle East.[120] Then it is natural for the US to turn her attention to the only alternative major source of 'boundless' supply in Central Asia.

In between chaos and uncertainty, the Taliban regime commenced in 1996 and at the time the US government had no criticism of it, rather a State Department spokesperson told reporters that there was "nothing objectionable" about the Taliban's coming to power.[121] In fact the US hoped that the Taliban would provide stability. They were expected to provide security for roads and, potentially oil and gas pipelines that would link the states of Central Asia to the international market through Pakistan rather than through Iran.[122] Between 1994 and 1997, the US was supporting the Taliban in the sense that it was allowing Pakistan and Saudi Arabia, its two allies in the region, to back the Taliban. This was because the US and US oil companies were interested in building oil and gas pipelines from Central Asia across Afghanistan, through Pakistan to the Gulf. In January 1998, the Taliban signed an agreement that would allow a proposed natural gas pineline project led by Unocal oil company of the US. For the realisation of other projects the US financed and encouraged the Taliban through its surrogates in Saudi Arabia and Pakistan. At that time the US was least bothered about the human rights record of the Taliban.

The victory of Taliban in Afghanistan opened a new chapter in its history. During Taliban's days in power another version of the great game was being played–there were efforts to create a world of fundamentalist Islam. Both state and non-state actors for mutual advantage used religion. The interests of Pakistan and the fundamentalist groups converged. The world that was to be created in this region would provide mutual depth to both fundamentalist Islam and Pakistan and other states that were willing to be integrated to this project. The key to this project, however, lay in converting Central Asia into a zone of instability and religious fundamentalism. In the calculation of religious radicals and their backers, Central Asia with vast resources like oil and natural gas, uranium and other rare metals was critical to their global plan. This apart, the nexus between drug trafficking and terrorism in the golden crescent became a major reason for political and social instability in the region. Afghanistan during the last decade emerged as the second largest producer of drugs in the world. From a relatively modest level of around 200-300 tons in 1979, opium production in that country went up to 4,500 tons by 1999. This gave the Taliban government enormous financial benefits that went to training, arming and campaign of the militant groups. The attempt of religious forces has been to identify nation with religion.

However, the US dislikes towards the Taliban began only when they realised that Taliban could not be a dependable instrument for the realisation of their interests in Central Asia. As early as 1997 Madeleine Albright was already publicly expressing her distaste for the Taliban. It indicated that an influential section in and out of the US government were becoming convinced that the Taliban were not going to deliver what was required of them. Further the US-Taliban relationship went into some rough waters after the bombing of US embassies in Africa in August 1998. In retaliation the US attacked on Sudan and Afghanistan. The attacks on US embassies were allegedly organised by Osama bin Laden. After the event of 9/11 the US attitude towards international terrorism emanating from Afghanistan changed dramatically and it successfully led the campaign to oust Taliban from power and destroy terrorist training centres. The fate of Taliban was finally sealed the day terrorists bombed the World Trade Centre building and the Pentagon on 11 September, 2001. In response to the attack the war in Afghanistan began on 7 October, 2001 and this marked the beginning of US's campaign known as the "War on Terrorism".

TERRORISM IN BANGLADESH

East Bengal or East Pakistan as called so far, emerged as an independent, sovereign state of Bangladesh in the comity of nations. The disintegration of Pakistan and the emergence of Bangladesh in 1971 dealt the first blow to the two-nation theory. The emergence of Bangladesh proved a milestone, as it reinforced the aspirations of many ethnic movements in the region. Since its independence in 1971, Bangladesh has experienced successive coups and the consequent establishment of martial law regimes, with intermittent suspension of the Constitution. The first Constitution of Bangladesh was enacted in 1972 which moulded the state into a parliamentary democracy, with the principles of nationalism, democracy, socialism and secularism set out as guidelines for running the newly independent state.[123] Later the consolidation of the military regime coincided with the abandonment of Mujib's secular commitment, and in April 1977, Islam was made one of the tenets of the Bangladesh state. Legislation discriminating against Hindus had already existed in East Pakistan before 1971. This was tightened after May 1977, and a policy of weeding out Hindus from the army, police and civil services was adopted. Making Islam the basis of the state, brought Bangladesh one step closer to Pakistan, and it has been suggested that the change was in fact instituted at the behest of Pakistan and Saudi Arabia.[124]

Bangladesh is the largest Muslim country in the world with over 85% of its population being the followers of Islam. It is a multi-religious society constituting about 12% Hindus, 1-2 Buddhists, and .01 Christians. Muslims are dominant in all parts of the country, excepting Chittagong Hill Tracks where Buddhists are pre-dominant. In general Hindus are present in all regions, though they constitute a majority in some parts of Khulna division. Religiously, Sufism is essentially a popular movement in Bangladesh with its three orders–The Qadiri, Naqshbandi and Chishti. The beliefs and practices of the first two are quite close to those of orthodox Islam, the third founded in Ajmer, India, is peculiar to the subcontinent and has a number of orthodox practices.[125] In spite of being a Muslim country it emphasised secularism in the Constitution of 1972 but it was changed in 1977 and 1988. General Ershad inserted an article in the constitution in 1988 which declared that 'the state religion of the Republic is Islam, but other religions may be practised in peace and harmony in the Republic. As a result a number of religious parties have emerged which press the government to implement Islamic principles in governance. The political scenario in Bangladesh indicates that religious fanaticism is on rise and the development has affected socio-economic life of the country.[126] In Bangladesh there is an intense and at times violent political rivalry between the country's two main political parties–the Bangladesh National Party (BNP) and the Awami League (AL) and the presence of radical Islamist parties and groups have defined the further political course of the country in recent years. It has presented the crisis in governance.

However, the crisis in governance is the result of the circumstances in which the new nation was born. In Pre-independence days the undivided Pakistan's inability to come to terms with the electoral verdict exposed the flaws in the political system. Mujib's own authoritarian tendencies led to unrest and dissatisfaction with the masses, military rule and the elections that lacked legitimacy further exposed the weakness of constitutional government. In recent years the rivalry and competitive politics of the two major parties under Sheikh Hasina and Khaleda Zia resulted in frequent hartals and strikes, disturbing civic life. Low literacy and state controlled media forces the opposition parties to take the issues to streets to mobilise masses to win their support to their programmes. As Patricia Butenis, the former US Ambassador stated that Bangladesh 'has suffered because the political parties could not agree on the basic rules of game— the hard part is actually creating political parties that are genuinely democratic in practice and outlook, parties that focus on issues and the national interest instead of personalities'.[127] The situation has given Islamist parties, some of which have ties to violent Islamist radicals, a disproportionate voice in Bangladesh's government and politics. With increased influence by Islamist extremists it could increasingly serve as a base of operations for terrorist activity.

In addition, the shape and size of terror in Bangladesh have largely been determined by domestic political change and the changes that are taking place in the country. In over three decades, millions of its workers have returned from West Asia infected by the austere Sunni and Wahabi Islam they found practised there. About three million Bangladesh work there and a large proportion come back changed almost beyond recognition: They go as ordinary men but come back completely different. They bear different clothes, cut their beards differently, put their women in burqas and profess an intolerant Wahabi type of Islam that is completely alien to other countrymen.[128] The percolation of this imported Islam into Bangladeshi society has turned the Jamaat-i-Islami into a potent political force. An allied cause of this is the failure of the State education system. This has sent more and more children to

Madrassas which are founded by private donations, and by liberal inflows of funds from religious trusts in Saudi Arabia and other West Asian countries.[129] These changes have led to the emergence of an intolerant aggressive, messianic fringe of reformed Sunni Muslims, who are bent upon purifying Bangladesh on the lines of the Taliban in Afghanistan.

The situation in Bangladesh has fast deteriorated after 11 September, 2001, than is normally understood. When Pakistan and Afghanistan came under pressure, a good number of terrorists, reportedly with Pak intelligence support, found Bangladesh as safe haven. Using Islam card for political gains, the Bangladesh society stands highly radicalised–most local groups working on the franchise of Pak-Afghan terrorist outfits including Al-Qaeda. The collective strength of terrorist groups like Harkat-ul- Jihadi Islami, Harkat-ul-Ansar, Okiyya Jote etc. now estimated in several thousands. While India is the principal target the anti-US and anti-West outbursts are too shrill to be ignored. The proximity to arm bazaars in Pacific Rim countries has enabled them to procure sophisticated weapons and explosives. Illustratively, in April 2004 at Chittagong port, 1,790 rifles, 150 rocket launchers, 2,700 grenades, one million rounds of ammunition etc. were seized while being loaded in ten trucks. The two trawlers who brought the consignment from Malaysia were owned by the brother of then ruling Bangladesh Nationalist Party (BNP) leader.[130] Frank Pallone, the Democratic Congressman from New Jersey in May 2004 drew attention of the US House of Representatives to the plight of the Hindus who he called a disappearing minority and it was confirmed by electronic media and the US State Department as well.

Religious fundamentalism and effects of the outside Muslim world gave birth to several terrorist and militant extremist groups in Bangladesh that include Harkat-ul-Jihad Al Islami (HuJI), Jagrata Muslim Janata Bangladesh (JMJB), and Jamaatul Mujahideen Bangladesh (JMB). In this context it is the general view of analysts and media observers that the presence of two Islamist parties, the Islamiya Okiyya Jote (IOJ) and the Jamaat-e-Islami as a coalition partner in the former ruling Bangladesh Nationalist Party had expanded Islamist influence in the country and created space within which terrorist and extremist groups could operate, Islami Okiyya Jote is thought to have ties to the radical Harkat-ul-Jihad-Al-Islami (HuJI).[131] With the fast radicalisation of Afghanistan, Pakistan and Bangladesh on one hand and erosion in the will and capability of the governments in power there the overall security scenario in the region stands highly vitiated.

Another coalition partner the Jamaat-e-Islami has also ties to Harkat-ul-Jihad-Al-Islami which has ties to Al-Qaeda and the former's leader Fazlul Rahman signed an Osama bin Laden holy war declaration in 1998.[132] The JMB seeks the imposition of Sharia law for Bangladesh and is thought responsible for the widespread and coordinated August 2005 bombings, while HuJI has been implicated in the January 2002 attack on the American Center in Calcutta, India. HuJI is on the US State Department's list of 'other terrorist organisations' and has links to Pakistani militant groups with a cadre strength of several thousand of its own. The JMJB is an unabashedly terrorist organisation in Bangladesh which claims more than 10,000 full-time cadres and 300,000 part-timers and helpers in the country and has been killing cadres of extremist groups like the Purbo Banglar Communist Party, whom the police has not been able to control. By doing these the organisation is gaining a spurious legitimacy with not only the key members of the BNP but also the police. It has openly modelled itself on the Taliban and claims that its aim is to build a society based on the Islamic model laid out in the 'Holy Hadith'.

However, for the present Bangladesh's political parties and intelligentsia, in comparison to Awami League of Sheikh Hasina the reportcard of BNP headed by Begam Khaleda Zia is painful. Under the BNP Bangladesh has recognised the ubiquity of the madrassas and opted to recognise their degrees and to modernise their curricula. Recognising the growing strength of a terrorist organisation and realising that it is concentrated in the western border belt alongside India, the BNP was quick to form an alliance with it. And BNP's alliance played a decisive role in its stunning and unexpected victory in 2001. At the time Awami League leader Sheikh Hasina had accused the government of 'letting loose communal extremist forces'. It was also reported that some international extremists are using Bangladeshi passports and some are obtaining them with the assistance of sympathetic officials at various Bangladesh Embassies.[133] Although the BNP government of Bangladesh had also taken some steps against the terrorist and extremist groups, but the opposition leader Sheikh Hasina stated, 'militants are partners of the government – the government catches a few militants whenever foreign guests visit Bangladesh.[134] She charged that the Jamaat has 15,000 guerillas and its own training camps. Steps are only the tip of the iceberg.

The foundation of terrorist and extremist groups in Bangladesh gradually became a concern for the world in larger context. Selig Harrison, a prominent South Asian analyst, expressed his view and noted in August 2006 that 'a growing Islamic fundamentalist movement linked to Al-Qaeda and Pakistani intelligence agencies is steadily converting the strategically located nation of Bangladesh into a new regional hub for terrorist operations that reach into India and South-east Asia. He argued that BNP's coalition alliance with Jamaat have allowed Taliban–styled squads to operate with increasing impunity and reportedly led to fundamentalist control over large parts of the Bangladesh economy, Islamist madrassas schools that act as fronts for terrorist activities.[135]

The facts and views on the issue failed to convince the US authorities and the State Department continues to consider the Government of Bangladesh as working to thwart terrorist activities. Hopefully, the new government headed by Sheikh Hasina had taken over at the beginning of the year 2009 and made a firm declaration that Bangladesh government would eliminate all forms of terrorism and would not allow Bangladesh territory to conduct terrorism in other countries.[136] It however, still continues to recognise the degrees awarded by religious institutions and madrassas as equivalent to the degrees in Bangladesh given by colleges and universities making religious education equal to secular education.

References

1. N.R. Madhava Menon, 'Combating Terrorism, and Some Management Issues,' *The Hindu,* 12 January, 2009.
2. A.S. Kalkat, 'Ensuring Security in the Age of Global Terror', in *Ibid*., 13 September, 2006.
3. Prem Shankar Jha, 'Sowing Dragon Seed,' *The Hindustan Times*, 13 September, 2003.
4. *Ibid.*
5. Sanjay Joshi, 'Many Faces of a Fanatic,' in *Ibid*., 26 September, 2002.
6. *Ibid.*
7. Sumanta Banerjee, 'The Politics of Violence in the Indian State and Society,' in Kumar Rupesinghe and Khawar Mumtaz (eds.), *Internal Conflicts in South Asia* (New Delhi: Sage Publications, 1996), pp. 81-82.
8. Pradhan H. Prasad, *Lopsided Growth: Political Economy of Indian Development* (Bombay: Oxford University Press, 1989), as quoted in *Ibid*., p. 85.

9. *Ibid.*, pp. 85-86.
10. Shivananda, 'Ethnicity, Conflict and Security of North East India,' *South Asia Politics*, Vol. 8, No. 7, November 2009 (New Delhi : 2009), pp. 29-31.
11. *Ibid.*
12. P.P. Rao, 'Working the Constitution,' in *Ibid.*, Vol. 9, No. 6, October 2010 (New Delhi : 2010), p. 11.
13. Verghese Koithara, *Society State and Security – The Indian Experience* (New Delhi: Sage Publications, 1999), pp. 104-05.
14. Madhumita, 'Naxalism – Development or Discontent – A Study of Jharkhand', *South Asia Politics*, October 2010, pp. 27-29.
15. *Ibid.*
16. Sumanta Banerjee, 'The Politics of Violence in Indian State and Society,' *Internal Conflicts in South Asia*, p. 87.
17. *Ibid.*, p. 88.
18. Verghese Koithara, *Society, State and Security – The Indian Experience*, pp. 108-10.
19. Barbara Crosette, 'Death Toll in India After Heavy Floods is Reported at 1000', *The Newyork Times*, 30 October, 1988.
20. United States Department of State, *Patterns of Global Terrorism : 1987* (Department of State Publication, August 1988), p. 4.
21. M.K. Narayanan, National Security : The Internal Dimention (New Delhi : RGICS, 1994), quoted in Verghese Koithara - *Society, State and Security: The Indian Experience*, p.110.
22. Shekhar Gupta, 'India Redefines its Role, 'Adelphi Paper 293, IISS (London : 1995), p. 28.
23. Paul Leventhal and Brahma Chellaney, 'Nuclear Terrorism - Threat, Perception and Response in South Asia,' paper presented to the Institute for Defence Studies and Analysis, 10 October, 1988 (New Delhi: 1988), p. 3.
24. K.F. Rustamji, 'Threat of Terrorism,' *The Hindustan Times*, 6 August, 1999.
25. N.R. Madhava Menon, 'Combating Terrorism, and Some Management Issues.'
26. Ajit Doval, 'Islamic Terrorism in South Asia and India's Strategic Response' (OUP, 2007), p. 2.
27. Jagdish Prasad Verma, 'Islamic Terrorism and the Indian Experience,' *South Asia Politics*, Vol. 7, No. 8, December 2008 (New Delhi : 2008), p. 23.
28. Myron Weiner, *Sons of the Soil: Migration and Ethnic Conflict in India* (Princeton : Princeton University Press, 1978).

29. Siddharth, 'Anti – Terrorism Laws in India & the Need of 'POTA', pp. 1-16.
30. *Ibid.*
31. *Ibid.*
32. N.R. Madhava Menon, 'Combating Terrorism, and Some Management Issues'.
33. *Ibid.*
34. Dr. Arvind Shukla, 'Impact of Terrorism on Social, Economic and Legal Structure of the Countries', Invertis Institute of Management Studies (Bareilly, UP), pp. 3-4.
35. *The Hindu*, 24 July, 2011.
36. *Ibid.*
37. Jagdish Prasad Verma, 'Islamic Terrorism and the Indian Experience,' p. 23.
38. Harish Khare, 'Terrors Challenge to the Indian Imagination', *The Hindu*, 18 July, 2007.
39. *Ibid.*
40. C. Uday Bhaskar, 'Strategic Implications of the Proxy War', *The Hindustan Times*, 18 August, 1998.
41. *Ibid.*
42. V.R. Raghavan, 'Response to Terror,' in *Ibid.*, 6 January, 1999.
43. Rajkumar Singh, *Contemporary India with Controversial Neighbours* (New Delhi:Gyan Publishing House, 2011), pp. 128-29.
44. Verghese Koithara, *Society, State and Security : The Indian Experience*, p. 113.
45. Manvendra Singh, 'Threshold of Patience,' *The Hindustan Times*, 15 January 2002.
46. D.C. Pathak, 'India's Role in the War on Terror,' *South Asia Politics*, Vol. 9, No. 10, February 2011 (New Delhi : 2011), p. 4.
47. *Ibid.*
48. N.C. Menon, 'Terrorism as an Epidemic,' *The Hindustan Times*, 18 August, 1998.
49. V.P. Dutt, *India's Foreign Policy in a Changing World* (New Delhi: Vikas Publishing House, 1999), pp. 121-22.
50. *The Indian Express*, 25 March, 1993.
51. Prem Shankar Jha, 'Sowing Dragon Seed,' *The Hindustan Times*, 13 September 2003.
52. C.V. Sukumaran, 'Let's Stop the Blame Game and Start Addressing the Grievances,' *The Hindu*, 7 August, 2011.
53. *Ibid.*

54. *Ibid.*
55. Rajkumar Singh, *Relations of NDA & UPA with Neighbour* (New Delhi: Gyan Publishing House, 2010), p. 94.
56. *The Hindustan Times*, editorial, 29 December, 1999.
57. *Ibid.*
58. V.R. Raghavan, 'Response to Terror.'
59. *Ibid.*
60. Michael Krepon, 'Forbearance is the Key Word', *The Hindustan Times*, 14 October, 2001.
61. Veena Kukreja, '*Contemporary Pakistan: Political Processes, Conflicts and Crises* (New Delhi: Sage Publications, 2008), p. 288.
62. C. Uday Bhaskar, 'New Rules for the New War', in *Ibid.*, 7 October, 2001.
63. Dilara Chowdhury, 'Toying with Weapons of Mass Destruction: What are India and Pakistan Up To?,' *The Daily Star*, 14 March, 2002.
64. Atal Bihari Vajpayee, 'We Shall Triumph Against Terrorism', *The Hindustan Times*, 1 January, 2002.
65. Veena Kukreja, *Contemporary Pakistan: Political Processes, Conflicts and Crises*, p. 290.
66. Ajit Doval, 'Outsourcing Terror,' *The Times of India*, 18 July 2011.
67. R.V.S. Mani, 'We Can Tackle Terror and Save Mumbai,' *The Hindu*, 7 August, 2011.
68. *Ibid.*, editorial, 27 December, 2008.
69. Rajkumar Singh, *Relations of NDA & UPA with Neighbours*, p. 144.
70. D.C. Pathak, 'India's Role in the War on Terror,' p. 4.
71. Ajit Doval, 'Outsourcing Terror.'
72. *Ibid.*
73. Shishir Gupta, 'Target for Terror,' *The Hindustan Times*, 7 September, 2011.
74. Abbas Rashid, 'Pakistan: the Politics of Fundamentalism' in Kumar Rupesinghe and Khawar Mumtaz (eds.), *Internal Conflicts in South Asia*, p. 59.
75. Uddipan Mukherjee, 'Jinnah's Tottering Pakistan', *South Asia Politics*, Vol. 8, No. 10, February 2010 (New Delhi: 2010), p. 3.
76. Abbas Rashid, 'Pakistan: the Politics of Fundamentalism', pp. 58-59.
77. Maulana Abul Kalam Azad, *India Wins Freedom* (New Delhi: 1988), p. 248.
78. Rajkumar Singh, *India and Pakistan–Social, Political and Military Perspectives* (New Delhi: Regal Publications, 2009), pp. 120-21.

79. Abbot Freeland, *Islam and Pakistan* (Newyork: 1968), p. 188.
80. Evrand Abrahamian, 'Khomeini: Fundamentalist or Populist?', *New Left Review*, No. 186, March/April (1991), pp. 102-119, as quoted in Abbas Rashid, 'Pakistan: the Politics of Fundamentalism,' pp. 55-56.
81. Vyacheslav Ya. Belokrenitsky, 'Islamic Radicalism in Pakistan: Evolution and Regional Role,' in Mahavir Singh (ed.), *International Terrorism and Religious Extremism–Challenges to Central and South Asia*, (New Delhi: Anamika Publishers, 2004), pp. 83-84.
82. Aziz Ahmad, *Islamic Modernism in India and Pakistan* (London: Oxford University Press, 1967), p. 238.
83. Rajkumar Singh, *India and Pakistan–Social, Political and Military Perspectives*, p. 226.
84. Mubashir Zaidi, 'Jehad in Retreat,' *The Hindustan Times*, 20 January, 2002.
85. Shaukat Hassan, 'Problems of Internal Stability in South Asia,' in Shelton U. Kodikara (ed.), *External Compulsions of South Asian Politics* (New Delhi: Sage Publications, 1993), pp. 262-63.
86. Shireen M. Mazari, 'The Militarisation of Pakistan's Civil Society,' in Kumar Rupesinghe and Khawar Mumtaz (eds.), *Internal Conflicts in South Asia*, pp. 101-2.
87. General Mirza Aslam Beg, 'Pakistan's Nuclear Programme: A National Security Perspective,' in Jorn Gjelstad and Olav Njolstad (eds.), *Nuclear Rivalry and International Order* (London: 1996), p. 158.
88. *Indian Recorder*, Vol. IV, No. 11, 22-28 March, 1997 (New Delhi: 1997), p. 2658.
89. *Newsline*, September 1998, p. 17,
90. *The Herald* (Karachi), May 2000, pp. 50-52.
91. Ziagham Khan, 'Allah's Armies,' in *Ibid.*, January 1998, p. 28.
92. Rajkumar Singh, *India and Pakistan–Social, Political and Military Perspectives*, p. 253.
93. Veena Kukreja, *Contemporary Pakistan–Political Processes, Conflicts and Crises*, pp. XII–XIII.
94. *Ibid.*
95. Vyacheslav Ya. Belokrenitsky, 'Islamic Radicalism in Pakistan: Evolution and Regional Role,' p. 89.
96. Dhrubajyoti Bhattacharjee, 'India–Pakistan Relations–A Troubled History With A Bright Future?,' *South Asia Politics*, Vol. 6, No. 9, January 2008 (New Delhi: 2008), p. 25.
97. *Ibid.*

98. United States Department of State, *Patterns of Global Terrorism: 1987*, pp. 1-2.
99. Walter Laqueur, *The Age of Terrorism* (Boston: Little Brown, 1987).
100. Aabha Dixit, 'Narco–Power: Threatening the Very Roots of Pak Society,' *Strategic Analysis*, Vol. XIII, No. 15, May 1991, p. 191.
101. *The News*, 13 September, 1994.
102. *The New Islamist International*, 1 February, 1993.
103. Prem Shankar Jha, 'Drop the Sarcasm,' *The Hindustan Times*, 2 January, 2004.
104. C. Uday Bhaskar, 'New Rules for the New War,' in *Ibid.*, 7 October, 2001.
105. Veena Kukreja, *Contemporary Pakistan–Political Processes, Conflicts and Crises*, pp. 186-87.
106. Bir Good Gill, 'India and the Problem of Cross-Border Terrorism,' in Mahavir Singh (ed.), *International Terrorism and Religious Extremism–Challenges to Central and South Asia*, pp. 179-81.
107. Kuldip Nayar, 'Not Enough in it for India,' *The Hindu*, 16 February, 2002.
108. Prakash Chandra Adhikary and Pranab Karmakar, 'State of Afghan Economy during Taliban Period and the Aftermath,' *South Asia Politics*, Vol. 9, No. 1, May, 2010 (New Delhi: 2010), p. 13.
109. Dilip Kumar, 'The Resurgence of the Taliban–Lessons Learned,' in *Ibid.*, Vol. 6, No. 1, May 2007 (New Delhi: 2007), p. 50.
110. K.T. Thomas, 'The Economic Roots of US Intervention in Afghanistan,' Proceedings of the Indian History Congress, 68th Session Delhi, 2007 (Delhi: 2008), pp. 1216-17.
111. Rajkumar Singh, *'India and Pakistan–Social, Political and Military Perspectives*, pp. 235-36.
112. Alison Jamieson, 'Global Drug Trafficking,' *Conflict Studies*, No. CCXXXIV, September 1990, p. 3.
113. Ivelaw L. Griffith, 'From Cold War Geopolitics to Post-Cold War Geonarcotics,' *International Journal*, Vol. XLIX, No. 1 (Winter 1993-94), p. 21.
114. Yang Shu, 'Afghanistan–Buffer State and Centre for Terrorism', in Mahavir Singh (ed.), *International Terrorism and Religious Extremism–Challenges to Central and South Asia*, pp. 101-2.
115. Ajit Doval, 'Islamic Terrorism in South Asia and India's Strategic Response' (Oxford University Press, 2007).
116. Ahmed Rashid, *Taliban, Islam, Oil and the New Great Game in Central Asia* (London: 2000).
117. *Ibid.*

118. Noam Chomsky, 'Mirror Crack'd,' *Outlook*, 29 October, 2001.
119. *Third Concept*, Vol. 4, No. 50-51, April-May 1991 (New Delhi: 1991), p. 70.
120. Anand Telumbde, 'War on Iraq: Dollar Dominance and Doom of America', in S.M. Daud (ed.), *War Against Iraq*, (2003), p. 92.
121. K.T. Thomas, 'The Economic Roots of US Intervention in Afghanistan,'pp.1219-20.
122. Madan Lal Sharma, 'World After 9/11,' *Third Concept*, September 2007 (New Delhi: 2007).
123. T. Maniruzzaman, *The Bangladesh Revolution and Its Aftermath* (Dhaka: UPL, 1980).
124. *The Canberra Times*, 31 October, 1977.
125. Rajkumar Singh, *Relations of NDA and UPA with Neighbours*, pp. 277-78.
126. Kshitij Prabha, 'Terrorism Challenges Secular Fabric of South Asia,' in Mahavir Singh (ed.), *International Terrorism and Religious Extremism–Challenges to Central and South Asia*, pp. 272-73.
127. Patricia Butenis, 'Elections the Road Ahead,' Dhaka University, 17 December 2006.
128. Prem Shankar Jha, 'That Other Neighbour,' *The Hindustan Times*, 13 August 2002.
129. *Ibid.*
130. Ajit Doval, 'Islamic Terrorism in South Asia and India's Strategic Response (Oxford University Press), 2007.
131. *BBC News*, 25 February 2005.
132. *The Hindustan Times*, 3 August, 2006.
133. *The Indian Express*, 29 August, 2006.
134. *The Hindustan Times*, 4 August, 2006.
135. Selig Harrison, 'A New Hub for Terrorism? In Bangladesh, An Islamic Movement with Al-Qaeda Ties is on the Rise', *The Washington Post*, 2 August 2006.
136. Kazi Anwarul Masud, 'Terrorism in South Asia And US Foreign Policy,' Paper No. 3292, 5 July, 2009 (New Delhi: South Asia Analysis Group, 2009), p. 1.

5

Cross-Border Terrorism in Jammu and Kashmir

The root cause of cross-border terrorism, continuing in the Indian State of Jammu and Kashmir lies in the partition of India in August 1947 as a result of which Pakistan came into existence. Competition, rivalry and enmity between India and Pakistan witnessed four declared wars between the two–the last one in 1999 at Kargil. Apart from wars Pakistan, on number of occasions, tried to hurt india's national and international interests at large. However, the loss of Bangladesh and failure in the insurgency in Punjab were the events which Pakistan could never reconcile to. Islamabad needed a different outlet for outpouring its grievances against its childhood enemy–India. Although the anti-India feeling and partial activity, from the beginning, has been integral part of Jammu-Kashmir's daily life, it took an alarming proportion at the close of eighties and early nineties due to engagement of a large number of terrorists who where earlier fighting in Afghanistan against the Soviet forces. Dozens of militant groups and thousands of terrorists began to take part in terror activities in Jammu and Kashmir. These terror organisations and militants were/are getting assistance and substantive support from Pakistan and its mentor the ISI. Since 1989 till day the Valley has seen a 'real' insurgency and has surely inflated to be one of India's internal security threats. Pakistan's proxy war against India through the Jihadis has been a persistent programme, irrespective of the regimes–military or otherwise at Islamabad.

Differing Perceptions

In past the border areas had served as a safe haven for terrorists, who after obtaining training and arms in Pakistan, crossed over into India and fanned out all over the country. There has been a steady one-way traffic of illegal immigrants from Pakistan to the border areas. The importance of the problem lies in the fact that not only human traffic but arms and narcotics find easy access into India. Reports from various parts of the country confirm that they smuggle arms and narcotics in large quantities. Unfortunately, there are many godfathers, agents, touts, etc. on the Indian side who not only provide shelter and food to the illegal migrants but all help needed to remain unnoticed. The defence forces with the help of local people and the police must break up these gangs, round up the agents and touts and send the godfathers to prison. What is needed is not a fence along the border but a highly efficient intelligence machinery capable enough to identify the illegal migrants and stop the trans-border commerce in humans, drugs and arms.[1] In August 1986 the Indian Parliament adopted a resolution in pursuance of Article 249 of the constitution whereby the Centre assumed special powers to create a security belt to deal directly and swiftly against large scale infiltration, illegal traffic in arms, drugs and secessionist and terrorist activities on international borders. Not only the entire border of Pakistan from Kashmir to Kutch but borders with Bangladesh and China also need to be protected. It is time India told its people the real and full story about Pakistan's role in the unrecognised war in Jammu and Kashmir which the latter has been waging since its first invasion in October 1947.

Terrorism, it is said, has become endemic to modern society. It continues to be generated by recurrent social crises, arising from the increasing marginalisation of some sections of society caused by the indescriminate spread of capitalism and the free market economy, through the much vaunted process of globalisation. At its root the terrorist movement is born out of frustration and despair. Despair caused by social marginalisation, economic decline and political defeat. Someone once said that 'young hope betrayed, transforms itself into bombs'. Perceived injustice if allowed to continue unresolved, would transform into despair and then violence. According to Leon Trotsky the two emotions central to terrorism, are despair and vengeance.[2] The causes of these issues and the form they take, whether it be terrorism or otherwise, must be studied and understood in a scientific and objective manner.

With the start of cross-border terrorism by Pakistan the Kashmir dispute assumed alarming proportions. Pakistan's historical record of its commitment to honour its agreements and treaty obligations, which it freely entered into, not only with India, but also with other countries has been extremely poor. The 1947 Standstill Agreement with Jammu and Kashmir, the 1948 UN Resolution, 1949 Karachi Agreement, 1954 SEATO and CENTO agreements, 1966 Tashkent Declaration, 1972 Simla Agreement, 1988 Geneva Accords with Afghanistan, 1999 Lahore Declaration, and so on stand out. When the Kashmir agitation picked up steam the Berlin Wall was being pulled down, the mighty Red Army had been forced out of Afghanistan by rag-tag bands of Islamic guerillas a year earlier and geographical boundaries were being redrawn across Eastern Europe and Central Asia.[3] Thus it was no surprise then that the votaries of azadi thought that India, too, would close shop in Kashmir. But this did not happen.

However, Pakistan's waging a covert war through trans-national terrorism has a strong religious base. It was during the regime of General Zia-ul-Haq that Islamabad began to use terror as a weapon to fight war. The strategy had found a sound footing from a book *Quranic Concept of War* written by Brigadier S. K. Malik (Lahore, 1979). In it, the Holy Quran was interpreted as requiring the believers to use terror as weapon of war. Unfortunately, the military dictator at that time, strongly recommended the book and its conclusions by stating that it brings out the 'Quranic philosophy' on the application of military force, within the context of the totality that is "JIHAD". The volume concluded that "jihad", the Quranic concept of total strategy, demands the preparation and application of total manpower and military instrument is one of its elements. It went on to say further that 'The holy Quran lays the highest emphasis on the preparation of war. The test of utmost preparation lies in our capability to instil terror into the hearts of the enemies'. The merging of the concept of jihad, war and terrorism has also been pursued by Pakistan in the trans-national terrorism it imposes in Jammu and Kashmir. Incidentally, a combination of jihad terrorism war has also been pursued by Pakistan in Afghanistan for nearly three decades.

There can be no doubt that India is the victim of sustained low-level aggression by secessionist forces encouraged and abetted by Pakistan. The present thinking on terrorism can be divided into two schools of thought. One school of thought places the terrorist beyond the pale of civilized society and considers him anathema to civilization and stigmatises him as a plain murderer who needs to be eliminated. But the second school of thought encourages an in-depth study of, and a systematic approach to understand and eradicate, the reasons that bring about such upheavals. The rational political, social and economic aspirations of peoples which when frustrated continuously give rise to full blown terrorism of the modern day, must be sifted out of the process of terroristic actions and looked at separately. Those political aspirations must be addressed honestly and seriously. The solutions that are employed must be made effective–legally and constitutionally, politically, economically and socially. The overall gained impression from the cross-border terrorism is that it relates to the second school of thought. Peace is more than the simple absence of war. It entails active engagement in the battle for identifying and rectifying the root causes of conflict.

The problem of cross-border terrorism took an alarming shape during 1988-89 for which solid ground had been prepared by the parties concerned. First, on the part of New Delhi it was a time to face realities on the ground and examine carefully the causes for the sense of alienation that the Kashmiris feel. The government is well advised to go into the history of the Kashmir issue in order to understand and appreciate how and when things went wrong and how the impass of this particular type came about. It is an open fact that the Government of India has, from the beginning, been ignoring the political, social, economical as well as cultural needs of the people of Jammu and Kashmir. The successive governments of the National Conference well alternated by the direct rule of New Delhi proved a disaster in real sense of the term. Farooq Abdullah's behaviour during his curtailed first term in 1983-84, has been described as that of 'a little boy with a toy', and during the second as 'a virtual abdication of governance.'[4] He acquired the sobriquet 'disco chief minister' because he was frequently sighted in discotheques in Indian cities, and he spent much of the rest of his time playing golf or vocationing abroad. His colleagues in government earned a reputation for corrupt practices. In nutshell, the Kashmiris feel that Delhi's behaviour has been atrocious in that it has chosen to ignore them completely.

The wars of 1965 and 1971 had succeeded in freezing the problem of Kashmir, however, the post-war agreements with Pakistan failed to keep the promises inherent in those documents. The Simla Agreement of 1972 in particular provided that the two would respect the ceasefire line of December 17, 1971, and that neither side would seek to alter it unilaterally irrespective of mutual differences and legal interpretations. They also agreed to refrain from a threat or a use of force as the agreement itself was based on the principles of bilateral diplomacy and durable peace. Notwithstanding the benevolent spirit of Simla, Pakistan continued to raise the issue of Kashmir at various international fora. A little latter of the signing of the agreement, Zulfikar Ali Bhutto, the then Prime Minister of Pakistan, fad clearly stated that there would be no compromise on the principle of self-determination in Kashmir. General Zia-ul-Haq followed the same militant line on the matter and succeeded in keeping the issue alive at both, bilateral and international levels. However, the issue had become critical and closely related to it was Pakistan's perception regarding its role in the State of Jammu and Kashmir.

Domestic as well as international are the two important determinants that govern Pakistani action in the State. The period that was responsible for initiation and growth of cross-border terrorism largely witnessed the power rivalry between the democratically elected ruling elite and the military. Prime Minister Benazir Bhutto inherited a mixed economy. Tied to these were two experiments of democratic rule, one of which was carried out by her father; and populist Islamisation process that was used by all as a tool for legitimacy. Her task was not just to undo autocracy but build an economy and industry that had for long been propped up by external aid. Her success at keeping the army at bay had also been uncertain. Therefore, militant posture for her became a need of the hour and in such a situation Kashmir remained the most readymade tool.[5] In addition, it was just a chance that both India and Pakistan were embroiled in grim problems outside Kashmir–India in Punjab and Assam and Pakistan in the volatile steamy city of Karachi where armoured personnel carriers were now common sight in the streets. There were host of problems for Pakistan in other states as well apart from the continuing and running battle between the federal and Punjab government.[6] The then government of Pakistan was beholden to the army and to the President to remain in office.

At that time India, too, was ruled by a minority and weak government headed by V. P. Singh, supported by Bharatiya Janata Party and Hindu fundamentalism. The situation in India convinced Pakistan that this was the time to liberate Kashmir. Among the military stalwarts, General Chisti, Arif and Gul were of the view that when the government in India is weak it is vulnerable to military and political pressures in the valley along with direct and indirect international wish to settle the issue of Kashmir. Hence they calculated that the situation would either lead to the decapitation of India by the loss of Kashmir and parts of Punjab as a result of developments on the ground or to an Indo-Pak deal by a softened and chastened India, and a tough and principled Pakistan. Finally, they concluded that in either way, militarily or diplomatically, India would lose in Pakistani thinking and 1971 would be revenged and with Pakistani getting its parity with India.[7]

So far as the international determinants of the Pakistani action in Kashmir was concerned, it was tied to Islamabad's perception about India's position regarding the state of Jammu and Kashmir. In the first place, Pakistan must have reason to believe that India would be reluctant to mobilise itself into a war over the issue. Reason for such a reluctance would lie both in civilian and military thinking in India. Democratic systems are rarely tuned to instantaneous response in the face of crisis because it is linked to the decision-making process of the political system. In India, while the military would be consulted, the decision about the war would be basically political. Islamabad's second perception was related to the situation in Kashmir itself. As the Government of India had implemented democracy in Jammu and Kashmir half-heartedly and on the other Pakistan perceived the accession of Kashmir to India as one attained by force, the Kashmiri population would welcome intervention by Pakistan to liberate it from India.

But finally was the consideration of international support that Pakistan hoped, particularly from the US and China. Pakistan has reason to believe that both United States and China along with others would extend international sympathy. Given the religious dimension of the issue Pakistan also counted on the continued support of the West Asian countries. At that time the Soviet Union, India's only ally was in a state of internal influx and Gorbachov himself had been supporting freedom movements in Eastern Europe. The Soviet system was also trying to cope with demands for change from its own ethnic minorities and nationalities. In Pakistan's perception India would find it difficult to get international support over its position in Kashmir. However, Pakistan's initial efforts to project Kashmir on the world stage failed because the major Powers had other preoccupations and were loath to add a hoary contentious issue to their agenda.[8] The Simla agreement came in handy for the world to put away the issue of Kashmir as the world knows that there can not be a radical solution short of war.

Diplomatic Channels Reactivated

In case of cross-border terrorism Pakistan is pursuing its own brand of 'two track' policy. While it wants a dialogue with India, it has kept up the level of violence. In its latter part of the strategy, Afghanistan's utility is the greatest. To wage proxy war against India, Afghan heroin pays for the weapons and salaries of Kashmiri militants. To escape the "terrorist state" label Pakistan places its Jihadi camps across the Durand Line. As said by the official of the Foreign Ministry a good chunk of the militants are Afghans and 'Afghanistan is the fountainhead of militancy'.[9] In fact the movement of Kashmiri people was hijacked by the Afghan-based elements. And from the start the real thrust of Pakistani terrorism in Jammu and Kashmir is not to give a chance to the people of the state to vote for their future but to channel the overflow of arms and mercenaries from the war-ravaged areas of Afghanistan, which would flood Pakistan if not sent elsewhere. It is true that the idea has caught the imagination of the Pakistani people and become a sort of precondition to any "settlement" of India-Pakistan question. Even today this precondition exists in Pakistani establishment. In June 2001, on the eve of his arrival in Agra, Musharraf told the Karachi monthly, *The Herald* that violence would decline as talks on Kashmir made progress. After the collapse of the Agra summit, a noted Indian writer on military affairs realistically noted, 'The only real bargaining leverage that Pakistan wields in Jammu and Kashmir is through its proxies, the Jehadi groups operating in the state'. For Pakistan, therefore, cross-border terrorism has to be retained as a lever until the end of the peace process. While India depended entirely on the hope that a resumption of negotiations would end the problem.

In the meantime change of guards took place in Islamabad and New Delhi respectively. While a democratic government was sworn in under the premiership of Benazir Bhutto in Pakistan, it followed the taking over of the second non-Congress government of National Front headed by Vishwanath Pratap Singh in India. Though both the countries had been obsessed with an inexorable state of "new cold war" on the subcontinent in the light of Pakistan's covert or overt support to secessionists in Punjab and Jammu and Kashmir, the new Indian government adopted the policy of friendliness and mutual understanding with neighbouring countries, particularly with Pakistan. A foreign office spokesman said, 'It is our hope that Pakistan will exercise similar restraint and desist from giving encouragement to terrorism directed against

India. Such action violates bilateral, regional and international obligations including the terms of the Simla Agreement and is not conducive to peace in the region'.[10] The provocative statements of Pakistan and terrorist support by it were considered by India as "unfortunate" and despite threatening posture the new dispensation did not abandon normalisation process entirely. In three respects the National Front Government's record had been creditable. First, inspite of developments in the Kashmir valley and a certain amount of militancy[11] in Islamabad's attitude, V. P. Singh's Government considered it appropriate to keep the dialogue open. Secondly, when Benazir's Government was dismissed, New Delhi avoided making any comments except for wishing well for a strong and stable Pakistan.[12] Third, India's active diplomacy in the Arab countries and western world was instrumental, to a large extent, in containing Pakistani efforts to internationalise the Kashmir issue.[13]

Since January 1990 political atmosphere between the two countries was vitiated due to statements of Pakistani leaders, particularly the Prime Minister who maintained that no compromise would be done with India on the question of the right of self-determination for the people of Jammu and Kashmir. She also announced through a state-run television that a joint session of Parliament would be convened in the first week of February 1990 to discuss the 'deteriorating situation in Kashmir'. It added fuel to the fire and compelled India's ruling as well as opposition circles to react sharply. They all condemned the statement of Pakistan's Prime Minister and conveyed its resentments in a message communicated to Sahib Zada Yakub Khan, country's Foreign Minister. India's concern involved terrorist activities directed against India in Jammu and Kashmir. It reiterated that Jammu and Kashmir is an integral part of India and any interference in our internal affairs would be unacceptable.[14] In this tense situation a balanced statement of Pakistani President Ghulam Ishaq Khan appeared that Pakistan can not afford war and added that there was no immediate threat from India. Inder Kumar Gujral, India's Minister for External Affairs, stressed the need to resolve their differences through dialogue and Confidence Building Measures to promote peace and cooperation in South Asia.

Earlier, at the close of the 1980s in order to avoid war and normalise ties New Delhi and Islamabad agreed to take some concrete CBMs. The turning point came following the holding of the military exercises by India called "Brasstacks" along the borders of Pakistan during the winter of 1986-87. Taking cognisance of the situation, both governments belatedly called for a reduction in their military presence and talks were held in New Delhi on 30 January, 1987 between senior foreign ministry officials of the two countries. On 4 February, 1987 a memorandum of understanding was signed that provided over the withdrawal of forces from both sides to a peace time position over the next fifteen days.[15] The CBMs between the two countries strengthened further in December 1988 when on the occasion of the fourth SAARC summit held in Islamabad, Rajiv Gandhi, the then Prime Minister of India, as a gesture of goodwill, announced the cancellation of routine exercises by the Indian military along the Pakistani borders. Pakistan also responded to invite international observers, including those from India to see military exercises in December 1989 called "Zarb-i-Momin".[16] Such steps taken by India and Pakistan proved to be useful for building mutual trust and confidence and the de-escalation of tension. Now it became possible for New Delhi and Islamabad to communicate directly at the times of crisis along the border.

Concrete steps and bold decisions taken by the two countries relating to CBMs had reduced the risk of an accidental war. Given the success of military CMBs agreed to between New Delhi and Islamabad India and Pakistan could embark on adopting non-military CBMs. However, both sides undermined the necessity to simultaneously adopt military and non-military CBMs. India had its own reasons to emphasise the adoption of non-military CBMs before settling the Kashmir dispute, and Pakistanis feel it is meaningless to go for these CBMs without settling the dispute with India. In other words, Indo-Pakistan difference in perceptions concerning CBMs is two fold : First, New Delhi wants Pakistan to agree on applying CBMs related to political, economic and cultural fields and argues that outstanding disputes should either be frozen or left aside for future discussions. In this regard, India cites the Simla Agreement as a model for its normalisation of relations with Pakistan. But Pakistan feels that the entire process of CBMs can not render positive results unless some measures are not taken to settle the bilateral issues.[17] Apart from this Pakistan also needs a nuclear parity with India to cope effectively with the Indian threat and to use the capability as a deterrent to any future Indian designs against Pakistan's territorial sovereignty.

When in the summer of 1990, the Kashmir dispute threatened a new outbreak of hostilities in the subcontinent, the two had decided to launch bilateral talks at the foreign secretary level for de-escalation of tension and normalisation of relations. The readiness on the part of India and Pakistan to start foreign secretaries' talks despite escalation of Kashmir and other disputes could be termed as an 'exercise in confidence building'. As scheduled, Muchkund Dubey, India's foreign secretary, met Tanvir Ahmed Khan, his Pakistani counterpart in Islamabad on 18-20 July, 1990 for talks to defuse the year long tension between the two countries over Kashmir. Benazir Bhutto was happy with the development and described Indian response as "Positive".[18] But in the talks India and Pakistan failed to make much headway to defuse tensions between them with the two sides sticking to their different perceptions on the situation in Kashmir.[19] The meeting ended without agreeing on any confidence building measure but it was decided to continue the dialogue in Delhi in the second week of August 1990.

Several rounds of talks at both levels had been held since, and almost half a dozen CBMs have been adopted by the two countries. Admist the dismissal of Benazir Bhutto's Government and Organisation of Islamic Conference (OIC) not endorsing Pakistan's call on Kashmir, India, in August 1990 proposed five non-military CBMs which were directly related to the cross-border terrorism. They were :

I. Statements [should be] made by political and military leaders in Pakistan disassociating themselves from [acts of] terrorism and subversion in the [Indian states of] Punjab, Jammu and Kashmir.

II. The handing over of [ten] fugitives who have been operating from Pakistan. India also asked Pakistan to handover Jammu and Kashmir Liberation Front leader Amanullah Khan. Such request was promptly turned down by Pakistan.

III. Seizure [by Pakistan] of arms and ammunition [that are] being smuggled into India and the arrest of infiltrators [who have been] crossing into India.

IV. Cessation of official statements and pronouncements from Pakistan inciting violence and striking communal passion in India.

V. Closure of officially sponsored funds that have been put in Pakistan in connection with recent developments in Jammu and Kashmir.[20]

In 1991 when militancy was at its peak, on 16 April, two accords on CBMs of military significance were signed. In this connection two conclusions could be made from the Indo-Pak normalisation talks. First, these talks were held at the official level and agreements signed were merely restricted to military security matters. Second, because of Political reasons, progress achieved in these talks were not durable. For example, after the sixth round of talks held in August 1992 and the subsequent defence secretaries' talks held in November of the same year, political relations between the two countries deteriorated to an alarming extent. Therefore, gains achieved in Indo-Pakistan talks are lost when something goes wrong, quickly the two countries are back to square one.

In between the change of guards Pakistan formally proposed 'negotiations on the settlement of Jammu and Kashmir in terms of Article 6 of the Simla Agreement', India responded with two stipulations : Pakistan must be 'in a position to adopt an effective and practical approach' and next, it must end 'support for secessionist elements' in Kashmir. At a later date Narasimha Rao rebuffed Nawaz Sharif, but waived the stipulations when Benazir came to power. On 19 October, 1993, he himself proposed 'a comprehensive dialogue for discussing all matters of mutual concern, including issues related to Jammu and Kashmir'. Unfortunately, Bhutto adopted this time a hard line that wrecked the talks in January 1994.

In 1997 Nawaz Sharif returned to Power second time and the dialogue was resumed. A joint statement was issued in Islamabad on June 23, 1997, announcing a decision 'to set up a mechanism, including working groups to address eight issues'. Militancy was not absent when Vajpayee went to Lahore in February 1999. Kargil derailed the process. On 13 June, 1999, Vajpayee said, 'India is for the continuation of Lahore process.......but for that process it is absolutely necessary for the status quo ante to be restored on the LoC'. He added, 'You withdraw your troops from Kargil and then we are prepared for talks'. Of late when Abdul Majid Dar, the sacked commander of the Hizbul Mujahideen was asked, 'You talk about a peace process, but you do not call for an end to militancy, why ?' Dar replied : 'We want a political process, but unless we see a positive attitude from the Government of India we can not put the gun down'. According to press reports the unsigned Arga Declaration of July 16, 2001, also set up a similar mechanism to discuss precisely those eight issues. 'Jammu and Kashmir' and terrorism and drug-peddling were listed separately for talks on different levels.

Thus, implementation of military and non-military CBMs along with results of the peace talks have always been marred by the preconditions by either side. For Pakistan, the problem of Kashmir has become the 'core issue' without which there can never be any settlement between Islamabad and New Delhi. Likewise the Indian leaders have stressed, on times without number, that any fruitful peace talks must be preceded by the end of cross-border terrorism in Jammu and Kashmir. It seemed that the whole exercise of CBMs and peace talks were directed in scoring competitive points rather than anything else. In fact, India and Pakistan have not moved systematically towards the goal of tension free relations. There is lack of political will on the part of the regimes in power-past and present to institutionalise the normalisation process by giving serious consideration to non-military CBMs to which the problem of cross-border terrorism is closely related. The need to act against terrorist camps, their support bases and the Pakistani army posts near the LoC which assist the cross-border infiltration will form one dimension of Indian strategy.[21] However, the larger and lasting dimension of Indian strategy must remain with the people of Jammu and Kashmir. They will isolate the militants and the terrorists and leave them exposed to military action, if their aspirations are met through good governance.

Men

General Zia-ul-Haq, who became martial law administrator in July 1977, had not only exploited religion to the maximum for legitimisation of his rule but delayed the return of democratic government for eleven long years. When the US-Pakistan Mujahideen nexus was formed, he sold thousands of brainwashed to fight against the erstwhile USSR. He exploited this Jihad to strengthen religious parties with state's backing to marginalise the influence of political parties, particularly, the Pakistan's Peoples Party. The regime of Zia faced the Afghans inflow both as refugees and Mujahideens as well. The latter was provided all possible assistance on humanitarian grounds and in the spirit of Islamic brotherhood. Zia identified himself with the cause of the Mujahideen, stating that their sacrifices would be written in 'golden letters' in the annals of history, for 'the safety and security of Afghanistan and of Pakistan depended on them'.[22] With the increasing post-cold war surge in Islamic fundamentalism on India's western flank, the situation has become even more serious. Afghanistan, a long time friend of India since its independence had increasingly embraced Islamic fundamentalism and many violent movements in the Indian state of Jammu and Kashmir has apparently developed a 'dangerous nexus with the Afghan Mujahideen.'[23] They based on for their material and moral support to the emergence of what may be described as a militant Pan-Islamic Jehad. Moving across the state borders in clandestine manner, equipped with lethal armaments and owing allegiance to no flag except the paymasters of the moment, these groups have the ability to cause mayhem and disappear into the murky mist of subnationalism and religious zealotry. For India the stakes are high since what is threatened by this proxy war is not mere territoriality but a concerted attempt to hack at the roots of the often taken-for-granted Indian independence and nationhood, based on democratic principles and abiding secularism.

Originally, rumblings of discontent appeared in Jammu and Kashmir were perceived as the normal expression of legitimate demands from a rapidly changing India.[24] But a little later disaffected Kashmiri youths formed the bulk of the cannon fodder. They were members of the Jammu and Kashmir Liberation Front (JKLF). The dream of Azad, independent Kashmir seemed but not a short struggle away. However, the unravelling of the independence struggle started with the inter-faction killings. Pakistani agencies involved in formulating and running Pakistan's Kashmir strategy worked hard not just to build up the Hizbul Mujahideen and other client groups but to actively undermine and weaken the JKLF. The former had also an important advantage over JKLF within Kashmir. It is politically connected to the Jamaat-i-Islami, which has a well-organised, well-funded party apparatus in Jammu and Kashmir. Thus, the Hizbul Mujahideen could rely on the Jamaat's infrastructure in Kashmir, while nothing comparable was available to the JKLF. Nonetheless, the HM never succeeded in winning the kind of spontaneous mass support the JKLF enjoyed in its prime.[25]

The authorised and controlled use of violence which was earlier kept within the purview of state machinery barring stray criminal acts has undergone a radical transformation since World War II. The deliberate targetting of civilian populations by the principal interlocutors in that war had opened the door to extending the scope of 'war' and over the decades, the explosive cocktail of military technology and misplaced fundamentalism of different hues has abetted the myriad subterranean forces that have been unleashed in the aftermath of the cold war. The ability to inflict mass destruction is no longer the sole purview of the state and the non-state actor and fringe group zealot has emerged as a new challenge to state security and stability. A heady infusion of religious fervour and the proliferation of lethal small arms, the prefix being a complete contrast to the massive destruction possible have enhanced the profile of the practitioners of this proxy war. The terrorist / militant / proxy war waging group in the state of Jammu and Kashmir now, too, possess fire power capability including artillery pieces and anti-aircraft missiles that would normally be associated with a regular army brigade.

Other causes that had speeded up the momentum of proxy war included three events of 1980s that accelerated the process of fundamentalist terrorism in the Muslim world. First was the 1978-79 revolution in Iran. It had ripple effect which spread Shiite militancy throughout the Middle East. Second, there was the war in Lebanon, where terrorists, particularly of the Hizbullah group, achieved signal success against the Western and Israeli forces. And, third, the war in Afghanistan, where the Russian army was defeated by the Mujahideen, the Islamic warriors drawn from all over the Muslim world committed to fighting Western civilization. In due course, the Mujahideen spread to different parts of the world wherever Islam was considered to be in danger.[26] For decades, India is facing a multi-pronged attack from the fundamentalist forces through Afghanistan and Pakistan into Jammu and Kashmir. Islamic warriors from Afghanistan, Sudan, Algeria, Tajikistan, Saudi Arabia, Chechnya, Bosnia and several other countries have been spearheading the separatist movement in the valley. The fact was evident from The Pattern of Global Terrorism, 1996 of the US State Department that noted, 'Afghanistan remained a training ground for Islamic militants and terrorists' and that individuals trained in its camps were involved in insurgencies in several countries including Kashmir.

The greater challenge for India is that such acts are receiving purposeful state support from across the border and thereby straining state resources and societal tolerance. Certain sections of the Pakistani establishment have vowed that the liberation of Kashmir is a "sacred mission" and the steady attempt at bleeding Indian secularism by a "thousand cuts" as the ISI describes the mission to its mercenaries represents an entirely new challenge to state and society.[27] One of the reasons why Islamabad is reluctant to talk to India on the issue is that now Pakistan is in the grip of elements who not only lacks legitimacy but who seem to be driven by the medieval concept of jehad or holy war against infidels. The open manner in which various Jehadi groups operate in Pakistan uttering dire threats against India, and the close involvement of these militants with official Pakistani agencies like the ISI in organising acts of terrorism in Kashmir and elsewhere in India, leave little scope for any purposeful dialogue with Islamabad.

The whole episode took a new turn when hundreds of graduates from Pakistan's terror camps came to India, a battle for supremacy between the pro-Pakistan Hizbul Mujahideen and pro-independence JKLF began. After 1993 on account of Hazratbal crisis Kashmiri militants weakened that made Pakistan worried who soon shifted the focus with ISI. It gave the "Afghan alumni," the rag-tag mercenary remnants of that country's war against the Soviet's, a new cause. India believes that infiltration and other foreign groups are solely responsible for militancy in Jammu and Kashmir. In the post-Hazratbal phase, the Harkat-ul-Ansar with its Afghan alumni began to push into the state. They shifted their routes south of the Pir Panjal range, through Jammu's Poonch and Rajouri districts. These areas are mountainous too, but they receive less snowfall.

The way to peace is never easy and a straight one. Not at least in the troubled state of Jammu and Kashmir. The Indian establishment is aware that the biggest task in Kashmir today is of engaging and eliminating "fidayeens" and foreign mercenaries, which it is doing with incremental success. In fact militancy in Kashmir is profitable. Brigadier Mohan Bhandari terms it as a "blue-chip" industry. He reveals that apart from the millions of dollars that the ISI gets from the narcotics trade to fund militancy, many Islamic countries also give it liberal donations for jihad. Militancy actually makes for a good career. Most local militants are paid between Rs. 2,500 to Rs. 5000 per month. Foreign mercenaries are paid about Rs. 5000 to Rs. 8000 per month. A deceased militant's kin get a pension of Rs 1,500 to 3,000 per month. There are good rates for each strata in the militant's hierarchy. Apart from this foreign militants get Rs. 2 lakhs while entering India and another Rs. 5 lakhs at the end of the two-year contract period. The reward for killing an Indian is around Rs. 150. If it is a soldier upto the rank of major the reward is around Rs. 7,000. While Lieutenant Colonel carry a price of Rs. 50,000 the Brigadiers command over Rs. 1 lakh.[28] Perhaps no one would like to give up such a lucrative career easily.

Since 1989 in Jammu and Kashmir the conflict between assorted militant organisations and the security forces has been one of the most important internal security issues in India. While the armed forces are equipped with a number of extraordinary legislations, insurgency has shown no signs of declining in the affected states. There are some of the more active terrorist groups, apart from JKLF, who fought for the unification and independence of India-Pakistan held Kashmir.

Hizb-ul-Mujahideen (HM), originated in November 1989, stands for the integration of Jammu and Kashmir with Pakistan, but will not oppose independence of Kashmir. It was patronised by the InterServices Intelligence of Pakistan who use and guide it to counter the influence of the Jammu and Kashmir Liberation Front. Before its birth the ISI had been supporting the JKLF but the former had a golden opportunity in 1988 when Kashmiri youths agreed to take up arms against Indian rule. Unlike the activists of the HM, the JKLF, the agent and the vehicle of the uprising, was dogmatically committed to the ideology of an independent, reunited Jammu and Kashmir state, separate from both India and Pakistan – an ideology elaborated as early as 1970 by the movement's veteran ideologue Amanullah Khan. From 1991 the ISI cut off aid to the JKLF and adopted a twin-track strategy to mould the valley uprising to Pakistan's conception and interests. It was done to divide and weaken the JKLF.

As a part of its second strategy or to weaken the JKLF, a pro-Pakistan guerilla organisation the HM was not only formed but nourished with outside help and support. As the armed revolt rapidly acquired a popular character owing to the severe and indiscriminate nature of Indian repression during 1990, thousands of valley youths started to cross the Line of Control in search of weapons and training. Hizbul Mujahideen is militarily the strongest force among the guerilla groups presently operating in Indian-administered Jammu and Kashmir. More than 50 per cent of the militants operating in the valley are from this outfit. The number of foreign mercenaries in this group is estimated to be around 30 per cent. It comprises mainly of local militants but most of foreign militant outfits operating in the valley are dependent on it for logistics and internal support.

Since the early 1990s the leader of Hizbul Mujahideen has been Yusuf Shah of Muzaffarabad in Pakistan controlled 'Azad' Jammu and Kashmir', who now goes by his nom de guerre, Syed Salahuddin. Salahuddin was a legendary Muslim warrior who fought against the Christian Crusaders. At the sametime Syed Salahuddin, the commander in chief of Hizbul Mujahideen was critical of Indian rule in the state and said an interviewer in 1992 that he had chosen to fight for the cause of Pakistan in Kashmir because experience had convinced him that "slaves have no vote in the so-called democratic set-up of India.[29] The Mujahideen's halo of heroism was gradually giving way to a painful realisation among the public that because of the phenomenal expansion of the armed struggle the ranks of freedom fighters contained politically. Though in 1993-94 HM emerged as the leading guerilla organisation in the field, its ideology that Kashmir will become Pakistan remained a minority orientation. Its sacrifices in the cause of azadi were widely admired, but its political affiliate Jammaat-e-Islami's brand of orthodox Islam, preached in a network of religious schools run by the party, is regarded with distaste by most muslims in the valley and other Kashmir-speaking areas.

However, the Hizbul Mujahideen has a significant presence, especially in the Pir Panjal mountains, a range that traverses a massive east-west arc across the northern Kashmiri-speaking part of Poonch district, the southern part of the valley, the mountainous Gujjar and Kashmiri muslim dominated upper reaches of Jammu's Udhampur district, and finally Doda district. The HM's fighting units in the area are called the Hizb-ul-Mujahidden Pir Panjal Regiment and, as in the valley and Doda, are mostly recruited from the local population. It has no effect either of the threat of Indian war, American pressure or General Musharraf's curtailment of activities in Azad Jammu and Kashmir as HM sources pointed out, 'We have many mobile training camps in the hills and forests of Indian Kashmir where youths are trained... and we have munitions stockpiled over the years.'[30]

The HM is an alien guerilla organisation having a strong social base in the Indian Jammu and Kashmir. A prepared ground was provided to it by the Jamaat-e-Islami of Kashmir which also has branches in Pakistan and Bangladesh. The jamaat-e-Islami of Kashmir is not affiliated to the Indian jamaat and is known for anti-secular and anti-national character. It is doing the greatest damage in the state by preaching sentiments that go against the basic secular traditions of the Kashmir. Its followers are trying to poison the minds of Kashmiris in cities, towns and villages. If one listens to the sermons they preach in village mosques, attends their study circle and just go through some of their literature which they circulate so widely, one would be convinced that they are sowing the seeds of discord and hatred.[31] Initially its stronghold area in the valley was Sopore, but slowly, the organisation spread to Anantnag and Kulgam followed by Srinagar city where it has much larger support. They are also not scarved of fund and their money comes from Pakistan and Gulf countries, particularly Saudi Arabia. Today the jamaat has a network of about 200 fairly efficiently run schools in the valley, and study circles and mosques are used to propagate anti-secular and anti-national ideas.[32] Apart from the guerilla warfare alignments with jamaat-e-Islami, Hizb-ul Mujahideen owes a close link with other Jehadi groups dominated by Pakistan, such as, Lashkar-e-Toiba (LeT), Jaish-e-Mohammad (JeM), Al-Badar, Tehreek-ul-Mujahideen, Harkat-ul-Mujahideen and Harkat-ul-jehad-e-Islami which are active in the area.

Lashkar-e-Toiba (LeT), it is an insurgent group active in Indian Jammu and Kashmir since the mid-1990s, spawned by a Pakistan-based movement professing an ultra-orthodox variant of Sunni Islam. Like JeM, it is predominantly composed of Pakistani religious radicals, and its leader is Hafiz Muhammad Sayeed, a Pakistani academic-turned fundamentalist activist. Its peak period along with JeM is known as Fidayeen (suicidal) phase. Between mid 1999 and the end of 2002, at least 55 Fidayeen attacks were made, usually executed by two-men teams and were targeted against police, paramilitary and army camps, and government installations in Indian Jammu and Kashmir, mostly in the valley. Though the LeT denies that its raids are suicide mission-preferring to call them 'daredevil' actions – since the group follows an ultra-orthodox version of Sunni Islam that strictly prohibits suicide. However its attackers almost never return from these penetrate and kill missions – their aim is not to save their own lives but to maximize the frightening psychological impact on the enemy by inflicting death and destruction on their targets.[33] It is also evident from LeT's mouthpiece *Jehadi Times* published from Islamabad until 2001, which has always discussed the suicidal warfare in Kashmir.

Keeping in view the continuing acts of violence, engaged in by the Lashkar-e-Toiba, the United States Government had issued stern warning to Pakistan in January 2001. Further the LeT's squad managed to enter the compound of India's Parliament building in New Delhi and then attempted to enter the building itself, on 13 December, 2001 where hundreds of Parliamentarians and government ministers were present at the time. The attackers were killed by the security officers after a forty-five minute battle with guns and grenades. Its cadres have been responsible for the majority of fidayeen attacks in Indian Jammu and Kashmir since 1999, and are the prime suspects in a number of massacres of non-muslim civilians.[34] At the root of India's terrorism it is not the LeT, JeM or another group but their common father – the Pakistani military. The latter's alliance with narco-terrorism has criminalised even its top echelons, blurring the line between civilian and military terrorists cloaked as jehadi. Without reform of the Pakistani military, there can be no regional peace, or an end to transnational terrorism, or nation-building in Pakistan.[35]

India and the US share the goal to moderate the Pakistani state, where fundamentalism and militarism feed on each other. It might be far more effective if Pakistan is squarely held responsible for patronising and instigating the extremist outfits operating from its territory. These groups operate openly, protected by the military regime's umbrella. They train, arm and indoctrinate young men and turn them into dogmatic jehadis in well-established camps in Pakistan. Primarily in response to US pressure, in January 2002 General Musharraf announced a crackdown on jehadi groups operating across the LoC from Pakistani territory. It followed a formal banning of LeT and JeM along with several other violent sectarian groups active within Pakistan.

Jaish-e-Mohammad (JeM), formed in early 2000 by Maulana Masood Azhar, a Pakistani cleric, is another zealot group led by Islamabad. It has a predominantly Pakistani membership and is direct descendant of Harkat-ul-Ansar which was active in Indian Jammu and Kashmir in the mid-1990s. Like a number of other militant groups, Pakistan's Inter Services Intelligence (ISI) facilitated formation and promotion of Harkat-ul-Ansar. With material aid and indoctrinated cadre drawn largely from the madrass as in Pakistan and Afghanistan, this pro-Pakistan militant group has been instrumental in killing a number of armed personnel and civilians in the valley. After the US declared Harkat-ul-Ansar a terrorist organisation in 1995 after the kidnapping of five Westerners in Pahalgam, the group changed its name to Harkat-ul-Mujahideen.

Earlier Maulana Masood Azhar, the leader of JeM was captured by Indian forces in the Kashmir valley in 1994 but released in December 1999. He was one of three jailed militants released by the Indian government in exchange for the freedom of 160 hostages after a group of Pakistani religious radicals hijacked an Indian

Airlines plane flying from Kathmandu to Delhi to Kandahar. JeM's mouthpiece fortnightly Urdu journal also published from Pakistan but unlike LeT it refers to self sacrificing martyr's unit.[36] It was involved in suicidal raid on India's Parliament on 13 December 2001. Apart from this its members are also implicated in sectarian Sunni violence against minority Shia Muslims and Christians in Pakistan. Along with LeT, JeM was formally banned in Pakistan in January 2002.

Both the insurgent groups LeT and JeM and their suicidal attacks are known as the Fidayeen phase in Kashmir. However, three points can be made about their aim and strategy.[37] First, the use of suicidal tactics as a weapon of war is neither novel nor the monopoly of militant muslims. In recent past among the contemporary political movements, Palestinian militants – especially but not exclusively their Islamic wing – have resorted to the tactic with increasing frequency and decreasing discrimination. But the most effective and most deadly practitioners of suicidal warfare in the South Asian subcontinent – and possibly in the world have been the Tamil Tigers of Sri Lanka. Second, it is true that the main ideologues and practitioners of suicidal warfare in the Kashmir war are radical Islamist groups of Pakistani provenance, particularly in case of Kashmir, it is not exclusively a 'cross border' phenomenon, but rather it is the product of the incendiary infusion of the ideology and tactics of trans-national Islamist militancy into a brutalized, desperate local environment – that is, of a conjunction of internal and external factors. The third point to be noted is that its most spectacular and most publicized attacks have been directed against such high profile targets as the Indian army's cantonment and operational headquarters in Srinagar, the headquarters of the SOG in Srinagar, Srinagar's airport, and the legislature's premises in Srinagar. But the crucial theaters of war in this phase lie away from urban centres, in the rural areas of Rajouri and Poonch districts, Jammu and in the Kupwara region of Kashmir valley.

Inter-Services Intelligence (ISI), is Pakistan's military's premier intelligence agency which has coordinated the US backed war against the Soviet Union and its allies in Afghanistan. The ISI runs Pakistan's 'Kashmir Programme' and is deeply involved in supporting and controlling the insurgency in Indian Jammu and Kashmir. It got prominence during the 1980s military regime of General Zia-ul-Haq, acquired vast resources and autonomy as the nodal agency. By 1989 when the Soviet forces were on their way out of Afghanistan it was in a position to focus on the new war in Kashmir, Pakistan's sacred national cause since 1947. The passing time witnessed an unexpected windfall for the ISI as sizeable number of youths from Indian Kashmir were, for the first time since 1947, ready to take arms against their country. On the other hand, formerly Pakistan did assist the JKLF in launching the uprising but it soon demanded a price for continued support. When JKLF by and large refused to change its pro-independence line, Pakistani agencies, the ISI in particular, promptly terminated all aid to it. Further it set about engineering defections from the JKLF ranks, and began building the same with Hizb-ul-Mujahideen.

Thus, the ISI has opened a new horizon of proxy war in Kashmir from across the border. In a well-thought calculated move it divided and weakened the JKLF by encouraging its pliable elements to break away and form pro-Pakistan guerilla groups. By 1991 at least two such factions had emerged – Al-Umar Mujahideen and Ikhwan-ul-Muslimeen. Al-Umar was led by Mushtaq Ahmed Zargar, alias Latram, a Srinagar JKLF militant who had become notorious for executing suspected collaborators by exploding grenades tied to their bodies.[38] It promoted Hizb-ul-Mujahideen, a pro-Pakistan guerilla organisation to replace the JKLF from its centre place. However, it appears that Pakistan has been reluctant to place all its eggs even in the HM's basket. Since 1993 Pakistan has floated several new armed groups in Indian-administered Jammu and Kashmir. The ISI had further diversified its Kashmir portfolio by encouraging zealot Islamic groups in Pakistan, such as Harkat-ul-Ansar to enter the Kashmir war. India is affected by terrorism sponsored both by the Pakistani State agencies as well as by the fundamentalist Islamic organisations operating from Pakistani soil.

Mission

Pakistan's foreign policy has always revolved round the idea of annexing Kashmir. If anything, Islamabad's intentions have acquired greater urgency since the Bangladesh war for it to do to India what it believes India did to it in 1971. This is why Pakistanis do not hesitate to tell their Indian interlocutors that they feel insecured and incomplete without Jammu and Kashmir. Several US congressional studies, think tank reports, task-force-on-terrorism findings and CIA revelations have named Pakistan for aiding and abetting the proxy war. Yet, not a day passes without Pakistan passing strictures on India's management of Jammu and Kashmir. The proxy war waged by Pakistan has also falsified the latter's claim that it is interested in the plight of Kashmiri Muslims. Its true interests are geostrategic and economic. Although it is more than the truth that the proxy war is unwinable by either side, Pakistan's aim is to make the cost for India holding Jammu and Kashmir high, diplomatically, politically and militarily.

Traditionally, terrorism is a highly organised enterprise that fits into a clear political strategy. It has been filling the news for most of our lives, and will doubtless go on demanding the attention of our children and grand-children as well. Even in the past terrorism was almost a part of the strategy of an armed national liberation movement, and in the colonial context it usually worked in the end. The reason why it worked so well in anti-colonial struggles was that it did not have to defeat the imperial power's superior military forces in order to win. They were a long way from the home, and there was a limit to how many lives and how much money the imperial government would spend to hang into its possessions. But the early, easy successes of terror tactics in the anti-imperial context left everybody with a great inflated notion of what the technique could achieve against an established national government with local roots.[39] Governments and armies that can not 'go home' – because they are already at home – simply do not give in to terrorism. After several years and more than 80,000 deaths, the Islamic fundamentalists, terrorist war against Algeria's crypto-military regime is no closer to success. They are capable of doing much harm but they are not politically serious people.

While India has traditionally been on the defensive, Pakistan made Jammu and Kashmir the core issue and the root cause of India-Pakistan dispute. Pakistanis and the world are fed on a routine diet of propaganda on television, radio and print media about Indian Army atrocities and human rights violations in Jammu and Kashmir.[40] Pakistan's initial strategy in Kashmir has settled down to three-pronged mutually supportive thrust line:

(i) Work for negotiations with India in an agenda which would discuss the Kashmir issue on the basis of not only the Simla Agreement but also the UN Resolutions, thus bringing the issue of plebiscite/self-determination into bilateral/multi-lateral talks. So far Pakistan's own obligations under the UN Resolutions (the basic reason why the resolution could not be implemented) are not even alluded to;

(ii) Strategy of overt support and covert action for a low-intensity proxy war fought by non-regular forces constructed on the ideology of religion based subnational separatism, and

(iii) Prepare for, and if necessary escalate to a regular war preferably in a manner that creates perceptions of India being the initiator of such war.[41]

The above strategy was aimed to seek the Pakistan's objectives of destablising India and its developmental plans, undermine its secular policy and feudal structure, push the Indian states towards increasing dependence on force and damage India's standing in the international community particularly at a time when it is receiving added recognition and respect. Pakistan would actually be pursuing a low-cost high-benefit strategy where the real price would be paid by the Kashmiri and other Indians. The proxy war could be sustained by Pakistan for a long time as long as some Kashmiris are willing to keep the conflict alive. Pakistan would try to avoid war as long as it sees the basic objectives being met by the other elements of its strategy without paying a direct price which is bound to be heavy.[42] India can hardly hope to win the low-intensity proxy war being waged against her if she does not have the undoubted capacity to win a possible regular war, whether it is of short or long duration. Winning the proxy war was itself requires a cool assessment of the evolving situation and elements of the Pakistani strategy so as to evolve appropriate responses, political as well as military.

It is said that the situation in the valley could not have taken such a serious turn since 1989, had the government handled militancy more effectively in its earlier stages. The policy makers of India were knowing Pakistan's plan. The details of the Pakistani plan were given in "Operation Topaz", published in one of the issues of the India Defence Review in 1988. Later on the plan was put into operation in stages. At each stage it tested government's will and preparedness to fight it. First, a number of explosions, without causing much damage, took place in Srinagar. This was followed by attacks on police stations and selected killings to terrorise the people. The three main objectives before the militants were : I. to demoralise the state police by targeting those officers who dared to take action against them; II. to drive out the Kashmiri Pandits from the valley; and III. to create a communal divide between Hindus and Muslims.[43] The key to the Kashmir problem lies in controlling its internal situation.

India has been for years at the receiving end of cross-border terrorism in Kashmir and surrounding areas. Scores of innocent civilians are mercilessly gunned down at all to frequent intervals, and bomb explosions kill and maim hapless victims in buses and trains as well as in the market place. At this stage our own strategy will have to rest on five concurrent elements:

(i) Keep the avenues for peaceful solution of the conflict with Pakistan open;

(ii) Political and administrative measures to restore normality in Kashmir with the use of force where incapable;

(iii) Sustained politico-diplomatic efforts to mobilise international support in countering Pakistan's proxy war for sub-national separatism;

(iv) Active use of force against infiltration and terrorist activities which are an important component of the proxy war; and

(v) Adequate preparedness to deter imposition of a direct war.

Management

Pakistan has been using terrorism as an instrument of state policy, waging a low-intensity covertly planned conflict against India for over the last 30 years. This policy is predicated on the Pakistani calculation that as long as the levels of intrusive terrorist violence remains short of a threshold, Pakistan could inflict damage upon India without attracting any punitive action against itself. There is also the Pakistani assessment that important powers would be willing to tolerate the situation in Jammu and Kashmir as long as this terrorist violence does not expand into a general conflict between India and Pakistan. As a result the latter's collusion with jehadi groups operating in Kashmir has weakened Islamabad's ability to influence any future political dispensation in the Valley. Pakistan's chosen Kashmir policy has also exacerbated domestic problems in multiple ways that do not require retelling. This debilitating condition can only be changed if the Pakistani leaders come to accept the proposition that a principled position on the Kashmir dispute can not be successfully advanced through unprincipled means.[44] The real thrust of Pakistani terrorism in Jammu and Kashmir is not to give a chance to the people of the state to vote for their future but to channel the overflow of arms and mercenaries from the war-ravaged areas of Afghanistan. The involvement of foreign mercenaries and international religious extremist organisations has become a challenge for the Indian agencies. Unfortunately these covert mercenaries are supported not only by Pakistan but by some other Islamic countries as well. Extraneous vested interests have developed in terms of Pan-Islamic agendas, narco-terrorism, arms sales and so on, which negatively affects the prospects of a reasonable dialogue focused on specific issues related to Kashmir.

Sporadic cross-border incidents along the Indo-Pak border were no surprise for New Delhi because it did not pose a threat to the either side. However, it got an alarming rate at the close of the eighties and especially with the Soviet's withdrawal from Afghanistan. The Pakistani military's Inter Services Intelligence (ISI) had, during the 1980s military regime of General Zia acquired resources and autonomy as well in co-ordination with the Central Intelligence Agency (CIA), who sponsored war against the Soviet take-over of Afghanistan. In the post-withdrawal phase the ISI was in a position to focus on the new war in Kashmir. It began to recruit Kashmiri youths for training and arming in Pak-controlled camps. It got, for the first time since 1947, a large number of Kashmiris' prepared to join the terrorist organisations managed and maintained by the ISI.[45] It was revealed in the recent book, *The Lost Rebellion*, written by Manoj Joshi, that once General Zia and Pakistan's ISI concocted the scheme of recruiting local disaffected Kashmiris, and arming and training them to become insurgents. Till 1987, Pakistan received only a trickle of recruits, but that turned into a flood after Rajiv Gandhi forced the National Conference into a shot-gun marriage with the Congress in 1987 and Farooq Abdullah allegedly rigged elections in the Valley to ensure his return to power. What followed then was a genuine insurgency.

The whole story began in late 1986 when Farooq Abdullah concluded a rapprochement with the Congress regime at the centre. Under its terms, he was reinstalled as chief minister pending fresh Assembly elections in March 1987, which he undertook to contest in alliance with the Congress Party. This alliance was deadly opposed by the Muslim United Front (MUF) coalition. It was mainly represented by a new generation of young men who born in the 1960s. The organisation was formed as an independent, pro-people entity to fight NC's opportunistic alliance with the detested Congress at the polls. The process and its outcome irrevocably tainted Farooq Abdullah and his supporters in the eyes of their former voters as just another clique, serving as tools of the Indian state in return for the spoils of political office.[46] This was the moment when the valley and some of its contiguous areas lost all residual confidence in India's political system. With this, the Kashmir conflict witnessed a changed mood of the younger generation in the Valley.

Apart from this internal factor, there were international elements, too, that gave a helping hand to Pakistan and the ISI in spreading their network in the state of Jammu and Kashmir. International events, particularly that took place in late 1989 and early 1990, played an important role. The first Palestinian intifada against Israeli occupation was a significant reference point, as was the collapse of repressive one-Party regimes in central and eastern Europe after mass demonstrations in the autumn of 1989. It was noted by a Srinagar scholar, 'We felt that if the Berlin wall could be dismantled, so could be the Line of Control'.[47] The young Kashmiri guerillas, for their part, were inspired by the 1989 Soviet withdrawal from Afghanistan in the face of Afghan Mujahideen resistance and success of Tamil Tiger guerillas in Sri Lanka against the vastly superior Indian force. It also became clear soon that these foreign expeditions were fundamentally misguided and increasingly costly in terms of resources and combat causualities.

From here onwards, the ISI has successfully financed, cultivated and armed a powerful section of the Kashmiri people. By 1990 there were over 30 militant groups in Kashmir and 29 of these had been receiving assistance and shelter in Pakistan. A US task force on terrorism and unconventional warfare, set up by a House Republican Research Committee, covered, in its report, various aspects of Islamic terrorism, its origin and spread to Afghanistan, Sudan and Iraq. The report held ISI responsible along with Pakistan for abetting and sponsoring terrorism in Kashmir as part of its over all effort to promote Islamic international terrorism. It noted that in 1986 Pakistan expanded its operations to sponsor and promote separation, primarily in Kashmir, as a strategic long-term programme.[48] Among the most crucial activities of ISI were to propagate religious fundamentalism in small but lethal doses and train and indoctrinate selected leaders from Kashmir to create militant cadres. The report said that several youth from Kashmir valley and Poonch district in Jammu region were given extensive training in the use of automatic weapons, sabotage and attacks on security forces.[49] The US State Department and the various reports published by several agencies confirmed that the extent of the growing state support for terrorism and insurgency in Kashmir is clearly reflected in the evolution of the organisations operating there.

The relation between the two had undergone a sea change when they exploded nuclear devices in May-June 1998. After the explosion, Tariq Altaf, a Pakistani Foreign Office spokesman, reiterated Nawaz Sharif's assertion saying that Pakistan was ready to have a non-aggression pact with India but 'after just settlement of Kashmir dispute'. He urged India to take up the Kashmir issue on 'priority basis' as it was root cause of tension between the two neighbours. Despite the fact that Vajpayee had cautioned Pakistan not to internationalise the Kashmir issue, the militants–mostly from Afghanistan and Pakistan find it easier to shoot and kill the people in the mountainous parts of Jammu and Kashmir region. Further Pakistan's ISI wanted to involve the Jammu region in violence to show the international community that the entire Jammu and Kashmir was disturbed – to strengthen its points of plebiscite in the state.[50] In nutshell, the militants were doing what they had been assigned to do while Pakistan was claiming that it was not involved in any manner in the armed militancy in Jammu and Kashmir.

The net result of cross-border terrorism was the full-fledged war between the two at Kargil sector. It broke out in May-June 1999 which ended in a humiliating defeat of Pakistan at India's hand. Formerly Islamabad had fully expected the big powers to intervene because of the potential nuclear peril, thereby effectively internationalising the Kashmir dispute. When nothing of the short occurred, and the entire exercise became dangerously counter-productive, Islamabad decided to pull back the intruders from Kargil.[51] But the end of Kargil war did not mean the end of continuing hostility to India. The so-called withdrawal of Pakistani forces from Kargil the border had not regained normalcy and guns continue to boom. Added to this was the calculated revival by Pakistan of cross-border-terrorism, and resort to provocative anti-Indian action along various points across the LoC.

As an after-effect of Kargil the Government of Nawaz Sharif was overthrown in a military coup on 12 October, 1999. General Pervez Musharraf, Chief of Army Staff, took over the Administration and again a new chapter of military rule was opened in Pakistan. The new ruler, in a televised announcement on 17 October, 1999, as a gesture of goodwill towards India, declared unilateral military de-escalation along the border. His address also included an offer to resume 'result-oriented' talks with India on 'all issues' but said, 'Pakistan would continue its support to the Kashmiri people for their right to self determination' and added that India must honour all UN resolutions on Kashmir. At a later stage in July 2000 when Bharat Bhushan, a correspondent of *The Hindustan Times*, asked General Musharraf about different aspects of terrorism, the latter had replied that as far as the hardware and the weapons of terror were concerned, 'We certainly want to curb the uncontrolled display and holding of weapons and we are taking action in this direction. But this is easier said than done. To disarm and de-weaponised a region completely is next to impossible'.[52] On the ideological front he presented his own definition of jehad and distinguished it from terrorism. He refused to equate these two perhaps in reference to Kashmir and said, 'Jihad means struggle in the path of God, opposing victimisation against Muslims wherever it exists'. But the world at large did not share Musharraf's perception ofJihad.

In this context, on times without number Islamabad has been told by countries of the world and its leaders to stop cross-border terrorism and reminded the assurance that the former had given to world organisations. Recently in the year 2002, the two most powerful associations of nations–the Group of Eight and the European Union through their adopted statements agreed that 'Pakistan must put a permanent stop to terrorist activity organising from territory under its control. It called on Pakistan to take further concrete action in accordance with the assurances it has already given and with its international obligations, including UN Security Council Resolution 1373 (2001), to stop infiltration across the Line of Control and to prevent terrorist groups from operating from territory under its control, also through closing of training camps'.[53] What seems to be clear, and all agree, is that the General has not done enough to curb militants. As military head and President Musharraf would have no problem in ordering terror camps in PoK to be closed. Of the powerful nations, Washington and London even doubted the power the General has over the jehadi groups. They believe that Musharraf's influence is limited, that large numbers of ISI officers operate independent of him. They refer to the December 13, 2001, attacks on Indian Parliament and the Karachi suicide attack on French nationals as evidence that Musharraf is not the puppet master of all jehadis.

But despite many stresses and strains on the Pakistan military over the last few years, the present day regime's chain of command remains intact. The logistical and communication linkages between the ISI and the Pakistani army units on the one hand and terrorist cadres on the other continue. The pattern and number of infiltrations from Pakistan into India across the LoC have been more or less at the same level. The terrorist training and launching camps which were closed briefly after January 12, 2002, in which

Musharraf promised a crackdown on terror, have been reopened and relocated in other parts of Pakistan and PoK, the northern areas, the Punjab and the North-West Frontier Province. There are an estimated 70 to 75 such camps which continue to be active. India also has information that the Harkat-ul-Mujahideen and Lashkar-e-Toiba cadres are now located in PoK. There are at least 12 launching camps being used for funnelling terrorists across the LoC into India in Jammu and Kashmir. The estimate of the Indian security forces is that there are about 3,000 to 3,500 militants under training in Pakistan.

India and the US both were uncertain about the future course of action that Musharraf would like to take. But they need to keep the working closely on the goals they share in relation to Pakistan. Not only for the present but also in recent past India's threat of war and US diplomacy have worked well in conjunction, with each reinforcing the other's message to Pakistan. Recent revelations of Pakistan's help to Iran, North Korea and Libya in their nuclear weapons programmes have further fuelled American distrust and the latter had expressed its unhappiness. Equally on the other the Western world, including the Chinese should also pause and reflect on the consequences of supplying sophisticated arms and technology to Pakistan. Transferring the M-11 missiles to Islamabad, even in unassembled form, is to give into the hands of potential forces of destruction, the wherewithal to strike at civil society in the name of jihad.

One possible way to minimise Indo-US pressure on Islamabad to end the cross-border terrorism is to start a dialogue between the two and thereby improve relations. Difficulties are more with Pakistan than with India. Today there is a rare consensus on this in Pakistani civil society, born of very diverse reasons. The religious parties favour this on the ground that it would increase Pakistan's capacity to resist pressure by the US to get more deeply involved in the 'war against terror', Pakistan's liberals, both in politics and business, want it in order to further consolidate the economy. With its much smaller economy, it can not indefinitely continue to try and match India. While nuclear weapons now provide it security against any alleged Indian hegemonism, nuclear sabre-rattling of the Kargil war period will not work. Equally, it is no longer possible for Islamabad to back proxy forces, even in the name of religion. This is more so because such forces are now turning against their Pakistani army mentors.[54] The demands for public funds for education, public health and so are no less compelling.

Kashmir is the speed-breaker on the road connecting India and Pakistan. Kashmiri Muslims are unhappy with our presence, but they are also doubtful about having close relations with Pakistan. With its best chance ever to end the scourge of cross-border terrorism, India needs to closely monitor the ground situation, continue to breathe down Pakistan's neck, and speak up whenever the circumstances demand. India's insistence on deeds, not just words, reflects not only the emergent maturity in its foreign policy but also signals that war as an Indian policy option remains primed for exercise if the hostile country refuses to understand the matter in proper perspective.

References

1. S.K. Ghosh, *Muslim Politics in India* (New Delhi: 1987), pp. 113-17.
2. As quoted in Chandrika Bandaranaike Kumaratunga, 'Original Sins,' *The Hindustan Times*, 29 April, 2002.
3. Bharat Bhushan, 'Match Fixing Won't Help in Kashmir,' in *Ibid.*, 21 April, 2000.
4. R.K. Jain (ed.), *Soviet-South Asian Relations*, Vol. 1, 1947-1978 (Atlantic Highlands, 1979), pp. 3-4.
5. Shrikant Paranjpe, 'Dangers of Indo-Pak Confrontation on Kashmir', *The Times of India*, 21 February, 1990.
6. *The Tribune*, 17 April, 1990.
7. *The Indian Express*, 26 July, 1990.
8. Pramit Pal Chaudhuri, 'The Return of the Great Game,' *The Hindustan Times*, 14 October, 2001.
9. A. G. Noorani, 'The Blackwill Thesis,' in *Ibid.*, 12 November, 2002.
10. *The Hindu*, 15 January, 1990.
11. Manorama Kohli, 'Foreign Policy Initiatives of the National Front Government in India,' in Ramakant (ed.), *South Asian Studies*, Vol. 25, No. 1 and 2, January-December 1990 (Jaipur : 1990), p. 141.
12. *The Times of India*, 9 August, 1990.
13. Dileep Padgaonkar, 'Pak Crisis and India's Choices,' in *Ibid.*, 6 August, 1990.
14. *Foreign Affairs Record*, Vol. XXXVI, No. 1, January 1990 (New Delhi: 1990), pp. 18-19.
15. Rikhye Ravi, *The War that Never Was: The Story of India's Strategic Failures* (New Delhi : 1988), p. 2.
16. Moonis Ahmar, 'The Role of CBMs in the Post Cold War Era,'

ACDIS, Occasional Papers, October 1993 (Pakistan : 1993), pp. 9-10.

17. *Ibid.*, p. 15.
18. *The National Herald*, 30 June, 1990.
19. *The Hindustan Times*, 19 July, 1990.
20. *The Indian Express*, 12 August, 1990.
21. V.R. Raghavan, 'The Right Kind of War,' *The Hindustan Times*, 22 March, 2002.
22. As quoted in *Pakistan Times Overseas Weekly*, 4 November, 1984.
23. *India Today*, 15 July, 1992.
24. Harish Kapur, *India's Foreign Policy, 1947-92, Shadow and Substance* (New Delhi : Sage Publications, 1994), p. 29.
25. Sumantra Bose, *The Challenge in Kashmir, Democracy, Self-Determination and a Just Peace* (New Delhi : Sage Publications, 1997), p. 194.
26. Prakash Singh, 'Militancy from Kashmir to Coimbatore' *The Hindustan Times*, 23 February, 1998.
27. C. Uday Bhaskar, 'Strategic Implications of the Proxy War,' in *Ibid.*, 18 August, 1998.
28. As quoted in Anita Kanungo, 'Peace Pangs', in *Ibid.*, 7 August, 2000.
29. *The Illustrated Weekly of India*, 10-16 October, 1992, p. 4.
30. Sumantra Bose, *Kashmir, Roots of Conflict, Paths to Peace* (New Delhi: Vistaar Publications, 2003), p. 163.
31. Udayan Sharma, 'Kashmir's Anti-National Jamaat-e-Islami,' *Sunday*, 2 December, 1979.
32. *Ibid.*
33. Sumantra Bose, *Kashmir, Roots of Conflict, Paths to Peace*, p. 142.
34. *Ibid.*, p. 295.
35. Brahma Chellaney, 'An Act of War,' *The Hindustan Times*, 18 December 2001.
36. *Kashmir Times*, 23 December, 2001.
37. Sumantra Bose, *Kashmir, Roots of Conflict, Paths to Peace*, pp. 145-47.
38. *Ibid.*, p. 126.
39. Gwynne Dyer, 'The Slow Decline of Terror,' *The Hindustan Times*, 24 August 1998.
40. Ashok K. Mehta, 'The Truth About the Proxy War,' in *Ibid.*, 11 August, 1998.
41. *The Hindu*, 15 May, 1990.
42. *Ibid.*

43. Ved Marwah, 'Hostage to Misrule,' *The Hindustan Times*, 16 July, 1998.
44. Michael Krepon, 'Forbearance is the Key Word,' in *Ibid.*, 14 October, 2001.
45. Sumantra Bose, *Kashmir, Roots of Conflicts, Paths to Peace*, pp. 125-26.
46. *Ibid.*, p. 94.
47. As quoted in Victoria Schofield, *Kashmir in Conflict* (London : 1996), p. 231.
48. *The Indian Express*, 23 February, 1997.
49. *Indian Recorder*, Vol. IV, No. 15, April 9-15, 1997 (New Delhi : 1997), p. 2726.
50. Rajkumar Singh, *Indo-Pak Nuclear Tension 1974-1998* (New Delhi: Samiksha Prakashan, 2001), pp. 103-4.
51. *Ibid.*, p. 126.
52. *The Hindustan Times*, 3 July, 2000.
53. Brahma Chellaney, 'Pakistan as Problemistan,' in *Ibid.*, 8 July, 2002.
54. Manoj Joshi, 'The Marathon Begins,' in *Ibid.*, 30 June, 2004.

6

Ethnic Terrorism in Sri Lanka

Sri Lanka is suffering the problem of ethnicity and struggling to establish peace and social stability since independence. The communal and ethnic conflicts, the separatist tendencies, inter-state terrorism and the practice of militarisation are the prolong challenges to the nation. The ethnic tension in Sri Lanka is between the Sinhalese and the Lanka Tamils. The present tragedy is the result of political and cultural rivalry between them, and the ineptitude of the national leadership in reconciling their differences.[1] The chauvinistic and obstinate attitude of both the sides aggravated the ethnic problem which led to the creation of space for the secessionist tendencies against the unity and integrity of Sri Lanka and demand of independent state. The conflict is manifested in a variety of ways ranging from political protest to ethnic violence and terrorist insurgencies to guerilla warfare. Ethnic conflicts arise when the multi-ethnic personality of such a state-centric nation is not adequately expressed in its power structure and its political system. If it is reduced to the virtual dominance of the major ethnic group, then the very rationale of the 'nation' is jeopardised and provokes political self-assertion of minority ethnic groups.[2] Despite its small size, the island of Sri Lanka is marked by a relatively wide diversity of ethnic groups, divided by language, religion, and to a lesser extent by caste.

Ethnicity With Different Dimensions

The terms 'ethnic and ethnicity' are used to include religious, racial, linguistic, tribal and similar divides which have been activated in socio-political conflict in the present age. It is associated with a sense of identity arising from shared customs, language and culture, physical characteristics, and so on, and would appear to be far removed from the material categories of economic and social life. As a category in modern political system conflict exists at the level of consciousness; but it is a reflection in consciousness of very real, concrete and material circumstances.[3] In modern world there is a wealth of literature attempting to define and discuss ethnicity. Anthony D. Smith places ethnicity in the context of modernisation and Cynthia Enloe examines the issue in the context of power and authority, while John Saul looks at the issues of tribe in relation to imperialism and the modes of production debate.[4] The ethnic conflicts have assumed major proportions and have become an important feature of political life in the final quarter of this century. The scale, intensity and persistence of these conflicts provide persuasive evidence that we are not dealing with these conflicts as fundamental determinants of history.

The first exposure in ethnic identity came from consciousness and material circumstances. Consciousness does not reflect material reality in some mechanistic way; and indeed a consciousness of ethnic identity can persist long after the material foundations that endangered it have withered away, or it can emerge in advance of the proper consolidation of an immanent identity. In general the material circumstance that underlies an ethnic unit is illustrated by drawing attention to the periphery, or boundary of a socio-economic unit which possesses its own internal structures or mode of production. Though ethnicity as a category in political conflict and the concomitant consciousness of identity are linked in this way to material life, yet slowly and tortuously, ethnicities disappear or become politically irrelevant.[5] For example, the Boers and the blacks of South Africa do not even today co-habit the same material socio-economic entity, their material transformations ultimately led them finally align itself with reality, but not until it has exhausted its own tortuous and extended life span. Its natural outcome is ethnic war and negotiation processes.

Ethnic war is a large-scale violent incident entailing an organised and prolonged military engagement and confrontation between regular (government) forces and highly mobilised insurgent or militant group(s). There is continuity in fighting; military attacks/operations are extended over a considerable part of the country's territory. Importantly, the warring parties and their grievances and goals are solely defined in ethnic terms. Whereas the government represents the dominant/majority ethnic group, civilians belonging to the minority/weaker ethnic community invariably constitute the insurgent or militant forces.[6] Like inter-state wars, internal ethnic wars are serious hostile events. Hostility does not develop in vacuum or automatically, but stems from deep-rooted socio-economic and political grievances that can not be redressed by normal political means. In most cases, grievances are genuine and serious. Even ethnic fear of extinction does not always evolve itself in a direct form to become a major source of ethnic war.[7] A long history of denial of legitimacy to or lack of recognition of, a group's identity in relation to its ethnic territoriality and its growing sense of relative deprivation, defined as a perceived gap between value expectations and value capabilities, may initially appear to be a mere ethnic grievance but, in the long run, creates a fear of its extinction.

However, grievance-formation as a principal source of ethnic war is a dynamic process in which each ethnic group with seemingly different ethno-ideological and value structures try to consolidate and promote its identity and material interests from a threat or invalidating behaviour of other groups. Ethnic war is deep-rooted in a situation, where one group's core sense of self interest is perceivably or in reality threatened by the demands of or denial by another group, thereby eliciting the former group's defensive response.[8] Ethnic wars are not fought over ordinary issues or for limited goals. Fighting a war is fundamentally the decision of the concerned group in pursuit of its own interests in that gains and losses are borne by its members. The warring parties belong to two different ethnic groups with strong identities based on distinct historical antecedents, heritage, culture, language and religion, but both of them form part of the same political system at least in the legal sense.

Ethnicity has gained prominence in South Asian politics today for two additional reasons. First, the growth of sectarian political parties throughout the region has amplified and redirected ethnic issues to the political limelight. These parties have arisen, or have been resurrected by parochial interests, because of the government's inadequacy or inability to remove ethnic grievances. These parties differ from national parties in that they have a narrow political base; represent the interests of only particular ethnic groups or segments thereof; and are dedicated to achieving political ends through violence. Second, the ethnic factor in South Asian politics is sustained also by the international role of the regional countries. For example, the Pakhtunistan movement in the NWFP has been inspired and sustained by successive Afghan governments and the Lanka-Tamil secessionist movement received full support from the neighbouring Indian state Tamil Nadu.[9] Likewise, the tribal in the Bangladesh CHT are deriving sustenance from the neighbouring Indian tribal movements in Mizoram, Tripura and Manipur.

Especially in the case of ethnicity in South Asia, the pursuit of colonial policies inevitably led to discrimination against certain ethnic groups which remained unresolved during that period. When the colonial masters withdrew they did not leave behind them a society with a strong potential ruling class in place. The other side of the same coin is the economic backwardness and the weakness and distortion of the productive forces in these countries. Hence, the nature of the state in newly independent countries and its interaction with class formation is unstable and tottering. Earlier, it was in the interest of the colonial authorities to encourage internal differentiation within the subject population. The positive impact of this policy was that the rich cultural diversities in the subcontinent were preserved and endangered, while its negative impact was that these gave rise to numerous parochial attachments. Although the national policies of the new ruling elites in post-independence period attempted to rectify historical anomalies or reorder political realities, it, however, only aggravated ethnic feelings or created new ethnic tension.

At large the issue of ethnicity is closely related to nation building and internal stability. Initially the pattern of political development was on the line of Western notions of modernisation and its leaders hoped that with the ongoing process of modernisation, parochial attachments would simply disappear. In course of time and with the rapid expansion of communication and transportation networks, the ethnicity in the region has invalidated most of these assumptions associated with the national development process. As a result within each country, the separate cultural identities of regions, far from losing social significance and becoming blurred, have in fact reasserted their cultural/regional identities by politically mobilising themselves in order to confront the state system which has failed to recognise or protect their interests. They have rejected the continued validity of national symbols and values and have redirected their allegiance to ethnic symbols and values in order to fight for greater influence within their societies.[10] In most cases the discriminatory policies of the national leadership have made ethnic communities to rise above parochial attachments to form a unified political order.

In the context of ethnicity, instability is a condition in which the established political order is under challenge because of policies that directly and adversely affect certain ethnic interests. In extreme situations this may lead to partial disintegration of the polity while in less serious instances, primordial sentiments tend to reassert themselves. In the circumstances, the best that can be hoped for is to contain them.[11] But we must recognise the fact that often the premordial sentiments are not necessarily obstacles to internal stability; rather institutionalised discriminations that lead to ethnic cleavages are the actual causes of instability within a polity. To attain any measure of permanence in internal stability in political systems, structural and attitudinal changes are a must. The first structural change in this direction should be the restoration of a democratic set up where it is absent as in Pakistan, and, where it is present, its redefinition be in manner that the majority tyranny does not become the order of the day as has been in the case of Bangladesh and Sri Lanka. Above all a sense of fairness and justice must also prevail among those who exercise effective decision making power, so that they are not perceived to represent the exclusive interests of a particular ethnic group. They must transcend narrow interests and formulate policy options that seek to benefit all groups within the polity.

Ethnicity in Sri Lankan Context

The ethnic peace is eluding in Sri Lanka as divergence exists in trying to date the ethnic conflict between the Sinhalese majority community and the Tamil minority. Recently the victory has been achieved on the military front, but there is no advance on the political front. The country is multi-ethnic in nature with varied racial and religious groups inhabiting the island. In Sri Lanka, there is no Christian or Buddhist ethnicity: there are Sinhalese and Tamil ones. It is also an interesting part of the history of Sri Lanka that the two principal communities, Sinhalese and Tamil, originated from India. The first to come in the island were the Sinhalese. Later the Tamils attacked the Sinhalese and ruled a part of Sri Lanka and maintained there supremacy in the northern part of the country. The rivalry between these two communities has not died out yet and has an important bearing on the political life and history of the country.[12] Thus, the root of the present long bloody ethnic conflict that the nation has seen in recent times is the result of historical competition and enmity. In addition, the linguistic and religious cleavages tend to reinforce each other, that is, the members of each major linguistic group tend to share the same religion. For instance, the Tamils including Tamil Christians take one side and Sinhalese including Christians, the other one. It is because the Tamil Christians were internal to and a part of Tamil or Jaffna society, economy, trade, agriculture and so on. Similarly Sinhalese Christians were internal to another cohesive socio-economic unit.[13] Physical structures of the island nation have contributed to the widening chasm between the two ethnic communities in Sri Lanka, the Sinhalese and the Tamils.

The two major ethnic communities of Sri Lanka–the Sinhalese and the Tamils are poles apart from language, religion and cultural points of view. The Sinhalese are a distinct ethnic group speaking the Indo-Aryan language Sinhala. They trace their origin to north India, claiming to be the earliest civilised inhabitants on the island. Most of the Sinhalese practise a variant of Theravada Buddhism which had received continuous support from the rulers since it was introduced on the island in the 3rd century B.C. Most Sinhalese consider themselves today to be the protectors of Buddhism. While the Tamils as a minority group have a distinct identity in racial and cultural terms. They trace their ancestry to the same period as that of the Sinhalese arrival. They are mostly Hindus and speak the south Indian Dravidian language Tamil. A significant number of them have converted to Christianity after the arrival of European powers. However, they both had the same legal status in Sri Lanka during the British rule.

The origin of ethnicity can be traced back in the 1920s when the Indian Tamils started first in the form of a cooperative movement and later under the Jaffna Youth Congress a social movement against caste distinctions in Sri Lanka.[14] It was the result of the reluctance of the Sinhalese to take to the regimented life of the estates. The period also witnessed arising of a political question relating to the representation in legislature. It posed a threat to the Sinhalese who were opposed to giving the large numbers of Indians the right to vote as recommended by the Donoughmore Commision in 1928. From the view of Sinhalese it meant I. a dilution of the electoral strength of the Kandyan Sinhalese in most of the constituencies in the Kandyan areas; II. the possibility of Indian Tamils being returned as representatives of Kandyan Sinhalese constituencies in the event of the splitting of the Kandyan Sinhalese vote between rival candidates ; and III. the likelihood, especially at the time of the Donoughmore reforms of British planters, and/or Indian state Kanganies herding the Indian vote in favour of the candidate of their choice. Later in 1929 the report of the Commission was debated in the Ceylon Legislative Council and the provision relating to the franchise of the Indian immigrants was modified by imposing several restrictions and the communal character of representation continued even thereafter.

Earlier the changes effected in the composition of the Legislative Council in 1909 and 1920 did not go far enough to satisfy the Ceylonese reforms, but in 1923 the Legislative Council was expanded so as to have a majority of Ceylonese unofficial members with a large elective element.[15] At this stage a cleavage occurred between the Sinhalese and the Ceylon Tamils. While the latter with the support from other majority groups, namely Indians, Muslims, Burghers and Europeans, wished communal representation to be maintained, the Sinhalese reformers asked for the introduction of the territorial principle. In other words, both communities–the Sinhalese and the Tamils became principal rivals in establishing their cultural superiority and administrative hegemony over the other. Family and familiar locality is often of central significance in the nourishment of loyalty to group and its associated territorial space.[16] Thus in most instances a Sri Lankan's patriotism to his island entity is built upon local experiences and sentimentalities.

In the history and politics of Sri Lanka the Sinhalese and the Tamil communities are fragmented through customs and separate higher from lower orders. There is nearly a complete absence of inter-caste marriages. Several members of the lower status caste groups have seized the opportunities provided by the modern economic system, and have become wealthy. These differences in wealth have created wide class cleavages that cut across boundaries of caste, religion, and language. Because of all these divisions, Sri Lankan society is complex, with numerous points of conflict. The uneven capitalist development that was characteristic of the plantation raj created serious socio-economic divisions within the Sri Lankan society.

The ethnic identities in Sri Lanka strengthened especially in response to the growing influence of Christian religion and English language in matters of social and cultural living in the middle of 19th century. In the period Buddhist revivalist movement started in the country as it is the only nation in the world where Theravada Buddhism had the largest following. There was a Buddhist cultural movement to assert the rightful place of Buddhism and it established a special relationship between Buddhism, the Sinhalese people and the island. The central theme of the movement was that Sinhala Buddhists alone had the original rights to Sinhaladvipa and Dhammadvipa–the land of the Sinhalese and the land of Buddhism respectively. By the time of independence this type of Sinhalese-Buddhists ethno-nationalism had become a part of the popular thinking. This apart, a fear of Indian domination, particularly of being swamped by the Tamils from across the Palk Strait, figured prominently in the Sinhala-Buddhist discourse.

Almost by the same time in response to the evolution of ethnic identities in Sinhalese, the Tamils of the island felt threatened. In the line of Sinhala thinking, Tamils, Muslims, Christians or other non-Sinhalese did not have a place. Although decades before independence there was no such feeling and initially English educated Sinhalese and Tamil elites worked together for constitutional reforms. In 1919 they came together under the banner of Ceylon National Congress whose first president was Sir Ponnambalam, a prominent Tamil. But soon the differences between the two communities surfaced in 1920 following the constitutional reforms which introduced territorial representation. These differences centered on the question of communal representation. While the Sinhalese insisted upon representation according to population strength, the Sri Lankan Tamil wanted representation in excess of their numbers. The divergent racial-religious-linguistic congruence of the two communities of Sinhalese and Tamils is further accentuated by a territorial factor. The northern Tamil district being proximate to Tamil Nadu provided for easy inter-state contact and to worsen ethnic strife. This factor may lead to Tamil secessionist demands which posed a threat to the territorial integrity of Sri Lanka.[17] Inevitably along with such domestic factors that influenced the ethnic conflict in Sri Lanka, external forces have played a critical role in aggravating the conflict.

The Sinhalese and the Tamils are not separated by ethnic divide only, but educationally, psychologically and geographically, too. A recent study on the subject of national harmony revealed that there is no school in Ceylon where there is a positive, well-integrated and gradual programme for racial integration, working hand in hand with the community agencies, for the realisation of the aim of making the children better Ceylonese citizens. Under the psychological factor the Sinhalese tend on occasion to group the indigenous Tamils with the Tamils of south India and view them in their entirety as 'the Dravidian peril'. Geographically Tamils, in general, reside in the northern and eastern part of island

and the latter are conservative and community-conscious. Even when opportunities for employment and commerce took them to the Sinhalese areas, they developed there flourishing self-contained settlements of their own. These parting tendencies in both the communities developed and strengthened further due to the defective or biased progress in constitutional history of the nation.

Even culturally, the island Sri Lanka is divided into two nations, namely, Tamil and Sinhala. They have been rivals in the past; they are rivals in the present; and are likely to continue to be rivals in future. It is a mosaic of self aware communities distinguished from one another along ethnic, religious or linguistic basis. The political life of Sri Lanka has been closely bound up with these communal and other social differentiations. These traditional groupings formed the basis of politically most significant loyalties, interests and demands. The Sinhalese and Ceylon's Tamil communities could associate these loyalties with past kingdoms and with specific territories. Because of the force of historical traditions there emerged within Sri Lanka forms of identity among the majority Sinhalese and the minority Tamil communities of the country.[18] Although the policies of the British were guided by the objective of creating a homogeneous society in the island, advancement of social mobilisation generated new aspirations and demands and widened concerns with educational opportunities, urban employment and government services heighting the potential for communal conflict.[19] In fact, the nation building experiment in Sri Lanka was based on the language of the majority community, namely Sinhala and religion of the majority, namely Buddhism that further paved the direction of nationalism on the basis of communal identity.

The deterioration of relations between the two communities of Sri Lanka continued as before after independence of the island nation in 1948, but especially after 1956 when the 'Sinhala Only' policy was adopted by the then government. Earlier the Sinhalese and the Tamils were self-conscious about their differences and were mutually suspicious, they were not hostile prior to the language issue. It was the political controversy surrounding the language dispute in the first decade of independence that generated the most severe regional feelings among the Ceylon Tamils. Consequently, communal antagonism became sharper than they had been for generations. After the language controversy the Federal Party (FP) became the principal spokesman of the Ceylon Tamils, replacing its rival the Tamil Congress (TC) which had advocated responsive cooperation with United National Party (UNP) government. Years after independence the government of the day initiated discriminatory policies harming the interests of Tamils at large, creating vacuum for conflicts and antagonism between Sinhalese and Tamils. The issues of discrimination responsible for bringing tussle and bickering were language, administration, education, employment, colonisation of land and the power devolution.

Soon after independence, the island nation had adopted a Presidential system which was found unsuitable to the heterogeneous nature of Sri Lankan society pushing the country into ethnic mess. In fact, the unitary system in Sri Lanka had completely failed on account of the parochial and inhuman attitudes of the Sinhalese political society in satisfying the preserved aspirations of the multi-ethnic people and therefore, the demand of decentralisation and democratic processes had been raised continuously in order to accomplish socio-political equity. The Tamils claimed that due to Sinhalese majority, the Tamil minority can not get access in the political activities and participation in the governance and the decision making process of the country.[20] A strong section of the people believe even today that if Sri Lanka had been provided with the federal constitution at the time of independence, the Sinhalese and the Tamil leaders might have been able to bargain with each other from their political power bases at the centre and the region and the prolonged ethnic conflict could have been prevented.

The grievance-formation on the part of Tamils from the beginning led the making of Federal Party in Sri Lanka in 1949. It was totally devoted to the cause of a separate state for Tamil Eelam and in fact laid the foundation of two-nation theory in the country. It strongly pleaded in favour of a Tamil Eelam and stated in Party's resolution of 1951, 'The Tamil-speaking people of Sri Lanka constitute a nation distinct from that of Sinhalese by every fundamental test of nationhood ; firstly that of a separate historical past, in this island at least as ancient and glorious as that of Sinhalese ; secondly by the fact of their being a linguistic entity, entirely different from that of Sinhalese with as unsurpassed classical heritage and a modern development of language which makes Tamil fully adequate for all present day needs ; and finally by reason of their territorial habitation of definite areas, which constitute over one-third of the island.[21] The political failure of democratic system and chief political parties in resolving Tamil grievances led to the demand of a separate Tamil state, the Tamil Eelam.

Actually, the dysfunctional nature of island's democracy remained unable to make a convincing argument that all the problems that might arise within this could be resolved within the framework of democratic institutions. As a result of the politically active young people it had created a sense of nihilism, which considers everything as permissive. In the political field, it means a belief in violence for its own sake. In that kind of situation the whole young generation would have no political aspirations except for protest for its own sake reflects as to how deeply the dysfunctional nature of Sri Lankan democracy has affected the entire nation and particularly the young.[22] The abandonment of the rule of law and the authority of institutions which was already visible in 1958, became a much greater problem in the years that followed, with a similar political approach by subsequent governments and even radical experiments to undermine democracy and rule of law.

For the deteriorating ethnic situation of Sri Lanka, the political system adopted in 1948 and the succeeding governments that enjoyed power in a discriminatory manner were responsible. It is said that the history of relations between the Tamils and central government has been a succession of missed opportunities. Even before Independence under the self-government allowed by the British government since 1931, communalist attitudes dominated political life, culminating in the Tamil claim for parity of Parliamentary representation between the Sinhalese majority and the minorities. Almost in the span of thirty years the political life of the island nation was run by two major political parties– UNP and SLFP. In the first phase each of these parties had a nine-year tenure-the UNP from 1947 to 1956 and SLFP from 1956 to 1965. In the second the UNP with its allies had a five-year-run, 1965-1970, while the SLFP, with its partners completed its 1970-1977 term. Despite their long and repeated innings UNP and SLFP governments, which were clearly Sinhalese dominated, had toyed with the idea of concessions, and all promises came to nothing for the minorities of Sri Lanka.

The decade 1970s was a decisive one in the political life of Sri Lanka. Sinhalese-Tamil relations deteriorated considerably during the period of United Front rule 1970-77. The Federal Party withdrew in June 1971 from the proceedings of the Constituent Assembly when the latter voted out its resolution on language rights. In 1972, the majority of Tamil political groupings including the powerful Indian Tamil CWC formed the Tamil United Front (TUF) under the leadership of FP leader SJV Chelvanayagam for purposes of joint political action. In the same year Chelvanayagam on behalf of the TUF resigned his parliamentary seat to obtain a mandate for the establishment of a sovereign 'Eelam Tamil' nation. The TUF, in its convention in May 1976, changed its name to the Tamil United Liberation Front (TULF) resolving the restoration and reconstruction of free and sovereign, secular, socialist state of Tamil Eelam in order to safeguard the very existence of Tamil nation in this country. The Sinhalese paradigm of one country, one nation, one language and one people compelled Tamil youths to rise against Sinhalese chauvinism.

As a result of the policies of pro-Sinhala governments in Sri Lanka the two dominant sections of Tamil parties–the Federal Party and Tamil Congress united to form the Tamil United Liberation Front (TULF) in 1975 and it, in its Vaddukoddai resolution, adopted in 14 May, 1976, called for the creation of a separate Tamil state of Eelam. Besides citing the existence of historical Tamil Kingdom in the southern Jaffna districts as the legal basis for a claim to the Eelam state, nine additional reasons were given: the disfranchisement of Indian Tamils (1948 and 1949); Sinhalese colonisation of traditional Tamil lands; the Sinhala Only Act; the favoured position of Buddhism: inequality of opportunity; severance of ties with South India; permitting and unleashing communal violence against Tamils; terrorism against Tamil youth; and the 1972 constitution.[23] In reaction to the long biased policy of pro-Sinhala government Tamil militancy emerged in Tamil areas with plenty of Tamil militant organisations to fight for their rights against the unending oppressive rule.

With the Tamil political leaders, failure in political bargaining and power politics, Tamil youths raised arms against the government. The armed uprising gave birth to political violence as the only means. The armed struggle for the establishment of Tamil Eelam manifested in a variety of ways ranging from political protest to ethnic violence and terrorist insurgencies to guerilla warfare and ultimately the ethnic conflict became a central problem in Sri Lankan politics. It was the failure of many years of peaceful demonstration by Tamil leaders in order to win their freedom from the successive Sinhala majority governments, who showed no concern for the Tamil grievances. In addition, it was the result of political and cultural rivalry between the Sinhalese and the Lankan Tamils and the ineptitude of the national leadership in reconciling their differences.[24] While some have interpreted this ethnic rivalry as a clash between two 'subnationalism' that of the dominated Buddhist elite and of the minority Tamil elite of the northern peninsula,[25] more often it has been in political terms in which the Sinhalese have consistently sought to diminish the cultural and political salience of the Tamils in post-Independence Sri Lanka.

Entrance of Violence and Birth of LTTE

Terrorism in Sri Lanka began in 1970 with the formation of a militant student body called the Tamil Students Movement to protest government plans to limit access of Tamil students to universities. Very soon this movement went underground and turned to avert terrorist activities. Violence escalated in Jaffna from 1972 onwards, beginning with the publication of new constitution seen by the Tamil United Liberation Front (TULF) as anti-Tamil. The year 1972 witnessed the formation of two Tamil terrorist groups such as, the Tamil New Tigers (TNT) and Tamil Eelam Liberation Organisation (TELO), while other active Tamil guerilla groups included the People's Liberation Organisation of Tamil Eelam (PLOTE), the Tamil Eelam Liberation Army (TELA), the Eelam Peoples Revolutionary Front (EPRLF), and the Eelam Revolutionary Organisation of Students (EROS). They all were averse to political bargaining and sought an armed solution to the Tamil problem.

The political frustration had finally resulted in support for separatism, these same chauvinists were able to say that they had been right all along. Historically, each of the political parties–the UNP and the SLFP, while in opposition, had played the role of a spoilsport. Ever since 1948 whenever the Government had taken an initiative to offer some accommodation to the Tamils, the then opposition had sought to politicise the issue by whipping up chauvinistic sentiments among the majority Sinhalese population.[26] The evolution of Tamil extremism around the mid seventies was of crucial importance and also developed due to the passing away of two important politicians of Jaffna, namely, SJV Chelvanayagam, the founder leader of Federal Party, and G.G. Ponnambalam, founder of Tamil Congress. They both had been a great integrative and moderating force among the Tamils.

In the initial years, following the independence of Sri Lanka, it was believed that the country would soon attain political stability and the major ethnic groups would get integrated into one nation. But the chasm between the Sinhalese and the Tamil–the two major ethnic groups in Sri Lanka has widened since then and a fundamental shift took place in state society relations. Some in the country believe that elements within the ruling party actively promoted violence, partly to destabilise their own government in order to enhance their position in a factional struggle for control, and partly to embitter relations between Sinhalese and Tamils in order to promote Sinhalese hegemony. The government maintained that the riots were caused by violent separatist elements within the Tamil minority and by Marxists seeking to overthrow the regime and to promote a general conflagration.[27] The anti-Tamil riots of 1958 and the insurrection of 1971 were viewed by the government in this context.

The anti-Tamil riots of 1958 were remarkable for the manner in which Sinhalese society accepted them as triumphant violence. In the Sinhalese political consciousness, the violence of 1958 is regarded with pride. Violence was the means by which Tamils who had exceeded the behavioural limits of an ethnic minority could be put back in their proper subordinate place. In a society where ethnic relations are hierarchically ordered, ethnic violence then was also a structural mechanism of re-establishing domination and submission.[28] The aftermath of 1971 insurrection also witnessed how even a confrontation of limited violence between the state and anti-state forces could ultimately strengthen and expand the institutional bases of state violence. It was indeed during this confrontation that the state argument for political violence expanded to include the moralistic argument that the state had a legitimate right to exercise violence to protect the people, and that that right should be protected from public scrutiny.[29] In the post-1971 years, any minor political provocation was certain to evoke the violent responses of the state. In the face of a new situation, the character of the Sri Lankan police and armed forces had changed completely over the last decades. Whilst before 1971 they were simply a force for the maintenance of law and order, they later found themselves engaged in military operations, firstly in 1971 with the Janatha Vimukthi Peramuna (JVP) revolt and then, after 1974, with the increase in Tamil terrorist activity.

Around the mid-1970s the extremist Tamil groups had begun to demand a separate state of Tamil Eelam and had been carrying out a prolonged guerilla struggle. The violence unleashed by the Tamil guerillas and the counter violence by the Sri Lankan army had made Sri Lanka one of the notorious killing fields' of South Asia. To say that the state has increasingly become violent is both a truism and an understatement. Rather, violence no longer constitutes a hidden dimension of state power. Similarly, the way in which subordinate ethnic groups and social classes relate to each other and negotiate with the state has come to be characterised by a recurrent propensity to use collective violence as a means of articulating their demands. The tendency to use violence for political purposes now exists alongside conventional adherence to the rules of parliamentary competition and electoral bargaining. State-centric and counter-state violence represent a qualitative shift in the dominant mode of political bargaining in South Asian societies today. In this sense violence is also a means by which the contending parties are engaged in the negotiating process.

Especially in the case of Sri Lanka the process of violence is being normalised in individual as well as social relations. The militarisation of social and individual relations in Sri Lanka has also been accompanied by militarisation of political conflicts. For instance, the pattern of the ethnic conflict in the 1980s was that the state, Sinhalese nationalist forces and Tamil nationalist groups came to regard armed confrontation as the only plausible mechanism to resolve ethnic antagonism. Even in the early 1990s irrespective of occasional utterances to the contrary by parties to the conflict, the advocacy and practice of a military solution remained so pervasive that there was very little social space for a non-militaristic alternative to the ethnic war.[30] It demonstrated, first of all, that the outcome of the conflict would depend largely on the capacity and willingness of the protagonists to be ruthlessly brutal and violent, not only against each other, but also against a society reduced to the status of a terrorised onlooker. It also showed that the capacity of the state to use violence against its domestic adversaries had virtually no bounds-material, political or moral.

In the situation, there has been a mass acceptance of political violence, practised by the state and anti-state forces alike in the recent history of Sri Lanka. Until the late 1970s, Sri Lanka experienced relative social peace, except on two occasions: the anti-Tamil riots of 1958 and the youth insurgency of April 1971. The ethnic riots of 1958 were fairly widespread; for the first time in independent Sri Lanka, both state violence and mob violence were deployed against Tamil civilians. The insurgency of 1971 was a different manifestation of political violence: an attempt made by a political movement of Sinhalese youth to capture state power through an armed rebellion. And now the Sri Lankan society has accepted political violence as a legitimate mode of political behaviour, whether by the state or anti-state forces. Contemporary Sinhalese Buddhism has moved towards openly advocating state violence of the ethnic kind; it has openly campaigned for intensifying the war effort of the state against Tamil separatist movements. Violence has become a norm in the present political culture, and it is a phenomenon normalised in all forms of political practices of the state as well as of counter-state formations. As a result of the ethnic conflicts the relations between the Sinhalese and the Tamils became militaristic, a development which was to have far-reaching implications for Sri Lankan politics. On the other hand, gradually, the state has also demonstrated that in the exercise of violence it could be far more brutally innovative than the rebels.

Among the ethnic terror organisations, formed so far in the whole history of Sri Lanka, was the Liberation Tigers of Tamil Eelam (LTTE). It was founded on 5 May, 1976 under the leadership of Velupillai Prabakaran. The LTTE was avowed to achieve a separate state or Eelam through bloody and violent confrontation with the Sri Lankan state what had become unachievable by peaceful methods in over 28 years after independence of the country. Prabakaran, keeping all the developments in view, became a strong believer in violence and in 1972 formed the Tamil New Tigers (TNT) when most of the Tamil youths lost their patience in reform methods adopted by the Tamil Parliamentarians. Soon Prabakaran became a wanted man known to the Jaffna police when he, in 1975 gunned down Alfred Duryappa, the mayor of Jaffna when he was on way to a Hindu temple. Prabakaran drew up the charter and helped design the LTTE crest, a roaring tiger at atop two crossed rifles and a halo of bullets set against a blood-red background. The Tiger had been the symbol of the Cholas, a Tamil dynasty which had dominated medieval South Asia.[31] For him no sacrifice was too great for the objective of Eelam.

The Liberation Tigers of Tamil Eelam was a separatist organisation, which from the beginning, waged a violent secessionist campaign and sought to create an independent Tamil state in the north and east of Sri Lanka. For its avowed purpose the LTTE had carried out civilian massacres, suicide bombings and various other high profile attacks, including the assassinations of several high ranking Sri Lankan and Indian politicians. They invented the suicide belt and pioneered the use of suicide bombing as a tactic. The world leader in suicide terrorism was the Tamil Tigers in Sri Lanka–they were a Marxist group, a secular group, a Hindu group. The Tamil Tigers have committed more suicide terrorist attacks than Hamas or Islamic Jihad. Instead, what more than 95 per cent of all suicide terrorist attacks since 1980 have in common is not religion, but a specific goal: to compel modern democracies to withdraw military forces from the territory the terrorists view as their homeland, From Lebanon to Chechnya to Kashmir to Sri Lanka to the West Bank, every suicide terrorist campaign since 1980s has had as its main objective to compel a democratic state to withdraw combat forces from territory that the terrorists prize.

In Sri Lanka, soon after its formation, the LTTE emerged as perhaps the most lethal, well organised and disciplined terrorist force in the world. Its operation area in Sri Lanka can be divided into three regions: I. In the northern threatre included Jaffna, Killinochchi and Mullaitivu districts and there the LTTE employed high and mid-intensity warfare. Since the mid-1990s, semi-conventional and unconventional insurgent and terrorist methods are also being used. With the loss of the peninsula in 1996 the LTTE had reverted to unconventional warfare, mostly sparrow tactics–hit and run methods. In the mainland, mostly in Wanni, the LTTE engaged the Sri Lankan troops semi-conventionally. This has become possible after the LTTE acquired artillery and heavy mortars. II. In the eastern threatre falls Batticaloa, Trincomalee and Amparai districts where the LTTE stationed high, mid and low intensity warfare. Dependent on the LTTE force level, it will engage the troops semi-conventionally or unconventionally. However, insurgent and terrorist tactics predominate. III. In southern threatre, LTTE's operations have been largely focussed on the Colombo, the capital. By targeting financial nerve centres and political leaders this divisionary tactic of the LTTE had been highly effective. After steadily shifting the threatre of terror into the seat of the country's administration, LTTE's elimination of political and military leaders has adversely affected the morale of the security forces.

Since its formation the LTTE had continued to pursue its objectives of a separate, independent Tamil Eelam through its policy of indiscriminate killing of all those the LTTE considered stood in its way, be they Sinhala or Tamil.[32] Soon after the formation LTTE had grown out to be massive army with the whole hearted support of the Tamil people and some years later it maintained thousand of brave soldiers, with a naval wing that had become a formidable in the subcontinent. In that kind of situation the LTTE had become the army that the Tamil people could look up to in order to put an end to all the troubles and win back the Tamil's homeland, Tamil Eelam. Barring a few terrorist attacks earlier, the LTTE carried out their first major attack on 23 July, 1983 when they ambushed a Sri Lanka army troop transport outside Jaffna in which 13 Sri Lankan soldiers were killed. The incident led to the Black July riots against the Tamil community of Sri Lanka. Large scale anti Tamil violence in the form of riots erupted in July-August 1983 in which at least several hundred people, almost all of whom were Tamils, were killed. It led many Tamils to spontaneously support all Tamil militant groups that came up in its wake.[33] In post-1983 period the subsequent anger amongst the Tamil community resulted in numerous Tamil youths joining Tamil militant groups to fight the Sri Lankan government, what is considered start of the insurgency in Sri Lanka.

From here onwards the LTTE had begun its armed conflict with Sri Lankan government and relied on guerilla strategy that included the use of terrorist tactics. The Tiger had integrated a battlefield insurgent strategy with a terrorist programme that targeted not only key personnel in the countryside but also senior Sri Lankan political and military leaders in Colombo and other urban centres. After it the LTTE had made its organisational structure wide and placed immense emphasis on the cult of martyrdom. It maintained a fleet known as Sea Tigers and carried out air raids using Czechoslovak-built propeller-engined trainers. Since the late 1980s the LTTE had conducted approximately two hundred suicide attacks. Targets have included transit hubs, Buddhist shrines, and office buildings. According to the Federal Bureau of Investigation (FBI), the LTTE invented the suicide belt and pioneered the use of women in suicide attacks. In later years the LTTE had strengthened itself significantly in Sri Lanka and abroad.

Viewing the gravity of ethnic situation in the country J.R. Jayawardene, the president of Sri Lanka, on 19 July, 1987 proposed the creation of an autonomous unit comprising the Northern and Eastern provinces and other related provisions were also made in the scheme. In post-1983 period India tried out all possibilities supporting the Tamil cause and militancy, helping the Sri Lanka government and the Tamils to resolve their differences across the table, working with Sri Lanka to help evolve a consensus on devolution of Tamils and lastly, underwriting an acceptable minimum package for Tamils in Sri Lanka through the accord.[34] On 29 July, 1987 an Accord was signed between India and Sri Lanka under which New Delhi committed to uphold Sri Lanka's sovereignty and territorial integrity on the condition that Colombo would grant a reasonable amount of autonomy to Tamils to their satisfaction. Following the provisions of the accord India sent a peace-keeping force to ensure that peace returned to strife-torn Tamil areas. In operational terms this meant the disarming of the LTTE cadres. Before India intervened in 1987, more than 37 Tamil militant groups came into being. All these groups except the LTTE surrendered arms after signing the accord in 1987.

The refusal of the LTTE made the accord irrelevant in context of establishing ethnic peace in the country. But processes-surrender of arms as well as cessation of hostilities were repudiated by the LTTE leadership on 7 October, 1987, when they retaliated against the capture at sea by Sri Lankan forces of thirteen of their senior cadres. The Indian Peace-keeping Force (IPKF) which came to the island nation as part of the Accord had to face a rough weather in the trouble-plagued Sri Lanka. The 1987 Accord ran into trouble within months after the LTTE took up arms against the IPKF. In response IPKF inaugurated their own military campaign against the Tigers on 10 October, 1987 which lasted for about two years. Now the IPKF got bogged down in a guerilla war against the Tamil Tigers which made essential a progressive increase in its numbers as well as in the number and range of its weaponary.[35] The operation which started off as a conventional one in 1987 quickly changed into a full-fledged country insurgency campaign. However, on this count the LTTE proved itself.

As a result of IPKF campaign against the LTTE, the latter confined to the Wanni jungles and within a year it became a spent force in Sri Lanka. Within a year of the IPKF completing Operation Checkmate-1, normal life was restored in the north-east. The direct fight of LTTE cadres against the Indian Peace-keeping Force caused the death of 1,255 Indian soldiers on Sri Lankan soil during their two years' stayal in the island nation. But it was not so good for the health of LTTE because its strength as the most powerful of the Tamil guerilla groups in the island had depended to a large extent on the moral and material support that it derived from Tamil Nadu state, at times both from the government and opposition ranks in the state, generally from the Tamil public and on occasion even from central government agencies such as Research and Analysis Wing (RAW). On the other the ruthlessness of Operation Pawan, launched to win control of the Jaffna from the LTTE, this campaign and the Indian army's subsequent anti-LTTE operations made the IPKF extremely unpopular among many Tamils in Sri Lanka.

Outside Support and Strategy

The freedom struggle of Tamil Eelam was not limited to the people of Tamil Eelam alone. Without the help of Tamil Diaspora spread around the world, it would become an uphill task for the Tamil people in Tamil Eelam to free themselves from the oppressive rule of the Sinhalese dominated Sri Lankan government. It is the responsibility of each Tamil world wide to ensure that the birth rights of the Tamils in Tamil Eelam are won to enable them to live in freedom and dignity. Realising this, the Tamil Diaspora is actively involved in various forms of nonviolent activities to expose the dark and ugly face of Sri Lankan state terrorism. Eelam web showcases some of these activities worldwide for the benefit of fair-minded people who care about the freedom of the Tamils of Tamil Eelam. The LTTE runs a wide network of publicity and propaganda activities with offices and cells located in at least 54 countries. The largest and most important centres are located in leading Western states with large Tamil expatriate communities, most notably the UK, France, Germany, Switzerland, Canada and Australia. In addition to these states they are also known to be represented in countries as far-flung as Cambodia, Burma, South Africa and Botswana. Its publicity networks covering Europe, Australia and North America also include radio and television.

The Liberation Tigers of Tamil Eelam received a substantial support in its avowed aim of achieving a separate Tamil state, called Tamil Eelam, from its narcotics business spread all over the world. The history of narcotics in the country goes back to the late 1970s when Tamil smugglers started carrying heroin into Sri Lanka from India. With the 1979 Soviet invasion of Afghanistan and the Fundamentalist revolution in Iran, the traditional smuggling routes used by many Afghan/Pakistan opium and heroin producers became severely disrupted, and the Sri Lankan Tamil soon provided a new way of getting their drugs to market elsewhere in the world. However, it also affected the society of the island nation and Sri Lanka found that the number of heroin addicts on the island was growing rapidly. Between 1983 and 1993, the number of addicts there grew to 50,000. Tamils also began running heroin into Western Europe by 1984 and in some significant incidents 204 Tamils were arrested in Italy during an investigation into a heroin smuggling ring. In the same year the Swiss police had found that Tamil refugees carried some 20 per cent of the heroin brought into their country. While by 1988, the Italian police had broken up four rings of Tamil heroin smugglers. In those days the business of narcotics proliferated easily in capitalist countries because the then Warsaw Pact nations were unwilling to ignore narcotics smuggling just because the intended market was inside the Capitalist West.

From 1985 until the early 1990s the intelligence estimate indicated that heroin from Pakistan and Afghanistan had risen from 20 to 65% of the Canadian market. Tamil traffickers had a part of that market and one ring was mentioned in 1991. One Tamil trafficker, Veeravagu Velmurugu, who entered Canada in 1984 as a refugee from the United States had been jailed in Canada for life for heroin trafficking. The Tigers also positioned themselves to be able to take advantage of heroin from South-east Asia. They established a naval base for themselves on the Island of Twante, offBurma–the worlds's leading source for herion from that part of the world. The LTTE also owned its own shipping line, and have reportedly used their own merchant ships to smuggle heroin into Europe. The American government was also aware of LTTE involvement with heroin in and around southern Thailand and Burma, but in the absence of any direct threat to the US from the Tigers, the resources of their Drug Enforcement Agency were focussed elsewhere. In addition, the Liberation Tigers of Tamil Eelam was also involved actively in human trafficking and people smuggling. The human trafficking and people smuggling were the common activity of the LTTE at international level. And by their illegal engagements worldwide, the terrorist outfit arrange for itself heavy amount in the form of foreign currency and invest the procured money in purchasing of arms and ammunitions for their cadres. It was the base or dependent source of their finance which led to various terrorist activities on Sri Lankan soil.

The LTTE had been greatly benefited by its sophisticated international support network from the decade 1980s. While some of the funding obtained by the LTTE was from legitimate fund raising and extortion among Tamil diaspora, a significant portion was obtained through criminal activities, involving sea piracy, human smuggling, drug trafficking and gunrunning. Apart from this the outfit, LTTE nourished and maintained a give and take relationship with other terrorist groups and the world terror groups including Al- Qaeda have learnt a lot from the LTTE in sphere of terrors' method and technique. The website 'South Asian Terrorism Portal' stated that there are increasing intelligence reports that the LTTE was smuggling arms to various terrorist organisations including Islamic groups in Pakistan and their counterparts in Philippines, using their covert smuggling network. The London-based International Institute for Strategic Studies found that the LTTE was building commercial links with Al-Qaeda and other militants in Afghanistan, and that several cadres were spotted in Afghan militant camps. According to Glen Jenvey, a specialist on international terrorism, the Al-Qaeda has copied most of its terror tactics from the LTTE. He highlighted the LTTE as the mastermind that sets the pattern for organisations like Al-Qaeda to pursue. Even the LTTE's ethnic cleansing campaigns against Muslims in northern Sri Lanka from 1985-1992 provided the inspiration for, and model by which, Kashmiri separatists evicted Hindus from Kashmir in late 1989-1990.

In the 1990s and thereafter the LTTE became a terrorist organisation of world-fame and in later years it had been listed by 32 countries as a terrorist organisation. The first country to ban the LTTE was its early ally, India. The Indian change of policy came gradually, starting with the IPKF-LTTE conflict, and culminating with the assassination of Rajiv Gandhi. It followed a chain of countries banning the outfit–United States (1997), United Kingdom (2000), Australia (2001), Europian Union (2006), Canada (2006). On 8 October, 1997 the United States of America included Sri Lanka's Liberation Tigers of Tamil Eelam in a list of 30 foreign terrorist organisations and barred from entering or collecting funds in the US. It was done under section 219 of the Immigration & Nationality Act as was re-evaluated on 2 November, 2001 and also in the light of a Specially Designated Global Terrorist (SDGT) under Executive Order 13224. The declaration said that the members of the designated group would be ineligible for US visas and their funds would be frozen under a new anti-terrorism law signed by President Bill Clinton in April 1996. As of today it is a crime to provide funds, weapons or other types of tangible support to any of the designed organisations.[36] Later in February 1999 US Assistant Secretary of State, when visited Colombo made it clear that the US would not like to be a mediator. It would, however, be quite happy to be a facilitator or be part of a group of facilitators, if it was called upon to assume that role by the two parties to the conflict.[37] According to the US Federal Bureau of Investigation the LTTE has perfected the use of suicide bombers, invented the suicide belt, pioneered the use of women in suicide attacks, murdered thousands of people and assassinated two world leaders– the only terrorist organisation to do so.

However, there was also the other side of the coin. Countries that provide a strong base of support for LTTE activities abroad include Canada, the US, and the UK. These countries are incidentally home to large Tamil immigrant communities and some of the parliamentarians in these countries opted to champion the ethnic problem to ensure votes to remain in parliament. Many of the Western countries viewed the ethnic problem in Sri Lanka a bigger combination involving caste/classdifferences between Jaffna Tamils and Eastern Tamils, the Christian factor–all forms of differentiations that actually divide the Tamils which are yet to be resolved. They considered it as the issue of self-determination along with human rights and humanitarian help without any extent. Many of the local and foreign NGOs/INGOs that sympathise with the LTTE are also of the view that the ethnic issue of Sri Lanka is closely related to their desire for self-determination and that they are really concerned with the welfare of the innocent people of the country. Perhaps it was the general opinion of the world at large that delayed Colombo to ban the LTTE only in January 1999. The same year in March the banning of LTTE by the US government was challenged in an American appeal court. In the district of Colombia court of appeal, Ramsey Clark, the LTTE lawyer, told the court that the LTTE would be able to refute the charges made against it, if given an opportunity, 'Millions of Tamils, who have a rich culture from an ancient civilisation and who are now fighting for self-determination and dignity, have come to the United States courts hoping that they will get justice'.[38] But the US government, and the Congress continue to view the LTTE as terrorist, and are keen on keeping it on the list of banned organisations.

After India signed the Indo-Sri Lanka Agreement in 1987, the LTTE had been functioning out of different parts of Southeast Asia. According to analysts, a base in South-east Asia offered several advantages to the LTTE. Given the extensive network of Sri Lankan Tamils living abroad, thousands of them becoming economic refugees, a lot of funds were also being collected around the world, from Canada and Australia to South Africa, Europe and the UK.

They channeled these funds, providing logistic support to the LTTE in eastern Sri Lanka and earning some profits out of the fleet of vessels that its front organisation owned. They also added that Singapore was the first choice of the Tamil Tigers but the outfit also realised that operating out of that city state involved a lot of restraint and regulation after the 1992-93 crack down of the Singapore Government and it was forced to shift the bulk of its operations to other centres.[39] In the circumstances, the Tamil Tigers found a congenial setting in both Myanmar and Thailand. The availability of a number of tiny islands between these two countries, some of them uninhabited, provided a convenient base for the LTTE to function.

Initially, the LTTE preferred to tie-up with the military junta in Myanmar and made use of the country's port as well as islands for its trade and transshipment. It was also the period when the Tamil Tigers were smuggling in a lot of weapons from the former Soviet Union states and procuring some from Cambodia and Thailand. The group had close links to the Khmer Rouge, the Cambodian army and the Government in Phnom Penh. It bought arms and ammunition from all three channels, because all of them were facing a resource crunch. The visa–on arrival facility, the high level of corruption and the French connection that Cambodia provided were all advantageous to the Tamil Tigers. When Myanmar applied some pressure on the LTTE to move out of its territory, the Tigers took refugee in small islands of Thailand, near Phuket. This provided a much more convenient link, because Phuket also had a fairly well-connected airport.[40] However, there was also a limit the Sri Lankan government could exert pressure on LTTE at abroad. Some of its commercial activities may even be legal and very profitable and the host government may not be able to halt them.

In June 1990 when the peaceful relations between the Government of Sri Lanka and LTTE ended, most probably, the Israeli experts have joined hands with the LTTE in the north-east and also supplied weapons, and trained their cadres. Earlier the same year in May a report published in *The Newyork Times* revealed Israeli connections with the outfit as early as 1984. The intermediary was Dr. Subramanian Swamy, a former Indian Member of Parliament, a top Israeli lobbyist and pro-Eelam activist.[41] He asserted that he had helped to establish contact between the LTTE and David Matnai, who was the head of the Israeli Interests Section in Colombo.

Later this information was confirmed by the controversial book written by Victor Ostrovsky and Claire Hoy, entitled, *By Way of Deception: The Making and Unmaking of a Mossad Officer*. It said that the Tamil militants were trained simultaneously with government security forces in the same military base at Kafar Sirkin.[42] The book claims that they trained elite forces for both sides without either side knowing about the other in 1984. The Israeli government supplied Sri Lanka with substantial military equipment including PT boats for coastal patrol. At the same time they were supplying the Tamil militants with anti-PT boat equipment to use in fighting the government forces. These revelations of Israeli connections with the government of Sri Lanka and the terrorist movement of the country have left a bad impression on the credibility of Israel as a "friend indeed".[43] It was a proved double game on the part of Israel–having dealing with the terrorists on the one hand and preaching against terrorism on the other.

Indian Connections

Among the outside supports that the terror outfit Eelam had received, the most heavyweight was from the Tamil Nadu state of India as well as its Central Government at New Delhi. The reasons for Indian support to the ethnic issue in Sri Lanka are well known–the Tamils in Tamil Nadu have close ethnic, cultural and religious links with the Tamils in Sri Lanka. Most of the Tamils in Sri Lanka were of South Indian origin especially from Tamil Nadu. Ethnic affinity between the Tamils of Tamil Nadu and the Indian Tamils in Sri Lanka is an important factor which influences the bilateral relations between India and Sri Lanka. A special emotional attachment was always between the residents of Tamils of Tamil Nadu and Tamils of Northern-Eastern province and Indian Tamils of central hills.[44] The Tamils of India and Sri Lanka not only belong to the same ethnic stock but also speak the same language and follow the same cultural pattern. Whenever communal riots between the Sinhalese and the Tamils take place, the Indian state of Tamil Nadu press the Government of India to take up the matter with Sri Lanka and do something or redress the wrong done to their brethren in that country.[45] Despite their internal differences and mutual hatred for each other, the Dravidian parties-Dravida Munnetra Kazhagam (DMK) and All India Anna Dravida Munnetra

Kazhagam (AIADMK) had taken a nearly common stand on the Sri Lankan-Tamilian issue.

More importantly, New Delhi attempted to use the Tamil problem in Sri Lanka to its advantage–to change Sri Lanka's pro-Western foreign policy to suit India's interests. Keeping in mind Sri Lanka's strategic location in the Indian Ocean, Indian policy makers have always advocated harmonious relations with Sri Lanka. There have been shifts and changes in the pattern of relationship marked by mutual differences, irritants, cooperation and friendship. After the Britishers, Indian policy makers were also very sensitive towards Sri Lanka. India's first Prime Minister Jawaharlal Nehru and Indian writer K.M. Pannikar advocated the strategic unity of India, Burma and Sri Lanka for India's defence. In addition, Ravi Kaul, a former Commander of Indian Navy stated, 'Sri Lanka is as important strategically to India as Eire is to the United Kingdom or Taiwan to China. As long as Sri Lanka is friendly or even neutral, India has nothing to worry, but if there be any danger of the island falling under the domination of a power hostile to India; India can not tolerate such a situation endangering her territorial integrity. He also added that fears were not about a threat from Sri Lanka, but that if anybody with inimical interests towards India gained a foothold in the island nation, India's security interests could be adversely affected.[46] Thus, both Tamil Nadu pressure on New Delhi as well as the security interests of India, have displayed equal importance in shaping Indian attitude towards Sri Lanka.

With the rise of the Tamil militancy and escalation of the ethnic conflict in Sri Lanka, the Sri Lankan government was seeking help from external powers for a military solution to the ethnic crisis. President J.R. Jayawardene Government in Sri Lanka sought military and political support from Israel, USA, UK and Pakistan. This was also inimical to India's security interests in the region. To win the US support, Sri Lankan government extended refueling and recreation facilities to visiting US naval ships. Jayawardene also tried to seek Britain's direct involvement in the ethnic conflict by giving a fresh lease of life to the 1947 defence agreement. Having their anti-India postures in foreign policy, China and Pakistan had given military support to Sri Lanka. What upset India was Sri Lankan government decision to grant a contract for leasing of oil storage tanks in Trincomalee to a Singapore based US company and its agreement with the US in December 1983 to set up a powerful Voice of America (VoA) station in the East.[47] India's firm and categorical stand against Sri Lanka's move to build up strategic relationship with external powers had serious implication for India's security. India has always opposed the presence of external powers in Sri Lanka and also tried to persuade Sri Lankan government to solve ethnic problem politically through negotiation.

From the beginning Indian interest in Sri Lankan Tamil problems has also been due to Congress Party's power politics in the state of Tamil Nadu. The Congress party ruled in Tamil Nadu from 1952-1967. During this period the Indian Tamil problem passed through various stages and in every stage the political parties as well as the Government of Tamil Nadu expressed their concern towards the welfare of the Indian Tamils to the Union Government. The pro-Tamil groups in India and particularly in Tamil Nadu have been consistently active right from the days of citizenship controversy and language issue in the first decade of Sri Lankan independence. The pressure by Tamil Nadu varied in accordance with the domestic situations in Sri Lanka and India. Whenever there was a problem or crisis in Sri Lanka affecting the welfare of the Tamils, the political parties of Tamil Nadu generally raised their voice in support of them. However, it also said that Tamil's struggle for independence has, to a certain extent, enabled India to preserve its superpower status in the South Asian region. It is worth noting that it is because of the effective control the LTTE exercised over the North-East of the Island, both in the sea and land, anti-Indian forces have not been able to penetrate India's corridor. If not for the presence of the LTTE, the Sri Lankan government would have sold out the island to anti-Indian forces long time ago.[48] Although India's involvement with militant groups in the Sri Lanka in 1981 and its intelligence agencies were actively engaged in the promotion of LTTE, the ethnic problem in Sri Lanka became acute and sensitive since the communal riots of 1983.

The racial riots of July 1983, was a watershed in the case of Tamil Nadu as far as the Tamil problem in Sri Lanka is concerned. It followed a wave of spontaneous indignation swept throughout Tamil Nadu, and life in that state came to a virtual standstill as all joined in public processions and meetings against the killing of Tamils in Sri Lanka. The leaders of two main political parties of Tamil Nadu–the DMK and the AIADMK tried their best to attract the attention of the public towards their individual efforts. The response of the both was motivated mainly by their desire to score debating points. Soon after the July 1983 riots the DMK leader M.

Karunanidhi and Anbazhagan resigned their seats in the Legislative Assembly to protest against New Delhi's lukewarm response to the sufferings of Sri Lankan Tamils. On 27 August, 1983, the DMK passed a resolution which stated that a separate Tamil Eelam shall be the only remedy and paramount solution. It also conducted a signature campaign and collected ten million signatures to send to the UNO requesting it to call upon the Government of Sri Lanka to grant right of self-determination to the Tamils in Sri Lanka.[49] The party formed an association with the help of pro-Eelam political parties in the state to help the Tamils in Sri Lanka, namely, the Tamil Eelam Supporters Association (TESA). TESA believed that only through the creation of Eelam, the problem of the Tamils in Sri Lanka could be solved.

In July 1983, the AIADMK was the ruling party of Tamil Nadu and its leader M. G. Ramachandran, convened an all-party meeting on 28 July in Madras and condemned, in no uncertain terms, the killing of Tamils in Sri Lanka.[50] In the meeting it was decided to send a delegation to New Delhi to seek India's intervention and in a telegram sent to Indira Gandhi, Ramachandran urged her to take up the matter in the United Nations Organisation (UNO). He also led a delegation to New Delhi which represented different political parties and it submitted a memorandom to the Prime Minister in which, among other things, stated, 'The grim and inhuman killings in Sri Lanka can not be dismissed as the internal affairs of the country. We definitely feel that the time has come for the Indian government to intervene effectively, actively and urgently to save the Tamils in Sri Lanka.[51]

As a result of July 1983 anti-Tamil riots, the Tamil Nadu government of AIADMK came under severe pressure from Tamil people and the Opposition Party DMK to take up the Sri Lankan Tamils issue with the Central Government of India. In opposition to the support of TELO by DMK, the ruling AIADMK had been supporting powerful LTTE led by Velupillai Prabakaran.[52] Writing on Tamil militants in July 1986, Marguerite Johnson observed that 'Tamil Nadu also harboured 39 rebel camps, in which an estimated 3,300 guerillas are undergoing training. New Delhi has not shut down the rebel camps, but Indian authorities keep a sharp eye on the guerilla organisations.'[53] In the politics of Tamil Nadu the period between 1983-1987 centered round as to who was the greater champion of the Sri Lankan Tamil interests.

In post-1983 period the Liberation Tigers of Tamil Eelam and its leader Prabakaran discovered a striking opportunity to convert the wide-ranging public sympathy for the Lankan Tamil cause that swept Tamil Nadu following the planned genocide of Tamils in Colombo in 1983, into support for his organisation. While the influx of thousands of refugees into the state exerted enormous economical and physical pressure on the State, the LTTE and other militant groups used the presence of so many Lankan Tamils to create a wide network of operation centres, bases and supporters. The Tigers realised that with both M.G. Ramachandran and M. Karunanidhi using the Tamil issue for their political one-upmanship it would be easier to manipulate them.[54] Where the others failed and the LTTE succeeded was in the manner that the Tigers could changes sides not out of any ideological leanings but merely for self preservation. Adapt and survive, became a term applicable to the Liberation Tigers. As long as Ramachandran was around, firmly entrenched in power, the Tigers treated Karunanidhi as if he did not exist. The LTTE used political parties and their leaders in the State to suit their ends–for fighting their military and propaganda war against successive Sri Lankan Governments.

Despite LTTE's leaning towards the AIADMK party, the DMK party and its leaders, too, were thinking that Tamil Eelam was round the corner. They hoped to be on the right side of the LTTE hoping that Prabakaran would be the de facto leader of new Tamil homeland of which they would be hailed as godfathers. A note prepared for the Home Ministry by an intelligence agencies underlined the similar view: 'For the local political parties, the slogan of Tamil solidarity became the catchword. The State as well as the Central Government machinery became active in Tamil Nadu and participated in the promotion of Sri Lankan Tamil groups. These groups consolidated themselves and flourished on Indian grants and donations.[55] The phase between 1984 and 1988 saw the Tigers consolidating their position in Tamil Nadu establishing their bases, and when the Government of Ramachandran announced a grant of rupees 4 crore to supply food and medicines to the Jaffna Tamils, the LTTE pocketed the complete cheque not giving a pie to other groups. However, the honeymoon between AIADMK and LTTE soured in November 1986 when Rajiv Gandhi hosted the SAARC summit in Bangalore and Sri Lankan President J.R. Jayawardene was one of the guests. The Research and Analysis Wing, apprehending the security risks, asked Tamil Nadu police to round up LTTE leaders and seize their arms.

When the Indian government signed an Indo-Sri Lanka Accord in July 1987, M.G. Ramachandran was with Central Government side and the LTTE, for its protection and support turned to the DMK, who made right noises against the Indian Peace-keeping Force posted in Sri Lanka and fighting against the LTTE. Now the Tigers had a new godfather, a new spokesman who would fight their political battle in the Tamil hinterland. M. Karunanidhi championed the cause of LTTE in Tamil Nadu even boycotted the reception given to the Indian troops after their withdrawal from Sri Lanka. He justified the opposition of IPKF in the Assembly and said, 'How could I welcome an army that killed 20,000 people of my race'? And when questions about LTTE's wide opposition in Tamil Nadu were raised he asked, 'Why should they come here, when they are ruling like kings in north-eastern Sri Lanka'.?[56] The DMK's sympathy and support for LTTE proved fatal for the Karunanidhi government and it was dismissed in January 1989, just two years into its new term.

Since the withdrawal of IPKF in March 1990 and especially after the assassination of Rajiv Gandhi, the former Prime Minister of India, on 21 May, 1991, India had adopted hands-off policy in the ethnic conflict of Sri Lanka. The brutal killing of Rajiv Gandhi alienated the popular support for Sri Lankan Tamils and militants in India. India declared LTTE to be an unlawful organisation and took severe action against its supporters. The sympathy and support that the Sri Lankans–militants, refugees and ordinary civilians enjoyed evaporated immediately. After this LTTE had emerged as the biggest threat to both India and Sri Lanka, it however, developed extensive contacts with terrorist groups all over the world.

In the larger perspectives, the strategic decision of the Government of India to sign an Accord with the Government of Sri Lanka and sending the Indian Peace-keeping Force as a follow up of its commitment, was justified on grounds more than one. As India is always for maintaining the unity and integrity of sovereign Sri Lanka, it remained against the demand of independent state of Tamil Eelam. India had understood that military intervention would create a milieu against Indian security and was reluctant to make any military intervention. Particularly in post-withdrawal phase, India remained aloof from any direct intervention in the Sri Lankan internal affairs leaving the entire developments on their fate. However, it decided to be confined to moral and external support to the developments and peace process in Sri Lanka. The

Jain Commission, which was set up to inquire the death of Rajiv Gandhi, also in its interim report, indicated that the training of Sri Lankan Tamil militancy operations are for encouraging internecine conflict. The commission stressed the point that prior to 1989 the militancy, particularly LTTE activity, was not anti-national in character. It also criticised the Sri Lankan government for making an unholy alliance with the LTTE that was a stab in the back of the Indo-Sri Lanka Accord.

As a result of an understanding between President Premadasa and the LTTE the Indian Peace-keeping Force withdrew in March 1990. But the honeymoon between them did not last long and in the final game plan, the LTTE proved gainer. With the departure of the Indian army Prabakaran, the leader, unleashed his vengenance against all perceived enemies internal and external. Earlier a number of small arms proliferated to the civilian population as a result of 1987 Accord and deployment of IPKF. A large number of army deserters with small arms have also been a source of criminal acts in the island following the withdrawal of Indian forces. Very soon in June 1990 a tricky situation arose with the resumption of violence in the Tamil dominated regions of Sri Lanka. It is also said that even withdrawal itself was ill- timed and it happened before the administration could consolidate itself in the north-east. Particularly since the LTTE had given nothing away, not even the arms it has collected. It had filled the military vacuum that the IPKF had left. In the new situation the LTTE gained control of the north and east systematically. The escalation of violence which broke out in June 1990 ended the dialogue which had gone on between the government and the LTTE. In the tense situation, however, political talks between the two continued and Sri Lankan authorities tried to bring the LTTE leadership into the mainstream of democratic politics in the island.

In the decade 1990s and particularly from 1995 onwards devastating attacks and talks for political solution and power sharing continued between the two. After failed peace talks with the government in 1994 the Sri Lankan authorities pursued a 'war for peace' line. In a series of military operations that followed the Sri Lankan Army re-captured the Jaffna peninsula, the heartland of Tamil in the country. With this the island was plunged into fresh war with the Tigers following a declaration that peace would be achieved through war. In late 1995, the Sri Lankan forces launched a massive campaign to retake the rebel–held north. The LTTE were expelled from Jaffna but 60,000 government troops found themselves hemmed in over the next few years as the Tigers captured large areas of the Wanni and the eastern province. The ongoing fighting between the LTTE and the Sri Lankan security forces was intensified in the first week of October 1997 which continued for years to come. Ultimately with the international initiation and effort a long-term Cease Fire Agreement (CFA) between the LTTE and the Sri Lankan government brokered by the Norwegian government was signed on 22 February, 2002.

The Last Eelam War and End of Terrorism

The LTTE's engagement at war with the Indian forces for more than two years in Sri Lanka and its assassination of Rajiv Gandhi in May 1991 gave the organisation a shattering blow to its strength and image as well. India trained the LTTE in the 1980s and created the Frankenstein monster. Despite enjoying India's hospitality for years and after welcoming the peace accord it teamed up with the Sinhala hard-liner, President R. Premadasa. It betrayed India by killing more than a thousand army personnel of the IPKF sent to the island to enforce the agreement. Thus, the LTTE needs to be dealt with as part of the problem-not part of the solution.[57] Gone are the days when the Tamil people of Sri Lanka, particularly who belonged to Jaffna region, felt that only the struggle of the type and magnitude waged by Prabakaran can assure us a life of dignity. We see no vested interest in the LTTE's struggle except our deliverance.[58] The anti-India activities of the LTTE made India its principal enemy and ensured that the gains of a decade unravelled in no time.

While in post-withdrawal phase and thereafter India was still hopeful that positive response and efforts would lead to meaningful and sustained negotiations with the participation of all concerned parties, the LTTE was on the opposite and thinking the strategy to concentrate all its energies on ensuring its own fascist control of northern Sri Lanka. As a consequence, it had been unable to provide sensitive and alert leadership which would necessarily include the capability to engage with the wider situation and respond in a timely manner to the opportunities to advance the Tamil cause as and when they arose.[59] Prabakaran's faith in a military solution, rather than a political one, prevented him from taking the easy way out. He continued to procure modern weapons and arms even as he spoke of peace. He did everything to scuttle the peace process and took advantage of the weaknesses of Sri Lanka's polity. Thus the LTTE's shortsighted and adventurist positions had cost the Tamil ethnic cause dearly even as valuable time had been lost in the failure to consolidate the gains achieved through political negotiations.

In total from the year 1998 the general population of Tamils in Sri Lanka began to be alienated from the LTTE and its dream 'Tamil Eelam'. It seemed that the Tamils needed liberation from both sides. They have to politically defeat LTTE if they want to regain the space to live in peace with dignity. Given the present scenario, with an internationally isolated LTTE ploughing a lonely furrow, the Tamils feel that Eelam is not attainable. The passion for Eelam is clearly dimming, though given the deep-seated suspicion plaguing Sinhalese Tamil-relations, Eelam is still seen as an 'ideal or permanent solution'. Even a pro-LTTE journalist admitted that 'there is no good support for it even in the Tiger heartland. People would settle for a unified Sri Lanka provided the North and East are merged and designated the Tamil Homeland. Land is the main issue.[60] In other words, the LTTE was suffering from a crisis of credibility.

The Cease Fire Agreement (CFA) signed between the LTTE and the Government of Sri Lanka in February 2002 was considered as an essential step towards finding a negotiated political solution to the ongoing ethnic conflict.[61] The basic objective behind the agreement was not a solution but to be a peace interval to move towards a negotiated settlement by pushing the Tigers to come under the scrutiny of the international community and to the negotiating table in the presence of international facilitators.[62] But unfortunately, after six rounds of talks in a period of just over a year, the LTTE withdrew from negotiations in April 2003, claiming 'certain critical issues relating to the ongoing peace process'. After LTTE's withdrawal from the peace negotiation talks the CFA continued for both the parties as a mere piece of paper and it was witnessed by the assassinations, bomb blasts and huge violations of the accord.

The initial years of ceasefire periods, as was widely believed, was used by the terror outfit–The Liberation Tigers of Tamil Eelam, under the leadership of Prabakaran, to attack its Tamil opponents and in acquiring sophisticated arms to strengthen itself. The former militant groups such as the EPDP, PLOTE and the Perumal wing of the EPRLF were almost eliminated by the LTTE. The TULF was now very much under LTTE control and its last independent leader Neelam Tiruchelvam had been killed by the LTTE. The outfit also used the opportunity of prolonged peace to build its warfare including airforce. It procured advanced arms to fight against government reviving civil war in a more powerful way and even started air attacks. At such juncture, negotiator Norway could not do anything positive in resolving civil war and therefore, Norway was blamed and criticised for being biased and prejudiced and unnecessarily interfering in government activities.

The ongoing situation aggravated and worsened further after the killing of Lakshman Kadirgamar, the Foreign Minister of Sri Lanka in August 2005 and coming of Mahinda Rajapaksa as the new President of Sri Lanka by the end of the year. Although the military and the LTTE were engaged in an undeclared war for over a year, the cycle of bloodshed that began with the assassination of foreign minister by suspected LTTE cadres had shown no sign of halting. Apart from this, all the killings in Colombo resulted from suicide missions, a dubious technique perfected by the LTTE.[63] But the entire envircnment began to change when Mahinda Rajapaksa took over as the president of Sri Lanka in November 2005. Not only on devolution of power and the continuing ethnic conflict, but on the Norwegian-brokered Cease Fire Agreement (CFA) of February 2002, the new ruler had a different approach and strategy to deal with.

Since 2006, when both sides resumed major military operations, the conflict had killed and wounded thousands of civilians and displaced hundreds of thousands, leaving many suffering from disease and hunger. After the breakdown of the peace process the Sri Lankan military launched a major offensive against the Tigers, bringing the entire country under their control and gradually defeating the LTTE militarily. In June 2006, the Deputy Chief of Army, Major General Parami Kulatunga, who was filling in for the recuperating Army Commander, was killed.[64] In the same month pursuing the LTTE's technique and planning on the propaganda front, the government borrowed liberally from its tactics and created the Media Centre for National Security (MCNS) with the sole aim of countering the pro-LTTE Portal Tamil Net. The Defence Minister revamped its own website and kept up a relentless campaign not only against the Tigers but against any one and every one who was critical of the war. On the battle front, the motto, in the words of army chief, was: Go for the kill, maximum casualties and destruction of infrastructure of the enemy with minimum possible damage to the troops.[65] This phase of hostilities witnessed the maximum use of air power.

The new wave of violence erupted in July 2006 which reached its worst level soon. With the deterioration of the security situation in North and East of Sri Lanka since the beginning of this year, and particularly after the suicide bomb attack on the Sri Lankan Army Commander in Colombo in April 2006 resulting in bombings of the LTTE controlled areas of the East by the Sri Lankan armed forces. Once the large scale fighting broke out, it dawned on Prabakaran that Colombo, too, had psychologically prepared itself for war. Rajapaksa was ready to pay back in a fitting manner, whatever the consequences. Now Sri Lanka unleashed its air force and artillery barrage on LTTE areas like never before. For once the state decided that it needed to be an LTTE to defeat the LTTE. The change of guard in the island nation proved a monumental blunder for the LTTE. Prabakaran felt the absence of Karuna group once the war started and picked up lethal speed from 2006 and the LTTE started losing one ship after another and suffering unprecedented battlefield reverses.

The ongoing struggle between the LTTE and the Sri Lankan forces intensified by the daredevil aerial raids carried out by the Tamil Tigers in a span of over a month from March 26 to April 29, 2007. Earlier the threats emanated either from land or sea but now even the skies were a source of horror. The current escalation of hostilities resulted in rebels staging a dramatic demonstration of their air-strike capabilities by using Czech-built Zin-143 aircraft in March 2007 they attacked the country's largest air force base at Katunayake. Another attack on the air base at Anuradhapura, a staging area for the Northern threatre of military operation, damaged or destroyed more than USD 30 million worth assets.[66] For the first time the LTTE had carried out an air attack. This meant it now possessed the capability to select a target anywhere in the country accessed by air-unopposed to destroy it. The LTTE air raid had raised fundamental questions about the strategy employed by the government. While publicly proclaiming that a politically negotiated settlement is the objective and putting forward the Cease Fire Agreement and the All Party Representatives' Committee process as evidence of this, the government had clearly chosen the military option with the avowed aim of annihilating the LTTE. In the year 2007 the Sri Lankan government took effective control of the Sri Lanka's eastern province, though it had trouble defeating LTTE combatants in the north. In the east the Sri Lankan forces recaptured almost all including large areas of rebel-dominated territory, south of the strategic eastern port city of Trincomalee. This area served as the lifeline for some 40,000 government troops deployed in the Northern Jaffna Peninsula. In the year although the LTTE made several devastating attacks on the Sri Lankan security forces, its overall position in the war was on decline. The year also witnessed the death of S.P. Tamilchelvan, LTTE's political wing chief on 2 November, 2007 in Sri Lanka Air Force bombing.

In the ongoing war with its intensification the LTTE had received remarkable reversal. Carefully coordinated action by the Sri Lankan security forces had seen the Tigers being targeted at many difficult levels. From destroying LTTE ships carrying arms to ambushing LTTE operations in landmine attacks, the forces had been hitting hard and consistently. The military establishment was gearing up to use a purely military approach. After decades of see saw fighting, Colombo took a visible upper hand vis-à-vis the LTTE, driving it away from the country's eastern province and crippling its shipping network. In the first week of January 2008 the Government of Mahinda Rajapaksa decided to withdraw from the CFA brokered by Norway in February 2002 and like earlier in 2008 the Government of Sri Lanka was determined to give a decisive blow to the LTTE ejecting it from territory it controlled and eliminating its leadership. With this objective in view Sri Lanka had acquired armaments-multi-barrel rocket launchers, heavier artillery precision guided missiles, and bunker busters and had recruited 30,000 new recruits into its armed forces. In response Prabakaran had directed attacks against hard military targets such as Air Force bases and soft political targets like ministers and civil guardsmen. The Tamil Tigers were using a combination of hit and run attacks, bombing and assassinations to deter and delay the government's impending assault. They had developed an air wing, an effective sea wing and have heavily infiltrated population centres in the Sinhala-dominated South.

The year 2008 proved a decisive one in the struggle between the LTTE and the Sri Lankan security forces and the latter had continued its all out offensive against the Tamil militant groups. It made several successful land air and navy attacks on LTTE strongholds and destroyed their training camps. In the month of March and April the LTTE had received heavy beating during clashes along the Wanni and the Jaffna Forward Defence Lines (FDLs). In November 2008 the Sri Lankan security forces got major success in destroying the outfits several training camps including the capture of LTTE's sea base Ponneryn which was considered as the last strategic stronghold. This phase of the military surge has forced the LTTE to retreat with heavy casualties. The LTTE was on the verge of losing its supply line along the western coast.[67] The terrorists were faced with fierce multipronged attacks from the military, which had left scores of terrorists killed and many bunkers abandoned. The terrorists had suffered serious damages in the fighting and unable to resist the military onslaught, terrorists had fled leaving the dead and a cache of weapons behind. The intense military assault and the small group operations had confined major movements of terrorists in the area.

The decisive fight that led to the fall/defeat of the Liberation Tigers of Tamil Eelam was fought in the early part of 2009, particularly in the month of January. On January 2, President Mahinda Rajapaksa announced that Sri Lankan troops had captured Kilinochchi, the island nation's northern town. The city Kilinochchi had been used by the LTTE for over a decade as its *de facto* administrative capital. Although small but strategically located that had served as the political hub of the once sprawling LTTE territory in the north and east of the island. Most importantly the town sat on a winding highway known as A-9 that linked Jaffna in the northern tip to the rest of Sri Lanka. It was stated that the loss of Kilinochchi had caused a substantial dent in the LTTE's image. It was also stated that after the fall of Kilinochchi the LTTE was likely to collapse soon under unbearable military pressure on multiple fronts. In August 2006 the LTTE controlled 1,500 square kilometres and at the start of the year 2009 it curtailed to 350 square kilometres with its fighting cadres strength believed to be down to about 1000. With this loss and all major bases in the district the Tigers have now confined to the jungles of Mullaithivu district. Rajapaksa considered it a major victory in the world's battle against terrorism.[68] It marked a turning point in the Tamil Tiger history.

After Kilinochchi, the armed forces were all set to zero in on the bases of the Tigers in Elephant Pass and Muhamalai across the Jaffna peninsula. On January 8, 2009, the LTTE was abandoning its positions on the Jaffna peninsula to make a last stand in the jungles of Mullaithivu. With the fall of Elephant Pass the Sri Lankan security forces were now poised to capture the remaining LTTE strong points at Mulliyan, Chempiyan-pattuwa, Chundikulama and Kaddaikadu. In line the entire Jaffna peninsula was captured by the Sri Lankan Army by January 14 and in a major success on 25th of this month the island's troops completely captured Mullaitivu town, the last major LTTE stronghold. It is an strategic town and capital of the district with the same name and the last bastion of the Tamil Tigers.

Now it appeared that the moment of truth had come for the LTTE when it received two major jolts further. In Chennai, Dravida Munnetra Kazagham leader and Chief Minister M. Karunanidhi reiterated that he does not support the LTTE that had weakened the Tamil resistence. In addition, the European Union, Japan, Norway, and the US, the four co-chairs of the Oslo peace process 2002, called upon the LTTE to lay down weapons and surrender after accepting the amnesty offer put forward by the Sri Lanka government and prevent further loss of civilian life.[69] In previous years the outfit, instead of vigorously pursuing the objective of getting the best devolution package through the talks, the LTTE focussed on building its armed strength with the trappings of a government–its own police, judiciary and administration. It was felt that the time has come for the LTTE to give up war.

In Sri Lanka and outside the country there was an increasing belief that the final military defeat of the LTTE was near. After capturing Mullaitivu the Sri Lankan troops, amid intense fighting further advanced into LTTE's remaining stronghold Puthukkudiyiruppu. In the area heavy fighting took place between the troops of I Sinha Regiment (ISR) and 9 Field Engineers intercepted group of terrorists trying to infiltrate army forward boundary east of the Nathikadal lagoon. In this war in a major set back for the tigers, the LTTE's financial wing chief Subarathnam, who handled the outfit's bank account, tax collection and all other financial matters, was killed in the confrontation. In the first week of April 2009 the Sri Lankan Defence Ministry claimed that it had gained total control over Puthukkudiyirippu. In the fighting LTTE's artillery wing head Manniwannan was killed and Adithyan, LTTE's former in-charge of Welioya, was also among the dead.

By the end of April 2009 the combat operations against the LTTE had reached their conclusion and in the light of developments the Sri Lankan government had instructed the troops to end the use of heavy weapons, which could harm civilian population. For the LTTE the beginning of May was a decisive one that proved a debacle and it accepted the defeat in principle. Now the Sri Lankan military was less than a kilometre from the remaining part of the

No-Fire Zone (NFZ) where the LTTE top brass and cadre had been held up holding an estimated 20,000 civilians as hostage. When about 80,000 civilians were to flee the LTTE-occupied zone on 10 May, 2009, the Tigers made a determination that they have lost the war and that no purpose would be achieved by holding on the civilians. The very next day the Tigers seemed to have deserted the sentry points, dismantled the defence lines and destroyed everything they could. The exodus of the last batch of civilians started on 12/13 May and perhaps by the night of 15th there was no civilians left in the 1.5 square-kilometre area the tigers were boxed into. In nutshell, the loss of LTTE's capabilities in the Tamil and non- Tamil areas was immense.

Decisive debacle for the LTTE started on 16 May, 2009 and lasted for two more days. The end-game inside the war zone began early with soldiers freeing the last remaining coastal stretch that the LTTE held. The link-up marked the first time that the military had total control of the island's coast lines in three decades. On 17 May, the military and the tigers were engaged in one of the most intense battles witnessed during the 33-month-old Eelam War- IV. The military operations began at 5 a.m. and loud explosions could be heard in the battle zone throughout the day.

However, the curtain came down on Eelam War IV in the early hours of 18 May, 2009 with the decimation of the LTTE's military capabilities in a 22-hour battle, which also resulted in the death of at least 18 of its top leaders. The intensity of the battle in the final hours to end the war could be gauged from the fact that the military had collected hundreds of bodies of the Tiger cadres. About the same time confirmation of the news that it was all over for the LTTE came on the pro-LTTE website, TamilNet titled, 'Long live human dignity, shame on the international community is exposed by its shameful conning, thousands of Tamil civilians and combatants are laying down their lives to uphold Tamil dignity and human dignity.'[70] The fighting with Prabakaran and his men erupted at 4 a.m. and was over within 90 minutes, leaving the man who had terrorised the country for over a quarter century dead near a lagoon in Mullaitivu district.[71] On the same day in the evening the three chiefs of the Sri Lanka, Army, Navy and the Air Force called on President Rajapaksa and informed him that the war against the LTTE had concluded and the forces had been successful in wiping out its entire leadership and either destroyed or captured its arms and ammunitions.

The death of Velupillai Prabakaran, the LTTE chief, was announced officially by the Sri Lankan government when the island's military had recovered his bullet-ridden body laying on the bank of the Nanthikadal lagoon. The dramatic collapse of the Tamil Tigers, accompanied by white flags and surrenders, is a sad commentary on the politics of uncompromising mayhem the rebels pursued for so long in Sri Lanka. When they were repeatedly called to go for negotiations, they decided to settle for nothing less than independence. Those who wanted to shake hands with the Sri Lankan state were dubbed traitors and killed. The LTTE set out to form an independent Tamil state by breaking up the north and east of Sri Lanka. They never fought any elections but prided themselves as the sole and authentic representative of the Tamils. By the time a quarter century of unceasing bloodlettings passed, more than 90,000 people lay dead, many thousands were injured and maimed, the Tamil were in ruins, and there was no trace of Tamil Eelam. Sri Lanka's decisive victory over the LTTE is the biggest success story in the world of anti-terrorism.

References

1. Inter-Racial Equity and Nationality in Sri Lanka (Colombo: Marga Institute, 1985), p. 13, as quoted in Shelton U. Kodikara (ed.), *External Compulsions of South Asian Politics* (New Delhi: Sage Publications, 1993), pp. 266-67.
2. Citha D. Maass, 'South Asia: Drawn Between Cooperation and Conflict', in Eric Gonsalves and Nancy Jetly (eds.), *The Dynamics of South Asia–Regional Cooperation and SAARC* (New Delhi: Sage Publications, 1999), p. 48.
3. Kumar David, 'Ethnic Conflict: Rethinking the Fundamentals', in Kumar Rupesinghe and Khawar Mumtaz (eds.), *Internal Conflicts in South Asia (*London : Sage Publications, 1996), pp. 1-2.
4. As quoted in *Ibid.*, p. 16.
5. Bernard M. Magubane, *The Political Economy of Race and Class in South Africa* (Newyork: Monthly Review Press, 1979), pp. 163-92.
6. Chaim Kaufman, 'Possible and Impossible Solutions to Ethnic Wars', *International Security*, Vol. 20, No. 4, pp. 136-75.
7. P. Sahadevan, 'Negotiating Peace in Ethnic Wars,' *International Studies*, Vol. 43, No. 3, July-September 2006 (New Delhi: School of International Studies, JNU, 2006), pp. 239-41.
8. *Ibid.*, pp. 41-42.
9. G.S. Bhargava, *South Asian Security after Afghanistan* (Lexington: D.C. Heath and Company, 1983), pp. 67-90.

10. Shaukat Hassan, 'Problems of Internal Stability in South Asia,' in Shelton U. Kodikara (ed.), *External Compulsions of South Asian Politics*, pp. 275-77.
11. Cynthia Enloe, *Ethnic Conflict and Political Development* (Boston: Little Brown and Co., 1973), as quoted in *Ibid.*, p. 78.
12. S.R. Chakravarti, Swaroop Rani Dubey, P.C. Mathur and Virendra Narain (authors), *Turmoil and Change in South Asia–Bangladesh, Sri Lanka, India and Pakistan* (Jaipur: Aalekh Publishers, 1978), p. 71.
13. Kumar David, 'Ethnic Conflict: Rethinking the Fundamentals,' in Kumar Rupesinghe and Khawar Mumtaz (eds.), *Internal Conflicts in South Asia*, p. 3.
14. V.N. Narayanan, 'Separating Tamils from the LTTE,' *The Hindustan Times*, 9 August, 1998.
15. Jeyaratnam Wilson, *Politics in Sri Lanka 1947-1979* (London: Macmillan Press, 1979), pp. 7-9.
16. Michael Roberts, 'Some Pillars for Lanka's Future,' *Frontline*, Vol. 26, No. 12, 6-19 June, 2009 (Chennai: 2009), p. 27.
17. *The Muslim* (Lahore), 30 April, 1987.
18. Lucy M. Jacob, 'Regionalism in Sri Lanka,' in Ramakant (ed.), *Regionalism in South Asia* (Jaipur: Aalekh Publishers, 1983), p. 175.
19. Vijaya Samaraweera, 'The Evolution of Plural Society,' in K.M. De Silva (ed.), *Sri Lanka: A Survey* (London: 1963), pp. 88-89.
20. Vinod F. Khobragade, 'Re-Thinking Power Devolution in Sri Lanka,' *South Asia Politics*, Vol. 6, No. 1, May 2007 (New Delhi: 2007), pp. 23-24.
21. Vinod F. Khobragade, 'Ethnic Politics in Sri Lanka–Political Solution to Tamil Cause and Military Solution to LTTE,' *South Asia Politics*, Vol. 7, No. 11, March 2009 (New Delhi: 2009), pp. 24-25.
22. B. Muralidhar Reddy, 'Democracy Deficit and Two Movements,' *Frontline*, pp. 22-23.
23. For the Vaddukoddai Resolution, see *Race Relations in Sri Lanka* (Colombo: Centre for Society and Religion, 1978), pp. 79-83.
24. *Inter-Racial Equity and Nationality in Sri Lanka* (Colombo: Marga Institute, 1985), p. 13.
25. Jeyaratnam Wilson, 'Race, Religion, Language and Caste in the Subnationalism of Sri Lanka,' in Michael Roberts (ed.), *Collective Identities, Nationalism and Protest in Modern Sri Lanka* (Colombo: Marga Institute, 1979), pp. 462-73.
26. *The Hindustan Times* editorial, 5 September, 1998.
27. James Manor (ed.), *Sri Lanka in Change and Crisis* (London: Croom Helm, 1984), pp. 1-2.

28. Jayadeva Uyangoda, 'Militarisation, Violent State, Violent Society: Sri Lanka,' in Kumar Rupesinghe and Khawar Mumtaz (eds.), *Internal Conflicts in South Asia*, pp. 118-19.
29. *Ibid.*
30. *Ibid.*, pp. 120-21.
31. Tom Farrell, 'For him no Sacrifice was too Great for the Objective of Eelam,' *The Hindu*, 24 April, 2009.
32. Jorge Heine, 'Misapplying Responsibility to Protect in Sri Lanka', in *Ibid.*, 27 June, 2009.
33. R. Hariharan, 'Sri Lanka: Need to Restore Trust,' in *Ibid.*, 18 May, 2010.
34. R. Hariharan, 'The Discarded Accord and the Unwanted War,' in *Ibid.*, 7 August, 2007.
35. Shelton U. Kodikara, 'Internal Politics and Foreign Policy : Prospects for Indo–Sri Lanka Relations in the Nineties', in *External Compulsions of South Asian Politics*, p. 233.
36. *The Hindustan Times*, 13 October, 1997.
37. *Ibid.*, 9 February, 1999.
38. *Ibid.*, 10 March, 1999.
39. *The Hindu*, 29 March, 2000.
40. *Ibid.*
41. *The Newyork Times*, 9 May, 1990.
42. *The Daily News*, 26 September, 1990.
43. G.P. V. Somaratne, 'Sri Lanka's Relations with Israel,' in Shelton U. Kodikara (ed.), *External Compulsions of South Asian Politics*, pp. 219-20.
44. Gurnam Chand, 'Influence of Tamil Nadu Politics on India-Sri Lanka Relationship,' *South Asia Politics*, Vol. 9, No. 11, March 2011 (New Delhi: 2011), p. 45.
45. Ahsan Ali Khan, 'The Tamil Question in Historical Perspective: Its Impact on Indo–Sri Lankan Relations,' *Pakistan Horizon Quarterly*, Vol. 2, p. 58.
46. Gurnam Chand, 'Growing Chinese Influence in Sri Lanka and India's Security Concerns,' *South Asia Politics*, Vol. 9, No. 9, January 2011 (New Delhi: 2011), p. 23.
47. *Ibid.*, p. 24.
48. Melbourne Broadcast of *Tamil Voice*, 22 December, 2003.
49. Tamil Nadu *Legislative Assembly*, Debate, Vol. III, No. 2, 25 October, 1983, p. 135.
50. *The Statesman*, 29 July, 1983.

51. A Sivarajah, 'Indo-Sri Lanka Relations and Sri Lanka's Ethnic Crisis: The Tamil Nadu Factor,' in Shelton U. Kodikara (ed.), *South Asian Strategic Issues–Sri Lankan Perspectives*, pp. 119-20.
52. *Ibid.*
53. Marguerite Johnson, 'Island at War,' *Lanka Guardian*, Vol. 9, as quoted in *Ibid.*, p. 121.
54. G.C. Shekhar, 'The Ones Who 'Rode' the Tigers,' *The Hindustan Times*, 16 November, 1997.
55. *Ibid.*
56. *Ibid.*
57. Subramanian Swamy, 'Sri Lanka Crisis and India's Options,' *The Hindu*, 29 November, 2006.
58. V.N. Narayanan, 'Between the Devil and Deep Blue Sea,' *The Hindustan Times*, 8 August, 1998.
59. Malini Parthasarathy, 'The Mirage of Eelam,' *The Hindu*, 24 April, 2009.
60. P.K. Balachanddran, 'Eelam a Receding Dream,' in *Ibid.*, 19 January, 1998.
61. Arti Bali, 'Enforcing Military Solution to Ethnic Conflicts,' *South Asia Politics* Vol. 7, No. 2, June, 2008 (New Delhi: 2008), p. 49.
62. B. Muralidhar Reddy, 'In Sri Lanka, a Ceasefire Under Siege,' *The Hindu*, 16 March, 2007.
63. *Ibid.*, editorial, 6 November, 2007.
64. *Ibid.*
65. B. Muralidhar Reddy, 'The War is Over,' *Frontline*, p. 8.
66. Arti Bali, 'Enforcing Military Solution to Ethnic Conflicts,' p. 49.
67. *The Hindu*, 3 November, 2008.
68. *Ibid.*, 3 January, 2009.
69. R. Hariharan, 'The Moment of Truth for the LTTE,' in *Ibid.*, 5 February 2009.
70. *Frontline*, 6-19 June, 2009, p. 14.
71. *Indo–Asian News Service*, 20 May, 2009.

Selected Bibliography

Documents

A Ministry of State Publication, *Sri Lanka: Who Wants a Separate State*? (Sri Lanka Government Press, 1983).

A Ministry of State Publication, *Tamil Eelam Terrorists Murder Again: Time Bomb Kill 30 at Madras Airport* (Sri Lanka Government Press, 1984).

Asian Balance of Power in the Seventies: Indian View (Institute for Defence Studies and Analysis, New Delhi, 1968).

Asian Relations Organisation, *Report of the Proceedings and Documents of the First Asian Relations Conference,* March-April 1947 (New Delhi, 1948).

Bangladesh and India's Security (Palit & Dutt, Dehradun, 1972).

Brar, K.S. Lt. General, *Operation Blue Star: The True Story* (New Delhi, 1993).

Bulganin, N.A., and Khrushchev, N.S., *Visit of Friendship to India, Burma and Afghanistan: Speeches and Official Documents, November-December 1995* (Foreign Languages Publishing House, Moscow, 1956).

Buzan, B. and Rizvi, *South Asian Insecurity and the Great Powers* (Macmillan, London, 1986).

Chari, P.R., 'The IPKF Experience in Sri Lanka', *ACDIS Occasional Paper* (University of Illinois at Urbana, Urbana, 1995).

Department of Information, *Peace for All, Prosperity for All and Envy Towards None* (Department of Government Printing, Sri Lanka).

Government of Pakistan, *The Constitution of Islamic Republic of Pakistan* (1973).

India, Kashmir and the United Nations (External Publicity Division, New Delhi, 1948).

India, Muslim's in India (Ministry of Information and Broadcasting, New Delhi, 1966).

India's Security Perspectives (ABC Publishing House, New Delhi, 1982).

India's Security: The North and North-East Dimension, Conflict Studies, 215 (Centre for Security and Conflict Studies, London, 1988).

International Institute for Strategic Studies, *Military Balance, 1992-93 to 1999-2000* (London, 1999).

Political Committee, *LTTE, Liberation Tigers of Tamil Eelam Freedom Struggle* (Madras, 1983).

Problems of Living in the Nuclear Age (Centre for Research in Rural and Industrial Development, Chandigarh, 1985).

Security Issues in South Asia, International Seminar on 'Regional Security in South Asia', Centre for Nepal and Asian Studies (Tribhuvan University, Nepal, 3-6 November, 1985, Kathmandu).

Sri Lanka: The Ethnic Conflict–A Collection of Writings edited by Committee for Rational Development (New Delhi, 1984).

Suhrawardy, H.S. *Statement on Foreign Relations and Defence* (Government of Pakistan, Karachi, 1957).

US Central Intelligence Agency, *Report on Heroin in Pakistan: Sowing the Wind* (September 1992).

US Foreign Policy for the 1970s: Shaping a Durable Peace: A Report of the Congress by Richard M. Nixon, President of the United States, 9 February, 1972 (Washington, 1972).

US Government, Department of State, *'Security Decision–Making in Pakistan,'* Report Prepared for the office of External Research, Department of State, September 1980.

World Armaments and Disarmaments SIPRI Year Book (Oxford 1974-2000).

Books

Ahmed, Akbar S., *Pakistan Society: Islam, Ethnicity and Leadership in South Asia* (Oxford University Press, Delhi, 1988).

Ahmed, Aziz, *Islamic Modernism in India and Pakistan 1957-1964* (Oxford University Press, London, 1967).

Ahmed, Ishtiaq, *The Concept of an Islamic State in Pakistan* (Vanguard, Lahore, 1991).

Ahmed, Kamruddin, *The Social History of East Pakistan* (Crescent Book Store, Dacca, 1967).

Allen, Douglas (ed.), *Religion and Political Conflict in South Asia* (Oxford University Press, New Delhi, 1993).

Ali Tariq, *Can Pakistan Survive: The Death of a State* (Penguin, Harmondsworth, 1983).

Ali Tariq, *Pakistan: Military Rule or People's Power* (Jonathan Cape, London, 1970).

Amin, Tahir, *Ethno–National Movements of Pakistan* (Institute of Policy Studies, Islamabad, 1988).

Ayub Khan, Mohammed, *Friends Not Masters: A Political Biography* (Oxford University Press, London, 1967).

Azar, Edward E., and Chung In Moon (eds.), *National Security in the Third World: The Management of Internal and External Threats* (Edward Elgar Publishing, Aldershot, 1988).

Bahadur, Kalim, *Democracy in Pakistan: Crises and Conflict* (Har–Anand Private, New Delhi, 1998).

Banuazizi, Ali and Weiner, Myron (eds.), *The State Religion and Ethnic Politics: Pakistan, Iran and Afghanistan* (Anguard Publishers, Lahore, 1987).

Bhaduri, Shankar and Afsir Karim, *The Sri Lankan Crisis* (Lancer International, New Delhi, 1990).

Bhuiyan, Abdul Wadud, *Emergence of Bangladesh and Role of Awami League* (Vikas Publishing House, New Delhi, 1982).

Bindra, S.S., *India and Her Neighbours–A Study of Political, Economic and Cultural Relations and Interactions* (Deep and Deep Publications, New Delhi, 1989).

Bose, Sugata and Jalal, Ayesha, *Modern South Asia–History Culture Political Economy* (Oxford University Press, New Delhi, 2004).

Bose, Sumantra, *Kashmir–Roots of Conflict and Paths to Peace* (Vistaar Publications, New Delhi, 2003).

Brecher, Michael, *The Struggle for Kashmir* (Oxford University Press, Newyork, 1953).

Brown, Michael E. and Ganguly, Sumit (eds.), *Government Policies and Ethnic Relations in Asia and the Pacific* (Cambridge, 1997).

Brown, W. Norman, *The United States and India and Pakistan* (Harvard University Press, Cambridge, 1953).

Buki, Shahid Javed and Baxter, Craig, *Pakistan Under the Military: Eleven Years of Zia-ul-Haq* (Westview Press, Boulder, 1991).

Carras Marry, C., *The Dynamics of Indian Political Faction* (Cambridge University Press, Cambridge, 1972).

Chakravarty, S.K., *The Evolution of Politics in Bangladesh 1947-1978* (Associate Publishing House, New Delhi, 1978).

Chakravarti S.R. Swaroop Rani Dubey, P.C. Mathur and Virendra Narain (Authors), *Turmoil and Political Change in South Asia–Bangladesh, Sri Lanka, India and Pakistan* (Aalekh Publishers, Jaipur, 1978).

Chaudhri, Muhammad Ali, *The Emergence of Pakistan* (Columbia University Press, Newyork, 1967).

Cheema, P.I., *Pakistan's Defence Policy, 1947-58* (Macmillan, London, 1990).

Chisti, General Faiz Ali, *Betrayals of Another Kind: Islam, Democracy and the Army in Pakistan* (Asia Publishing House, Cincinnati, 1990).

Chopra, Pran, *Uncertain India: A Political Profile of two Decades of Freedom* (Asia Publishing House, Bombay, 1968).

Cohen, Stephen P., *The Pakistan Army* (Himalayan Books, New Delhi, 1984).

Cohen, Stephen P., and Richard L. Park, *India: The Emergent Power* (Russak & Company, Newyork, 1978).

Cooper, Mary H., *The Business of Drugs* (Popular Prakashan, Bombay, 1993).

Cressey, George B., *Asia's Lands and Peoples* (McGraw-Hill, Newyork, 1951).

Davis, Kingsely, *The Population of India and Pakistan* (Princeton University Press, Princeton, 1951).

Dean, Vera Micheles, *New Patterns of Democracy in India* (Harvard University Press, Cambridge, 1969).

Dixit, Aabha, *Ethno-Nationalism in Pakistan* (Institute for Defence Studies and Analysis, Delhi, 1996).

Dixit, J.N., *Anatomy of a Flawed Inheritance: Indo–Pakistan Relations: 1970-94* (Konark Publishers, New Delhi, 1995).

Doorn, Jacques Van (ed.), *Armed Forces and Society* (Mouton: The Hague, 1968).

Dube, S.C., *India's Changing Villages–Human Factors in Community Development* (Routledge and Kegan Paul, London, 1958).

Easton, David, *The Political System: An Inquiry into the State of Political Science* (Scientific Book Agency, Calcutta, 1971).

Embree, Ainslie T. (ed.), *The Hindu Tradition* (Modern Library, Newyork, 1966).

Esposito, John L. (ed.), *Islam in Asia: Religion Politics and Society* (Oxford University Press, Oxford, 1987).

Falik, Richard A., *Global Approach to National Policy* (Harvard University Press, Cambridge, 1975).

Farmer, B.H., *Ceylon: A Divided Nation* (Delhi, 1963).

Feldman, Herbert, *Revolution in Pakistan* (Oxford University Press, 1967).

Gaige, Frederick H., *Regionalism and National Unity in Nepal* (Vikas Publishing House, New Delhi, 1975).

Gardezi, Hassan and Rashid Jamil (eds.), *Pakistan: The Roots of Dictatorship: The Political Economy of a Praetorian State* (Oxford University Press, Delhi, 1984)

Gough, Kathleen and Sharma, Hari P. (eds.), *Imperialism and Revolution in South Asia* (Monthly Review Press, New Delhi, 1973).

Gupta, R.C., *US Policy Towards India and Pakistan* (B.R. Publications, Delhi, 1977).

Gupta, Sisir, *India and Regional Integration in Asia* (Asia Publishing House, Bombay, 1964).

________, *Kashmir–A Study in India–Pakistan Relations* (Asia Publishing House, Bombay, 1966).

________, *India's Relations with Pakistan,* 1954–1957 (Indian Council of World Affairs, New Delhi, 1961).

Haq, Iqramul, *Pakistan: From Hash to Heroin* (Anoor Publisher, Lahore, 1991).

Harrison, Selig S., *India: The Most Dangerous Decade* (Princeton University Press, Princeton, 1960).

________, *In Afghanistan Shadow: Baluch Nationalism and Soviet Temptation* (Washington, 1981).

Hassnain, S.E., *Indian Muslims: Challenge and Opportunity* (Lalvani Publication House, Bombay, 1968).

Hussain, Asif, *Elite Politics in an Ideological State* (Dawson, Folkestone, 1979).

Islam, Nurul, *Development Planning in Bangladesh – A Study in Political Economy* (C. Hurst and Co., London, 1977).

Jackson, Robert, *South Asian Crisis: India, Pakistan, Bangladesh* (Chatto and Windus, London, 1975).

Jahan, Rounaq, *Pakistan: Failure in National Integration* (Columbia University Press, Newyork, 1972).

Jalal, Ayesha, *Democracy and Authoritarianism in South Asia: A Comparative and Political Perspective* (Cambridge University Press, Cambridge, 1995).

________, *The State of Martial Law: The Origins of Pakistan's Political Economy of Defence* (Cambridge University Press, Cambridge, 1990).

James, Manor (ed.), *Sri Lanka in Change and Crisis* (Croom Helm, London, 1984).

Jeyaratnam, Wilson, A., *Politics in Sri Lanka–1947-1979* (Macmillan Press, London, 1979).

Kodikara, Shelton U. (ed.), *South Asian Strategic Issues, Sri Lankan Perspective* (Sage Publications, New Delhi, 1993).

________, *External Compulsions of South Asian Politics* (Sage Publications, New Delhi, 1993).

Kukreja, Veena, *Contemporary Pakistan–Political Process, Conflict and Crises* (Sage Publications, New Delhi, 2003).

________, *Civil–Military Relations in South Asia: Pakistan, Bangladesh and India* (Sage Publications, New Delhi, 1991).

________, *Military Intervention in Politics: A Case Study of Pakistan* (NBO, New Delhi, 1985).

Kumar, Dharam, *Land and Caste in South India* (Cambridge, 1965).

Kumaraswamy, P.R. (ed.), *Security Beyond Survival* (Sage Publications, New Delhi, 2004).

Kumar, Satish, *The New Pakistan* (Vikas Publishing House, New Delhi, 1978).

Laxmi, Y., *Trends in India's Defence Expenditure* (ABC, New Delhi, 1988).

Madhu, Limaya, *India and the World* (New Delhi, 1979).

Malik, Iftikhar H., *State and Civil Society in Pakistan: Politics of Authority, Ideology and Ethnicity* (St. Martin's Press Inc., Newyork, 1997).

Mallik, Dev Narayan, *Post-War International Politics–A Quadripartite Survey* (Veena Mandir Publishers, Muzaffarpur, 1973).

Maniruzzaman, Talukdar, *Radical Politics and the Emergence of Bangladesh* (Bangladesh Book International, Dhaka, 1975).

________, *Bangladesh Revolution and Its Aftermath* (Bangladesh Book International, Dhaka, 1980).

Mittal, Nemisharan, *World Famous Drug Mafia* (Family Books, New Delhi, 1990).

Mishra, Pramod K., *South Asia in International Politics* (Udh Publishers, Delhi, 1984).

Naik, J.A., *The Pak Bomb and Rajiv's India* (National Publishing House, New Delhi, 1986).

Nath, Tribhuvan, *The Nepalese Dilemma 1960-74* (New Delhi, 1975).

Nayak, Pandav (ed.), *Pakistan: Society and Politics* (South Asia Publishers, New Delhi, 1984).

Nehru, Jawaharlal, *Glimpses of World History* (L. Drummond, Newyork, 1946).

Ohlson, T., and M. Brozska, *Arms Transfer to the Third World 1971-85* (Oxford University Press, Oxford, 1986).

Palmer, Norman D., *South Asia and United States Policy* (Houghton Miffliu, Boston, 1966).

_________, *Indian Political System* (Houghton Miffliu, Boston, 1961).

Pai Panandiker, V.A. (ed.), *Problems of Governance in South Asia* (Konark Publishers, 2000).

Phadnis, Urmila, *Ethnicity and Nation Building in South Asia* (Sage Publications, New Delhi, 1990).

Rosen, Stephen Peter, *Societies and Military Power: India and Its Armies* (Oxford University Press, Delhi, 1996).

Rupesinghe, Kumar and Mumtaz, Khawar (eds.), *Internal Conflicts in South Asia* (Sage Publications, London, 1996).

Roy, Asim, *Islam in South Asia: Regional Perspective* (South Asia Publishers, New Delhi, 1996).

_________, (ed.), *Dilemmas of a Developing State* (Aalekh Publishers, Jaipur, 1985).

Sathyamurthy, T.V. (ed.), *Region, Religion, Caste, Gender and Culture in Contemporary India* (Oxford University Press, Delhi, 1996).

Shaha, Rishikesh, *Nepali Politics: Retrospect and Prospect* (Delhi, 1975).

Shelly, Mizanur Rahman, *Emergence of a New Nation in a Multipolar World: Bangladesh* (University Press, Dhaka, 1979).

Singh, Jasjit (ed.), *Kargil 1999: Pakistan's Fourth War for Kashmir* (Knowledge World, New Delhi, 1999).

Singh, Mahavir (ed.), *International Terrorism and Religious Extremism – Challenges to Central and South Asia* (Anamica Publishers, New Delhi, 2004).

Singh, Rajkumar, *Less Tasty Indo–Nepal Political Relations 1947-1997* (Novelty & Co., Patna, 1998).

_________, *India – South Asia Minus Congress Regimes* (Novelty and Co., Patna, 2000).

________, *Indo-Pak Nuclear Tension 1947-1998* (Samiksha Prakashan, New Delhi, 2001).

________, *India's Foreign Policy: The First Study in Continuity and Change* (Samiksha Prakashan, New Delhi, 2001).

________, *Past, Present and Future of Kashmir* (Gyan Publishing House, New Delhi, 2008).

________, *India and Pakistan–Social, Political and Military Perspectives* (Regal Publications, New Delhi, 2009).

________, *Global Dimensions of Indo–Nepal Political Relations–Post-Independence* (Gyan Publishing House, New Delhi, 2009).

________, *Relations of NDA and UPA with Neighbours* (Gyan Publishing House, New Delhi, 2010).

________, *Contemporary India with Controversial Neighbours* (Gyan Publishing House, New Delhi, 2011).

________, *Ethnic Politics and LTTE in Sri Lanka* (Kalpaz Publications, New Delhi, 2012).

Smith, Chris, *The Diffusion of Small Arms and Light Weapons in Pakistan and Northern India* (Brassey's London, 1993).

Smith, Donald E., *India as a Secular State* (Princeton University Press, Princeton, 1963).

Smith Wilfred Cantwell, *Modern Islam in India: A Social Analysis* (Ripon Printing Press, Lahore, 1974).

Sobhan, Rahman, *The Crisis of External Dependence: The Political Economy of Foreign Aid to Bangladesh* (Dhaka University Press, 1982).

Spear, Percival, *India, Pakistan and the West* (Oxford University Press, London, 1958).

Subrahmanyam, K., *Security in Changing World* (B.R. Publishing Company, Delhi, 1990).

Sutton, John L., *Arms to Developing Countries, 1945-1965* (Institute of Strategic Studies, London, 1966).

Syed, Anwar Hussain, *Pakistan: Islam, Politics and National Solidarity* (Praeger, Newyork, 1982).

Tahir-Kheli, Shirin, *The United States and Pakistan: The Evolution of an Influence Relationship* (Praeger Special Studies, Newyork, 1982).

Thomas, Raju, G.C., *Indian Security Policy* (Princeton University Press, Princeton, 1986).

Varma, S.P., and Narain, V. (eds.), *Pakistan Political System in Crisis: Emergence of Bangladesh* (University of Rajasthan,

Jaipur, 1972).

Varma, S.P. and Misra, K.P. (eds.), *Foreign Policies in South Asia* (Orient Longmans, New Delhi, 1969).

Victor, Cecil, *India: The Security Dilemma* (Patriot Publishers, New Delhi, 1990).

Vital, David, *The Survival of Small States: Studies in Small Power/ Great Power Conflict* (Oxford University Press, London, 1971).

Vohra, Dewan, C., *India's Aid Diplomacy in the Third World* (Vikas Publishing House, New Delhi, 1980).

Waseem, Mohammad, *Politics and State in Pakistan* (National Institute of Historical and Cultural Research, Islamabad, 1994).

White, Lawrence J., *Industrial Concentration and Economic Power in Pakistan* (Princeton University Press, Princeton, 1974).

Zaidi, A.M. (ed.), *Evolution of Muslim Political Thought in India,* Vol.1 (New Delhi).

Zaidi, Akbar S. (ed.), *Regional Tribalances and Regional Questions in Pakistan* (Vanguard Books, Lahore, 1992).

Zingel, Wolfgang Peter and Zingel, Stephanie Lallemant (eds.), *Pakistan in the 1980s: Ideology Regionalism, Economy, Foreign Policy* (Vanguard Books, Lahore, 1985).

Articles in Books, Periodicals and Newspapers

Adhikary, 'Prakash Chandra and Pranab Karamakar, 'State of Afghan Economy during Taliban Period and the Aftermath', *South Asia Politics* Vol. 9, No. 1, May 2010 (New Delhi, 2010).

Ahmad, Emajuddin, 'Current Trends in Islam in Bangladesh,' *Economic and Political Weekly*, Vol. XVIII, No. 25, 18 June, 1983.

Ahmad, Kamaluddin, 'Six–Point Movement and Emergence of Bangladesh,' *South Asian Studies*, Vol. 13 (July–December 1978).

Ahmar, Moonis, 'Ethnicity and State Power in Pakistan: The Karachi Crisis,' *Asian Survey*, Vol. XXXVI, No. 10 (October 1996).

Ahmed, Eqbal, 'Islam and Politics in Mohammad Asghar Khan (ed.), *Islam, Politics and the State* (Zed Press, London, 1985).

Ahmed, Feroz, 'Ethnicity and Politics: The Rise of Muhajir Separatism,' *South Asia Bulletin*, Vol. 8 (1988).

Ahmed, Parveen, 'Bangladesh Political Alliance Threatens More Protests of Upcoming Election,' *Associated Press*, 18 December, 2006.

Ahmed, Samina, 'The United States and Terrorism in South Asia: The Lessons of History, *International Security* (2002).

Ali Khan, Ahsan, 'The Tamil Question in Historical Perspective: Its Impact on Indo-Sri Lanka Relations,' *Pakistan Horizon Quarterly*, Vol. 2.

Anand, Som, 'Islamism and Pakistan's Social Realities,' *Man and Development*, Vol. 2, No. 1 (March 1980).

Ayoob, Mohammed, 'Two Faces of Islam,' *Asian Survey*, Vol. 19, No. 6, June 1979.

Aziz, A., 'Problems of Stateless Workers in Ceylon,' *Blitz*, 30 October, 1982.

Babu, Ramesh B., 'The Liberal Capitalist West as the New Global State,' *International Studies*, Vol. 43, No. 3 July-September, 2006 (Sage Publications, New Delhi, 2006).

Bahadur, Kalim, 'Ethnic Problems in Pakistan,' *World Focus*, Vol. XV, Nos. 4-5 (April-May 1994).

Bains, J.S., 'India's International Disputes,' *Indian Journal of Politics*, Vol. 2, No. 1 (Aligarh, January-June 1968).

Bhadrakumar, M.K., 'Taliban's Return and India's Concerns,' *The Hindu,* 28 June 2011.

Bajpai, K. Shankar, 'Three in This Marriage,' *The Hindustan Times*, 15 March, 2005.

Balachanddran, P.K., 'TULF Seeks LTTE's Permission to Function,' *The Hindustan Times*, 6 January, 1999.

Bali, Arti, 'Enforcing Military Solutions to Ethnic Conflicts,' *South Asia Politics*, Vol. 7, No. 2 (New Delhi, June 2008).

Barabasi, Albert–Lazlo, 'Linked: The New Science of Networks (Perseus, 2002).

Barry, John and Michael Hirsh, 'The Real Tip of the Spear,' *Newsweek*, 8 October, 2001.

Baudrillard, Jean, 'The Spirit of Terrorism,' 2 November, 2001.

Barnds, William J., 'United States Policy towards South Asia: Shifting Perceptions and Policy Choices,' *Pacific Community*, Vol. 8, No. 4 (July 1977).

Bastiampillai Bertram, E.S.J., 'Ethnic Conflicts in South Asia and Inter-State Relations Especially in Relation to Sri Lanka,' in Shelton U. Kodikara (ed.), *South Asian Strategic Issues: Sri Lankan Perspectives* (Sage Publications, New Delhi, 1990).

Beg, General Mirza Aslam, 'Pakistan's Nuclear Programme: A National Security Perspective (London, 1996).

Beri, H.N., 'Pakistan and CENTO,' *Strategic Analysis* (New Delhi), Vol. 1, No. 3, January, 1977.

Bidwai, Praful, 'Lahore Verdict Opens New Phase in Pakistan,' *The Times of India*, 14 January, 1999.

________, 'Not in Our Name,' *The Hindustan Times*, 25 February, 2003.

Chakravarty, Sukha Ranjan, 'The Pakistan National Movement,' *Foreign Affairs Report*, Vol. XXV, No. 1 (1976).

Cheema, Pervez Iqbal, 'Impact of the Afghan War on Pakistan,' *Pakistan Horizon,* Vol. XXXI (1988).

Chellaney, Brahma, 'Hard Words Soft Actions,' *The Hindustan Times*, 29 February, 2000.

________, 'A Perilous Course,' in *Ibid.,* 11 January, 2001.

________, 'Jehad on Jehadi,' 20 September 2001.

________, 'LoC Stock and Barrel', 31 August, 2004.

________, 'Fighting Terrorism in South Asia: The Lessons of History,' *International Security* (2002).

Chopra, Surendra, 'Islamic Fundamentalism and Pakistan's Foreign Policy, *India Quarterly*, Vol. XLIX, Nos. 1-2 (January-June 1993).

Chowdhury, G.W., 'Bangladesh: Coup and Counter Coup: International Implications,' *ORBIS*, Vol. XIX, No. 4, Winter, 1976.

Dar, A.N., 'Need for Cautious Approach in Kashmir,' *The Hindustan Times*, 27 August, 1997.

Dash, P.L., 'Afghanistan: The epicentre of Terror' in Mahavir Singh (ed.), *International Terrorism and Religious Extremism– Challenges to Central and South Asia* (Anamica Publishers, New Delhi, 2004).

Dieter, Bram, 'Changes in South Asia Intra–regional and External Relationship, '*The World Today*, Vol. 34 (London, October 1978).

Dixit, J.N., 'In the General's Own Words,' *The Hindustan Times*, 2 February, 2000.

________, 'Calling on Neighbours, in *Ibid.*, 14 August 2002.

Doval, Ajit, 'Islamic Terrorism in South Asia and India's Strategic Response' (Oxford University Press, New Delhi, 2007).

________, 'Outsourcing Terror', *The Times of India*, 18 July 2011.

Dubhashi, P.R., 'Obama's US Presidency and India's Foreign Policy,' *South Asia Politics*, Vol. 1, No. 11, March 2009 (New Delhi, 2009).

Dutta, Vijay and Ninan Servanti, 'The Route of Discontent,' *India Today*,16-31 July (Living Media, New Delhi, 1978).

Dworkin, Anthony, 'Beyond the War on Terror: Towards a New Transatlantic Framework for Counterterrorism, 13, *European Countries on Foreign Relation* 1 (2009).

Engineer, Asghar Ali, 'Pakistan's Policy and its Viability,' *The Hindu*, 14 October, 2000.

Farrell, Tom, 'For him No Sacrifice was too Great for the Objective of Eelam,' in *Ibid.*, 20 May, 2009.

Galbraith, James K., 'Rising Inequality After 1980 is the Rule,' *Foreign Affairs*, July-August 2002 (Newyork, 2002).

Girardet, Edward, 'Corrupt Officials Reap Spoils of Afghan War, '*The Christian Science Monitor*, 7 September, 1988.

Glaberson, William, 'US Won't Label Terror Suspects as Combatants,' *The Newyork Times*, 14 March, 2009.

Goyal, D.R., 'International Terrorism: Challenge and Response,' in Mahavir Singh (ed.), *International Terrorism and Religious Extremism–Challenges to Central and South Asia* (Anamica Publishers, New Delhi, 2004).

Griffith, Ivelaw L., 'From Cold War Geopolitics to Post Cold War Geonarcotics,' *International Journal*, Vol. XLIX, No. 1 (Winter 1993-94).

Guha, Seema, 'The Lankan Tug of War,' *The Times of India*, 28 July 1997.

Hagerty, D.T., 'India's Regional Security Doctrine,' *Asian Survey*, Vol. 31, No. 4 (New Delhi, April 1991).

Halan, Y.C., 'A Blurning Pakistan: Causes and Cures,' *Third Concept*.

Hanlon, Michael E. O., 'A Flawed Masterpiece,' *Foreign Affairs*, May-June 2002.

Hariharan, R., 'Militancy and Small Arms Proliferation,' *The Hindu*, 20 April, 2007.

________, 'The Discarded Accord and the Unwanted War,' in *Ibid.*, 7 August, 2007.

________, 'The Moment of Truth for the LTTE,' 5 February, 2009.

________, 'Succession Squabble,' *Frontline*, Vol. 26, No. 12, 6-9 June, 2009 (Chennai, 2009).

________, 'Sri Lanka: Need to Restore Trust,' *The Hindu*, 18 May, 2010.

Harrison, Selig, 'A New Hub for Terrorism? In Bangladesh An Islamic Movement with Al- Qaeda Ties is on the Rise,' *The Washington Post*, 2 August, 2006.

Hassan, Shaukat, 'Problems of Internal Stability in South Asia', in Shelton U. Kodikara (ed.), *External Compulsions of South Asian Politics* (Sage Publications, New Delhi, 1993).

Heine, Jorge and Thakur Ramesh, 'The Darkside of Globalisation,' *The Hindu*, 10 January, 2011.

Huntington, Samuel, 'The Clash of Civilizations,' *Foreign Affairs* (Summer, 1993).

Huria, Sonali, 'War on Terrorism in South Asia–Af-Pak and Beyond,' *Institute of Peace and Conflict Studies*, No. 108 (New Delhi, 2009).

Iqbal, Anwar, 'Is the Tide Turning Against the MQM? *The Muslim* (Islamabad), 17 May, 1989.

Iqbal, Javid, 'Islamization in Pakistan,' *Journal of South Asian and Middle Eastern Studies*, Vol. 8, No. 5 (Spring, 1985).

Jacob, Lucy M., 'Regionalism in Sri Lanka,' in Ramakant (ed.), *Regionalism in South Asia* (Aalekh Publishers, Jaipur, 1983).

Jagunnathan, N.S., 'The End of a Misadventure,' *The Indian Express*, 2 April, 1990.

Janik, Anton I, Jr., 'Prosecuting Al-Qaeda: America's Foreign Policy Interests Are Best Served by Trying Terrorists Under International Tribunals,' *Denver Journal of International Law and Policy*, September 2002.

Jha, Prem Shankar, 'Where Next with Pakistan,' *The Hindustan Times*, 12 February, 2000.

________, 'That Other Neighbour,' in *Ibid.*, 13 August, 2002.

________, 'Fear and Loathing,' 27 September, 2004.

________, 'A Question of Trust,' 22 April, 2005.

Joshi, Manoj, 'A Tale of Two Countries,' *The Times of India*, 5 February, 2005.

Kalkat, A.S., 'Ensuring Security in the Age of Global Terror,' *The Hindu*, 13 September, 2006.

Kamal, A. Nazir, 'Karakoram Highway–A Nation Building Effort, *Strategic Studies*, Vol. 11, No, 3 (Islamabad, Spring 1979).

Karunaratne, Victor, 'Tamil Federalist in Ceylon,' *Eastern World* Vol. XVI (September 1962).

Kearney, Robert N., 'The New Political Crisis in Ceylon,' *Asian Survey*, Vol. II, No. 6 (June 1962).

________, 'Language and the Rise of Tamil Separation in Sri Lanka,' *Asian Survey*, Vol. XVIII, No. 5 (May 1978).

Khobragade, Vinod F., 'Re-Thinking Power Devolution in Sri Lanka,' *South Asia Politics*, Vol. 6, No. 1 (New Delhi, May 2007).

————, 'Sri Lankan Tamil Question–India's Paroxism,' Vol. 7, No. 8 (New Delhi, December 2008).

————, 'Ethnic Politics in Sri Lanka–Political Solution to Tamil Cause and Military Solution to LTTE,' Vol. 7, No. 11 (New Delhi, March 2009).

Kodikara, Shelton U., 'Persons of Indian Origin in Ceylon,' *Foreign Affairs*, Vol. XIII, No. 2 (February 1964).

————, 'Communalism and Political Modernisation in Ceylon,' *Modern Ceylon Studies*, Vol. 1, No. 1 (1970).

————, 'War and Peace Options for the LTTE,' *The Sunday Observers*, 1 July, 1990.

————, 'Internal Politics and Foreign Policy: Prospects for Indo-Sri Lanka Relations in the Nineties', in *External Compulsions of South Asian Politics* (Sage Publications, New Delhi, 1993).

Krishna, Shetty K.P., 'Ceylon's Foreign Policy: Emerging Patterns of Non-Alignment,' *South Asian Studies*, Vol. 1, No. 1 (April 1966).

Kumar, Dilip, 'The Resurgence of the Taliban–Lessons Learned,' *South Asia Politics*, Vol. 6, No. 1 (New Delhi, 2007).

Kumar, Satish, 'Militant Islam: The Nemesis of Pakistan,' *Strategic Digest*, Vol. XXX, No. 8 (August 2000).

Kumar, Sumit, 'Pakistan's Jehadi Apparatus: Goals and Methods', *Strategic Analysis*, Vol. XXIX, No. 12 (March 2001).

Kumaratunga, Bandaranaike Chandrika, 'Original Sins', *The Hindustan Times*, 29 April, 2002.

Laport, Jr. Robert, 'Pakistan in 1995: The Continuing Crisis,' *Asian Survey*, Vol. XXXVI, No. 2 (February 1996).

Low–Beer, Francis, 'The Concept of Neutralism,' *American Political Science Review*, Vol. LVIII (Washington, 1964).

Malkani, K.R., 'Inside the Muslim Mind,' *The Hindustan Times*, 13 October, 2001.

Maniruzzaman, T., 'The Bangladesh Revolution and Its Aftermath' (Dhaka, 1980).

Masud, Anwarul Kazi, 'Terrorism in South Asia and US Foreign Policy', Paper No. 3292, 5 July, 2009 (South Asia Analysis Group, New Delhi, 2009).

Mazari, Shireen M., 'The Militarization of Pakistan's Civil Society, in Kumar Rupesinghe and Khawar Mumtaz (eds.), *Internal Conflicts in South Asia* (Sage Publications, New Delhi, 1996).

Menon, Madhava N.R., 'Combating Terrorism, and Some Management Issues,' *The Hindu*, 12 January, 2009.

Mohanty, J.C., 'WTO and Implications for Indian Agriculture,' *Administrative Change*, Vol. XXX, No. 1 and Vol. XXXI, No. 2, January-December 2002 (Jaipur, 2002).

Mueller, John, 'Nine Propositions About the Historical Impact of Nuclear Weapons,' in Jorn Gjelstad and Olav Njolstad (eds.), *Nuclear Rivalry and International Order* (London, 1996).

Mukherjee, Uddipan, 'Jinnah's Tottering Pakistan,' *South Asia Politics*, Vol. 8, No. 10, February 2010 (New Delhi, 2010).

Muni, S.D., 'The United States and South Asia: The Strategic Dimension,' in Shelton U. Kodikara (ed.), *External Compulsions of South Asian Politics* (Sage Publications, New Delhi, 1993).

________, 'Terrorism, 'Tectonic Plates' and Strategic Equations in Asia,' in Mahavir Singh (ed.), *International Terrorism and Religious Extremism–Challenges to Central and South Asia* (Anamica Publishers, New Delhi, 2004).

________, 'A Common Destiny,' *The Times of India*, 23 April, 1989.

________, 'On a Hot Tin Roof,' *The Hindustan Times*, 30 August, 2003.

________, 'Dealing with a New Nepal, *The Hindu*, 15 September, 2008.

Muthiah, S., 'Legacy of a Dream,' in *Ibid.*, 24 January, 2010.

Nandy, A., 'The Sociology of Sati,' *The Indian Express*, 5 October, 1989.

Narain, Virendra, 'Bangladesh and Changing International Context: An Analysis of Perceptions,' in S.P. Verma and Virendra Narain (eds.), *Pakistan Political System in Crisis: Emergence of Bangladesh* (South Asia Publishers, New Delhi).

Nayar, Kuldip, 'Estranged Neighbour: The Arrogant India,' *The Indian Express*, 12 December, 1994.

________, 'Not Enough in it for India,' *The Hindu*, 16 February, 2002.

Narayanan, V.N., 'Between the Devil and Deep Blue Sea,' *The Hindustan Times*, 8 August, 1998.

________, 'Separating Tamils from the LTTE,' in *Ibid.*, 9 August, 1998.

Obeyesekere, Gananath, 'The Origins and Institutionalisation of Political Violence,' in James Manor (ed.), *Sri Lanka in Change and Crisis* (Croom Helm, London, 1984).

Padgaonkar, Dileep, 'Pak Crisis and India's Choices,' *The Times of India*, 19 August, 1990.

Pathak, Sukumar, 'Obstacles to Afghan War on Terror–Pak's Hesitancy and Karzai's Apostasy,' *South Asia Politics*, Vol. 9, No. 10, February 2011 (New Delhi, 2011).

Pattanaike, Smruti S., 'Islam and the Ideology of Pakistan,' *Strategic Analysis*, Vol. XXII, No. 9 (December 1998).

Poulose, T.T., 'The Politics of Nuclear Free Zone in South Asia', *Pacific Community,* Vol. 6 (Tokyo, April 1977).

Prabha, Kshitij, 'Terrorism Challenges Secular Fabric of South Asia,' in Mahavir Singh (ed.), *International Terrorism and Religious Extremism–Challenges to Central and South Asia* (Anamika Publishers, New Delhi, 2004).

Pylee, M.V., 'States Under Constitutional Emergency,' *Journal of Commonwealth Political Studies*, Vol. 1, No. 2 (1967).

Qureshi, S.M.M., 'Pakhtunistan: The Frontier Dispute Between Afghanistan and Pakistan,' *Pacific Affairs*, Vol. XXXIX, Nos. 1-2 (Spring-Summer, 1966).

Radyuhin, 'Russia's Tempered Response to Abbottabad,' *The Hindu,* 13 May, 2011.

Raghavan, V.R., 'Response to Terror,' *The Hindustan Times,* 6 January 1999.

Rahman, M. Anisur, 'East Pakistan: The Roots of Estrangement,' *South Asian Review*, Vol. 3, No. 3 (April 1970).

Rajan, M.S., 'Bangladesh and After,' *Pacific Affairs*, Summer, Vol. 45, No. 2.

Rashid, Abbas, 'Pakistan: The Ideological Dimensions in Mohammad Asghar Khan (ed.), *Islam, Politics and The State: The Pakistan Experience* (Zed Press, London, 1985).

_________, 'Pakistan: The Politics of Fundamentalism,' in Kumar Rupesinghe and Khawar Mumtaz (eds.), *Internal Conflicts in South Asia* (Sage Publications, New Delhi, 1996).

Rashid, Ahmed, 'Taliban, Islam, Oil and the New Great Game in Central Asia, (London, 2000).

_________, 'The Taliban Exporting Extremism,' *Foreign Affairs*, Vol. LXXVIII, No. 6 (November-December, 1999).

Reddy, Sheela C., 'Globalisation–A Human Rights Perspective,' *South Asia Politics*, Vol. 5, No. 2, March 2007 (New Delhi, 2007).

Rex, *Hudson A.*, 'The Sociology and Psychology of Terrorism: Who Becomes a Terrorist and Why ?,' *Federal Research Division, Library of Congress*, September 1999.

Rimington, Stella, 'Terrorism Did Not Begin on 9/11,' *The Hindustan Times*, 8 September, 2002.

Rothenberg, Richard, 'From Whole Cloth: Making up the Terrorist Network,' *Atlanta*, USA, 2 November, 2001.

Roy, Oliver, 'Why the War is Going on in Afghanistan: The Afghan Crisis in Perspective,' *Journal of International Affairs* Vol. 5, No. 4 December 2000-February 2001.

Rushdie, Salman, 'Saddam Impact,' *The Hindustan Times*, 3 September, 2002.

Sahadevan, P., 'Negotiating Peace in Ethnic Wars,' *International Studies*, Vol. 43, No. 3 (New Delhi, July-September 2006).

Sahay, Anand K., 'Kashmir As General Fodder,' *The Hindustan Times*, 29 January, 2002.

Saighal, Vinod, 'USA–PAK Potentially More Menacing Than AF–PAK,' *South Asia Politics*, Vol. 9, No. 1, May 2010 (New Delhi, 2010).

Sanghvi, Vir, 'An American Anniversary,' *The Hindustan Times*, 8 September, 2002.

________, 'US Since 9/11-Lessons and Conundrums,' in *Ibid.*, 15 September, 2002.

Sareen, Rajendra, 'Dimensions of Turmoil,' *The Tribune*, 5 February, 1990.

Sengupta, Bhabani, 'Waiting for India: India's Role as a Regional Power, *Journal of International Affairs*, Vol. 29, No. 2 (New York, 1975).

________, 'A Deeply Divided Nation,' in Pran Chopra (ed.), *Contemporary Pakistan–New Aims and Images* (Vikas Publishing House, New Delhi, 1979).

________, 'After IPKF is Out, '*The Hindustan Times*, 23 December, 1989.

________, 'How to Avoid War with Pakistan,' *The National Herald*, 13 February, 1990.

________, 'Global Change Cripples Pakistan,' in *Ibid.*, 22 February, 1990.

Sengupta, Jayshree, 'Threats to Globalisation,' *The Hindu,* 4 February, 2000.

Shane, Scott, 'CIA to Expand Use of Drones in Pakistan,' *The Newyork Times*, 4 December, 2009.

Sharma, Madan Lal, 'World After 9/11', *Third Concept*, September 2007 (New Delhi, 2007).

Shu, Yang, 'Afghanistan–Buffer State and Centre for Terrorism,' in Mahavir Singh (ed.), *International Terrorism and Religious Extremism–Challenges to Central and South Asia* (Anamica Publishers, New Delhi, 2004).

Singh, Manvendra, 'Threshold of Patience,' *The Hindustan Times*, 15 January, 2002.

Singh, Prakash, 'Militancy from Kashmir to Coimbatore,' *The Hindustan Times,* 23 February, 1998.

Singh, S.P., '11 September and America's Balance Sheet in South and Central Asia,' in Mahavir Singh (ed.), *International Terrorism and Religious Extremism–Challenges to Central and South Asia* (Anamica Publishers, New Delhi, 2004).

Singh, Suman, 'Terrorism in South Asia,' *South Asia Politics*, Vol. 9, No. 2, June 2010 (New Delhi, 2010).

Sood, Vikram, 'Policy Sans Frontiers,' *The Hindustan Times*, 5 December, 2011.

Steele, Jonathan, 'The Taliban's Wish List,' *The Hindu*, 22 January, 2011.

Sivarajah, A., 'Indo-Sri Lanka Relations and Sri Lanka's Ethnic Crisis: The Tamil Factor,' in Shelton U. Kodikara (ed.), *South Asian Strategic Issues–Sri Lankan Perspectives* (Sage Publications, New Delhi, 1990).

Subrahmanyam, K., 'Washington's Waiting–Islamabad's Tokenism Will Not Work,' *The Times of India*, 11 September, 2002.

________, 'Next Move, Next Door,' *The Hindustan Times*, 19 July, 2004.

Swami, Praveen, 'Osama's Death a Gift to Resurgent Al-Qaeda,' *The Hindu*, 3 May, 2011.

Swamy, Subramanian, 'Sri Lanka Crisis and India's Optious,' in *Ibid.*, 29 November, 2006.

Tehranian, Majid, 'Khomeini's Doctrine of Legitimacy,' in Anthony J. Parel and Ronald C. Keith (eds.), *Comparative Political Philosophy* (New Delhi, 1992).

Telumbde, Anand, 'War On Iraq: Dollar Dominance and Doom of America', in S.M. Daud (ed.), *War Against Iraq* (2003).

Thomas, K. T., 'The Economic Roots of US Intervention in Afghanistan,' *Proceedings of the Indian History Congress,* 68th Session, Delhi, 2007 (Delhi, 2008).

Varadarajan, Siddarth, 'A Fork in the Road for the US in South Asia, *The Hindu*, 3 May, 2011.

Verma, A. K., 'Radical Islam and Terror,' *South Asia Politics*, Vol. 7, No. 8 December, 2008 (New Delhi, 2008).

Verma, Jagdish Prasad, 'If You Wish for Peace, Understand Terrorism,' *South Asia Politics*, Vol. 9, No. 7, November 2010 (New Delhi, 2010).

Victor, Cecil, 'Busting Terrorist Bases no Solution,' *The Patriot*, 18 May, 1990.

Vohra, Pankaj, 'Prospects of a Full-scale Conflict in India's Backyard Are Real,' *The Hindustan Times*, 17 September, 2001.

Waxman, Mathew C., 'The Structure of Terrorism Threats the Laws of War,' *Duke Journal of Comparative and International Law*, Vol. 20, May 2010.

Weiner, Myron, 'The Politics of South Asia,' in Gabriel A. Almond and James S. Coleman, *The Politics of Developing Areas* (Princeton University Press, Princeton, 1960).

Williamson, John, 'The Washington Consensus and Beyond,' *Economic and Political Weekly*, Vol. XXXVIII, No. 15, 12-18 April 2003 (Mumbai, 2003).

Wriggins, Howard W., 'Pakistan's Search for a Foreign Policy After the Invasion of Afghanistan,' *Pacific Affairs*, Vol. 57, No, 2 (The University of British Columbia, 1984).

Zaidi, Mubashir, 'Jehad in Retreat,' *The Hindustan Times*, 20 January, 2002.

Zaman Uz Rashed, 'WMD Terrorism in South Asia: Trends and Implications' (University of Bangladesh, Dhaka).

Newspapers

Amrit Bazar Patrika (Calcutta)

The Ceylon Daily News (Ceylon)

Daily News (Colombo)

The Financial Times (London)

The Hindu (Madras)

The Hindustan Times (New Delhi)

The Indian Express (Delhi)

The National Herald (New Delhi)

The Newyork Times (Newyork)
The Pakistan Times (Lahore)
The Patriot (New Delhi)
The Statesman (Delhi)
The Sunday Standard (New Delhi)
The Times (London)
The Times of India (New Delhi)
The Tribune (Chandigarh)
The Washington Post (Washington)

Periodicals

American Political Science Review (Newyork)
Asian Affairs
Asian Survey (New Delhi)
Eastern Economists (Bombay)
Economic and Political Weekly (Bombay)
Foreign Affairs (Newyork)
Foreign Policy Report (New Delhi)
Frontline (Chennai)
India Today (New Delhi)
Indian Journal of Political Science (Hyderabad)
International Studies (New Delhi)
Journal of Commonwealth Political Studies
Pacific Affairs (Newyork)
Political Science Quarterly (Newyork)
South Asia Politics (New Delhi)
Tamil Times (London)
World Today (London)

Index

Q

R

S

T